D1568023

ROMAN SOURCES FOR THE

HISTORY OF AMERICAN CATHOLICISM,

1763–1939

ROMAN SOURCES

for the HISTORY

of AMERICAN

CATHOLICISM,

1763–1939

MATTEO BINASCO

Edited with a foreword by
KATHLEEN SPROWS CUMMINGS

University of Notre Dame Press
Notre Dame, Indiana

University of Notre Dame Press
Notre Dame, Indiana 46556
undpress.nd.edu

Published in the United States of America

Library of Congress Cataloging-in-Publication Data

Names: Binasco, Matteo, 1975– author.
Title: Roman sources for the history of American Catholicism, 1763–1939 /
Matteo Binasco ; edited with a foreword by Kathleen Sprows Cummings.
Description: Notre Dame : University of Notre Dame Press, 2018. |
Includes bibliographical references and index. |
Identifiers: LCCN 2018012506 (print) | LCCN 2018012583 (ebook) |
ISBN 9780268103835 (pdf) | ISBN 9780268103842 (epub) | ISBN 9780268103811
(hardcover : alk. paper) | ISBN 026810381X (hardcover : alk. paper)
Subjects: LCSH: Catholic Church—United States—History—Sources.
Classification: LCC BX1406.3 (ebook) | LCC BX1406.3 .B56 2018 (print) |
DDC 282/.7307204563—dc23
LC record available at https://lccn.loc.gov/2018012506

Contents

CHAPTER 4. Other Civil and Religious Archives

CHAPTER 5. Libraries

Foreword

Toward a Transatlantic Approach to US Catholic History

KATHLEEN SPROWS CUMMINGS

The idea for this volume surfaced at a seminar sponsored by Notre Dame's Cushwa Center for the Study of American Catholicism convened in June 2014 in collaboration with Matteo Sanfilippo (Università della Tuscia) at Notre Dame's Rome Global Gateway. The seminar focused on transatlantic approaches to writing US Catholic history, with a view to encouraging scholars of US Catholicism to make more use of the Vatican Secret Archives and other Roman repositories. To that end, seminar participants visited seven archives of the Holy See and throughout Rome for hands-on workshops exploring potentially relevant sources. Members of our group, which included graduate students and faculty from universities throughout the United States, were guided by Professor Sanfilippo and other Italian scholars, including, most notably, Professor Luca Codignola, then of the University of Genoa.

The seminar was an eye-opening experience, revealing the rich potential of Roman archives to enrich individual research projects and the field at large. The earliest generations of US Catholic historians did not need to be convinced of this. Most of them, after all, were clerics or members of religious congregations who had studied in Europe or had close connections there. They were conversant in multiple European languages and understood well the transatlantic flows of people, ideas, devotions, and beliefs that shaped the church in the United States. By the 1960s and 1970s, however, the prominence of the American exceptionalist paradigm, combined with the advent of the new social history, led many historians of the US church to adopt a tighter nationalist frame. As a result, these historians were, in the main, much less interested in identifying connections between the United States and the Holy See and less inclined to harness the potential of Roman archival repositories. There were, of course, exceptions to this rule. Foremost among them was Gerald P. Fogarty, SJ, who provided an enduring model of how to conduct research in Roman archives, both in his study of Denis O'Connell in Rome and in his magisterial *The Vatican and the American Hierarchy* (1985). There were other scholars, many of whom were also ordained or members of a religious community, who consulted Roman sources. Still, American exceptionalism carried the day, and most scholars insisted on emphasizing the autonomy of the US Church.

The late Peter D'Agostino played a significant role in changing this approach. In the late 1990s, D'Agostino emerged as a vociferous critic of US historians who ignored Roman archives, insisting that the story of Catholics in America simply cannot be told apart from their connections, real and symbolic, with the Holy See. D'Agostino's award-winning book, *Rome in America: Transnational Catholic Ideology from the Risorgimento to Fascism* (2004), relied on Roman sources to demonstrate the importance of papal politics for nineteenth- and early twentieth-century American Catholic life. His tragic death deprived Catholic historians of a gifted colleague, but his insistence that Roman archives should be accessible to, and regularly accessed by, lay Church historians is one of his lasting legacies.

The 2014 Cushwa Seminar in Rome represented an effort to respond to D'Agostino's exhortation. Three overlapping developments nurtured both the seminar and the initiatives it inspired, this resource included. The first of these was historiographical. The so-called transnational turn gripped the American historical profession during the 1990s, and many subfields of American history embraced the effort to situate the history of the United States in a global perspective. In 2003, the Cushwa Center sponsored a conference titled Re-Thinking US Catholic History: International and Comparative Frameworks, and ever since affiliated scholars have urged historians of Catholicism to adopt transnational approaches. Doing so, we argued, would not only offer a chance to better integrate Catholics as subjects in mainstream narratives but would also help render more accurately the history of the Roman Catholic Church, a body that Princeton historian David Bell recently characterized as "the world's most successful international organization."[1]

The second overlapping development might be described as personal in that it materialized out of my own particular research on American saints. In conceiving my project, I intended to structure it as a social history of reception, focusing exclusively on the context in which causes for canonization were promoted in the United States. My desire to take D'Agostino's exhortation to heart, combined with a trip to Rome in 2010 to attend the canonization of Brother André Bessette, CSC, changed all that. With the encouragement and guidance of Matteo Sanfilippo, I undertook research in the Vatican Secret Archives and discovered the rich array of sources available there. On that initial foray and on subsequent trips, I became increasingly convinced that canonization, and indeed US Catholic history more generally, could be properly interpreted only in a transatlantic context, with close attention given to archival sources at the Holy See and in Rome.

The life and afterlife of Elizabeth Ann Bayley Seton (1776–1821) offers a case in point. Seton was first proposed as a candidate for canonization in 1882, and she was canonized in 1975, the first American-born person so honored. Throughout her long journey to the altars of sainthood, the epicenter of Seton's story alternated between the United States and Europe, with axis points in Baltimore, Emmitsburg, Philadelphia, and New York in the former and France (by virtue of the Emmitsburg Sisters of Charity's formal alliance with the French Daughters of Charity in 1850), Italy, and the Holy See in the latter. See in the latter. In the Vatican Secret Archives alone, within the collections of the Congregation of Rites, there are twenty-four volumes of printed and manuscript material related to Seton's cause for canonization. A vast amount of additional material related to Seton's cause for canonization is housed in the General Archives of the Congregation of the Mission (Vincentians) on via dei Capasso in Rome.

The same is true in the cases of other canonized people from the United States, such as Philippine Duchesne, RSCJ, and John Neumann, CSsR. The causes for canonization of these European-born missionaries generated a tremendous amount of material both in the Vatican Secret Archives and in the archives of their respective congregations, the General Archives of the Society of the Sacred Heart, located in the Trastevere neighborhood of Rome, and the General Archives of the Redemptorists on via Merulana, as detailed in this guide. In consulting this material, I have been astounded by the ways that Roman sources help me understand my subjects better and prompt me to ask new questions about the Catholic experience in the United States.

The third overlapping development that inspired the 2014 seminar and, subsequently, this volume, might be described as institutional. Six months before our seminar convened, the University of Notre Dame opened its new Rome Global Gateway on via Ostilia, just steps away from the Colosseum. Theodore J. Cachey, professor of Italian and the Albert J. and Helen M. Ravarino Family Director of Dante and Italian Studies at Notre Dame, served as the Rome Global Gateway's first academic director, and guided by his vision the Gateway is becoming a hub of intellectual inquiry and scholarly conversations. The timing of this initiative on the part of the University of Notre Dame was fortuitous, as it provided me, in close collaboration with Italian colleagues, a base of operations for undertaking more systematic efforts to apprise other US-based scholars of the rich promise of Roman archives.

Once the 2014 seminar concluded, we searched for a means to build on its momentum. With support from Notre Dame International, the College of Arts and Letters, and Notre Dame's Office of Research, the Cushwa Center launched a more sustained effort to encourage research in Roman archives. On the recommendation of Professor Luca Codignola, we hired Matteo Binasco as a postdoctoral fellow at the Rome Global Gateway, who began his research in September 2014. From then until the summer of 2016, Binasco researched and prepared this comprehensive guide to almost sixty institutional archives in Rome—far more than we had expected—detailing their sources for American Catholic studies. He has uncovered a rich variety of archival gems, detailed throughout his engaging descriptions of relevant holdings. Binasco's preface cites several of these gems, which we deemed particularly illustrative. They also appear in the profiles of their respective archives. This repetition represents an editorial decision based on assessment of how scholars were likely to engage the volume.

Our plans for building bridges between Italian and US scholars of American Catholicism and for fostering research in Roman archives continue. Luca Codignola now serves as an honorary senior fellow at the Cushwa Center, and I am very grateful to him and to Matteo Sanfilippo for their advice and generous support in producing this volume and for other

Cushwa initiatives. Above all, thank you to Matteo Binasco for his superb and meticulous research, which we hope will serve scholars venturing to Rome for years to come.

Grazie mille to all the Cushwa Center staff members who worked on this volume, especially Shane Ulbrich, Peter Hlabse, and Deandra Lieberman. The Cushwa Center would not have been able to launch this project without the assistance and advice provided by Robert J. Bernhard and Hildegund Müller at Notre Dame's Office of Research, Nicholas Entrikin and Tom Guinan at Notre Dame International, and John McGreevy, I. A. O'Shaughnessy Dean of the College of Arts and Letters. Thanks, too, to Ted Cachey, whose tenure as academic director at the Rome Global Gateway coincided with the development of this volume. His ready support has immeasurably enriched this project and other initiatives of the Cushwa Center in Rome.

One final note: This volume will be most useful to US scholars who have a competency in ecclesiastical Latin and Italian. Although some documents are in English, French, or Spanish, many reports are in Latin or Italian. US Catholic historians in recent generations have not placed a high premium on developing linguistic abilities, and until they do so it will be difficult to adopt truly transnational approaches.

Finally, as proud as we are of the number and breadth of the profiles contained in this volume, we make no effort to claim that it is exhaustive. In some cases, repositories were unable or unwilling to cooperate with Matteo Binasco. Despite his admirable effort, to quote an anonymous reviewer, "to pound the pavements (cobblestones)" of Rome, it cannot be said to be entirely comprehensive. That said, we agree with the same reviewer's assessment that nothing of this scale has previously been attempted and that the copious information contained in this volume will make *la dolce vita romana* even sweeter.

NOTE

1. David A. Bell, "This Is What Happens When Historians Overuse the Idea of the Network," *New Republic*, October 25, 2013.

Acknowledgments

This guide has been completed thanks to the outstanding support of a series of institutions and people. First of all, I would like to thank Professor Kathleen Sprows Cummings, director of the Cushwa Center for the Study of American Catholicism at the University of Notre Dame, for her incredible support. She has been the key driving force behind this project, and not a single word of this guide would have been written without her supervision and help. I am grateful to Notre Dame Research for its essential financial support. I thank Professor John T. McGreevy, as through his books I learned much more about the "transnational" nature of American Catholicism. To Professor Luca Codignola and Professor Matteo Sanfilippo, my two mentors in Rome, I owe an immense debt of gratitude. During the course of this project—but also before it—I enjoyed their guidance, their thorough knowledge of the Roman archives, their expertise in North American history, and their sharp but constructive criticisms. At the Archives of the Congregation for the Doctrine of the Faith, I was fortunate to have the support of Professor Giovanni Pizzorusso, who has been my guide through this fascinating repository. I thank the two anonymous referees who read all of the manuscript and who gave illuminating advice on how to improve it. I am very grateful to Professor Joseph M. White, who read and revised the bibliography. Without his knowledge and his useful comments, it would have a been a chaotic and meaningless list of names and books.

The staff of the Cushwa Center in South Bend has always been ready to answer my queries. My thanks go to Shane Ulbrich, Pete Hlabse, Heather Grennan Gary, and Dr. Catherine R. Osborne. I owe a great debt to Deandra Lieberman and Mary Reardon, who revised my English and copyedited the volume as a whole. At the Rome Global Gateway, I had the good fortune to enjoy the support of its first academic director, Professor Theodore J. Cachey Jr. His continuous encouragement, combined with his irony, make the Rome Global Gateway a unique place for research and for meeting new scholars. A big *grazie* to Anthony Wingfield, Alice Bartolomei, Pamela Canavacci, Silvia Dall'Olio, PhD, Simone De Cristofaris, Krista Di Eleuterio, Danilo Domenici, Costanza Montanari, and Mallory Nardin for their constant and kind willingness to help me.

To complete this guide, I had to access many archives, where I benefited from the assistance of a series of wonderfully competent and extremely kind prefects and archivists. I would like to express my sincere thanks to the following: the Reverend Monsignor Alejandro Cifres and Daniele Ponziani, Archives of the Congregation for the Doctrine of the Faith; Fr. Alessandro Saraco, Archives of the Apostolic Penitentiary; Mauro Onorati, Archives of the Pontifical Lateran University; Maria Rita Giubilo and Eleonora Mosconi, Archives of the Pontifical Oriental Institute; the Reverend Monsignor Luis Manuel Cuña Ramos and Giovanni Fosci, Archives of the Sacred Congregation "de Propaganda Fide"; Domenico Rocciolo, Archives of the Vicariate of Rome; Cardinal Leonardo Sandri and Giampaolo Rigotti, Historical Archives of the Congregation for the Oriental Churches; Archbishop Paul Richard Gallagher and Professor Johan Ickx, Archives of the Secretariat of State, Section for Relations with States; Monsignor Guido Marini, Chiara Marangoni, and Chiara Rocciolo, Archives of the Liturgical Celebrations of the Supreme Pontiff; Cardinal Angelo Comastri, Assunta di Sante, and Simona Turriziani, Archives of the Fabbrica di San Pietro; Archbishop Jean-Louis Bruguès, OP, and Paolo Vian, Vatican Library; Bishop Sergio Pagano, B, Gianfranco Armando, and Luca Carboni, Vatican Secret Archives; Fabiana Spinelli, Archives of the Dominican Province of Saint Catherine of Siena (Santa Maria sopra Minerva); Fr. Brian Mac Cuarta, SJ, Roman Archives of the Society of Jesus; Fr. Luis Marín de San Martín, OSA, and Nico Ciampelli, General Archives of the Augustinians; Fr. Francis Ricousse, FSC, General Archives of the Brothers of the Christian Schools; Fr. Luigi Martignani, OFM Cap, and Fr. Lorenzo Declich, OFM Cap, General Archives of the Capuchins; Fr. Augustinu Heru, CM, General Archives of the Congregation of the Mission; Sr. Michela Carrozzino, DSMP, General Archives of the Daughters of Saint Mary of Providence; Fr. Angelo Lanfranchi, OCD, and Marcos Argüelles García, General Archives of the Discalced Carmelites; Fr. Gaspar de Roja Sigaya, OP, General Archives of the Order of Friars Preachers (Dominicans); Fr. Priamo Etzi, OFM, and Anna Grazia Petaccia, General Archives of the Franciscan Order (Curia Generalizia); Fr. Maciej Michalski, OMI, General Archives of the Missionary Oblates of Mary Immaculate; Alberto Bianco, Archives of the Congregation of the Oratory in Rome; Sr. Margaret Phelan, RSCJ, and Federica Palumbo, General Archives of the Missionary Sisters of the Sacred Heart of Jesus; Fr. Adam Owczarski, CSsR, General Archives of the Redemptorists; Odir Jacques Dias, General Archives of the Servants of Mary; Sr. Giuditta Pala, MSC (Cabrini), Sr. Michela Carrozzino, DSMP, and Fr. John Cunningham, OP, Archives of the Irish Dominican College, San Clemente; Fr. Mícheál Mac Craith, OFM, Donatella Bellardini, and Claudia Costacurta, Archives of the Irish Franciscan College of Saint Isidore; Professor Johan Ickx, Archives of the Pontifical Institute of Santa Maria dell'Anima; Monsignor Ciarán O'Carroll, rector, Archives of the Pontifical Irish College; Fr. Daniel Fitzpatrick, rector, and Fr. Gerald Sharkey, vice rector, Archives of the Pontifical Scots College; Monsignor Philip Whitmore, rector, Professor Maurice Whitehead, and Orietta Filippini, Archives of the Venerable English College; Alessandra Mercantini, Doria Pamphilj Archive; Fr. Francesco De Feo, OSB, Archives of the Abbey of San Paolo fuori le Mura; Rev. Augustin

K. Rios, Archives of Saint Paul's Within the Walls Episcopal Church; Luca Caddia, Archives of the Keats-Shelley House; Fabrizio Alberti, Archives of the Museo Centrale del Risorgimento; Dr. Amanda Thursfield, Archives of the Non-Catholic Cemetery of Rome; Eugenio Lo Sardo, Central Archives of the State; Paolo Bonora, Archives of the State of Rome; MariaRosaria Senofonte, Archives of the City of Rome; Rita Fioravanti, Casanatense Library; Cinzia Claudia Lafrate and Angelina Oliverio, Library of the Waldensian Faculty of Theology; Fr. Giovanni Terragni, CS, General Archives of the Scalabrinians; Fr. Luigi Cei, SDB, General Archives of the Salesians.

Last but not the least I thank my family (including my cats at home). My father, my mother (especially her, and she knows why), my sister, my two little rogue nephews, and my brother-in-law have always provided unique encouragement for all these years. I owe a big *grazie* to Marina, my girlfriend, and to her mother for their support.

This guide is dedicated to the memory of the late Peter D'Agostino, who had always been a keen promoter of the need to use the Roman sources to understand the transnational dimension of American Catholicism.

Abbreviations

AAES	Archivio degli Affari Ecclesiastici Straordinari (Archives of the Secretariat of State, Relations with States Section)
AAQ	Archives de l'Archevêché de Québec (Archives of the Archdiocese of Quebec)
ACDF	Archives for the Congregation for the Doctrine of the Faith (Archivio della Congregazione per la Dottrina della Fede)
ADASU	Archivio della Delegazione Apostolica degli Stati Uniti
AGC	Archivio Generale dei Cappuccini (General Archives of the Capuchins)
AGOFM-Storico	Archivio Storico Generale dell'Ordine dei Frati Minori (General Archives of the Franciscan Order)
AGOP	Archivum Generale Ordinis Praedicatorum (General Archives of the Order of Friars Preachers, another name for the Dominican Order)
AOCD	Archivio Generale Ordine dei Carmelitani Scalzi (General Archives of the Discalced Carmelites)
APF	Archives of the Sacred Congregation "de Propaganda Fide"
ARSI	Archivum Romanum Societatis Iesu
ASC	Archivio Storico Capitolino (Archives of the City of Rome)
ASSP	Archivio Storico di San Paolo fuori le Mura (Archives of Saint Paul Outside the Walls)
ASV	Archivio Segreto Vaticano (Vatican Secret Archives)
B	Barnabites; today mostly referred to as Clerics Regular of Saint Paul (CRSP)
b.	busta, or folder

bb.	buste, or folders
BAV	Biblioteca Apostolica Vaticana (Vatican Library)
CFX	Congregation of Saint Francis Xavier (Xaverian Brothers)
CGFSMP	Congregazione delle Figlie di S. Maria della Provvidenza (Daughters of Saint Mary of Providence, also known as Guanellians)
CM	Congregation of the Mission (Lazarists/Vincentians)
CPPS	Congregatio Pretiosissimi Sanguinis (Fathers of the Most Precious Blood)
CRSP	Clerici Regulares Sancti Paul (Clerics Regular of Saint Paul); formerly Barnabites (B)
CS	Congregatio Missionarium a S. Carolo (Scalabrinians)
CSC	Congregatio a Sancta Cruce (Congregation of Holy Cross)
CSJ	Congregation of the Sisters of Saint Joseph
CSsR	Congregazione del Santissimo Redentore (Redemptorists)
d.	died
DSMP	Daughters of Saint Mary of Providence
fasc.	fascicolo (pl., fascicoli), a division of a book, journal, or archival volume published or subdivided in parts
fol.	folio
FSC	Fratres Scholarum Christianarum (Brothers of the Christian Schools)
LDB	*Lettere e Decreti della Sacra Congregazione e Biglietti di Monsignor Segretario*
MCRR	Museo Centrale del Risorgimento
MS	manuscript
MSC	Missionarie del Sacro Cuore di Gesù (Missionaries of the Sacred Heart of Jesus)
OCD	Ordo Carmelitarum Discalceatorum (Order of Discalced Brothers of the Blessed Virgin Mary of Mount Carmel or Discalced Carmelites)
OFM	Order of Friars Minor (Franciscans)
OFM Cap	Order of Friars Minor (Capuchins)
OMI	Oblates of Mary Immaculate
OP	Order of Friars Preachers (Dominicans)
OSA	Order of Saint Augustine (Augustinians)

OSB	Ordo Sancti Benedicti (Benedictines)
r	recto
RSCJ	Religieuses du Sacré-Cœur de Jésus, or Religiosae Sanctissimi Cordis Jesu (Religious of the Sacred Heart of Jesus)
rubr.	rubrica (pl., rubriche), a text heading or section
SAC	Società dell'Apostolato Cattolico (Society of the Catholic Apostolate or Pallottines)
SDB	Salesians of Don Bosco
SJ	Societas Iesu (Jesuits)
SOCG	*Scritture Originali riferite nelle Congregazioni Generali*, APF
sottorubr.	sottorubrica (pl., sottorubriche), a subfolder
v	verso
WDA	Westminster Diocesan Archives
†	died

Introduction

A Key Tool for the Study of American Catholicism

Luca Codignola and Matteo Sanfilippo

PART 1

Matteo Binasco's *Roman Sources for the History of American Catholicism, 1763–1939* accompanies the curious reader on a tour through the mysteries of Roman archives.[1] Whether zooming in for a close-up of a known repository or perusing several entries in search of that particular document, the overall feeling of the reader is one of awe before the magnitude and the complexity of the task. While the sense of mystery will remain—a lifetime would not be enough to lift all veils from these rich archives—this guide allows any researcher to do many things. First, while at home, to establish objectives for a research project; then to select at what doors to knock once in Rome; next, to learn which series, volumes, or individual item to enter in the repository's application form; and finally, to get down to business—to see, touch, and read the actual document one needs, be it a private letter, a public memorandum, the proceedings of a meeting, or a bull appointing a bishop.

This guide is meant for students of the history of the United States from 1763 to 1939. It is not the first attempt to untangle the difficulties awaiting scholars unfamiliar with Roman archives and practices. In the early twentieth century, the Carnegie Institution of Washington attempted to help scholars in this predicament, publishing a number of guides to archival material for the history of the United States scattered around the Western world. In 1911, US diplomatic historian Carl Russell Fish (1876–1932) wrote a volume on "Roman and Other Italian Archives" meant as "a preliminary chart of a region still largely unexplored." Fish lived in Rome for less than a year (1908–9). Yet his century-old guide is still valuable for scholars embarking on a research trip to Rome. More recently (1996–2006), the Academy of American Franciscan History, mainly through the painstaking work of Slovenian archivist Anton Debevec (1897–1987) and his Italian assistant and successor, Giovanna Piscini, produced an eleven-volume "calendar" of the Archives of the Sacred Congregation "de Propaganda Fide." This was the Holy See's department in charge of all missions around the world, including, until 1908, the United States and Canada. Debeveč's *Calendar*, while a most useful finding aid, is therefore limited to one repository, albeit of vast importance for the history of the United States. It is this situation that Matteo Binasco's *Roman Sources* addresses. Having personally reconnoitered fifty-nine Roman repositories, Binasco moves well beyond where Fish's *Guide* left off over a century ago.[2]

Before taking the reader through a quick and selective survey of the relationship between the Holy See and the United States between 1763 and 1939, let us explain why these two dates were selected. The opening year, 1763, is the year that the Treaty of Paris ended the French and Indian War with Britain and France ceded its Canadian holdings to Britain. As a result, several provinces and colonies north of the Spanish Main came to constitute a vast British North America. As of 1776, most of them became part of the United States. It took another few decades before British North America (later Canada) and the United States agreed on their respective borders. In fact, many French-speaking Catholics later became citizens of the United States. During this early period, then, the borders between the two countries were blurred, and it would be a mistake to try to clearly distinguish between them; therefore, from the point of view of Catholic history, 1763 is a more useful opening date than 1776. As for 1939, at this time that year represents the official closing date for consultation of the Vatican archives. (Presently researchers are permitted access to documents extending through the pontificate of Pius XI, which ended with his death in 1939. Other material will become available in the future. The reason for this restriction of access is that the chronological limits for consultation are set by the popes. Each pope decides whether or not to extend the chronological limits.) For some time, Vatican archivists and international scholars have been whispering about the new accessibility of World War II and Cold War material. At this time, however, there are no set dates for the release of documents dated during the pontificate of Pius XII (1939–1958). As indicated by Binasco's *Roman Sources*, some post-1939 material, is, however, already available. For example, documents of the Second Vatican Council (1962–65), as well as those of the Ufficio Informazioni Vaticano and Prigionieri di Guerra (Vatican Information Office and Prisoners of War) dealing with the years 1939–47, are open to researchers. They are housed within the Vatican Secret Archives collections.

PART 2

Prior to the American War of Independence, the Catholic inhabitants of the British continental colonies, about 1 percent of the population, mostly lived in Maryland and Pennsylvania, with a few families in New Jersey and Virginia. Their only ministers were a handful of priests sent by the English Province of the Society of Jesus. Because the open practice of the Catholic religion was officially forbidden both at home and in the colonies, the activity of these priests was shrouded in secrecy. Very little of what took place in the British colonies made its way to Rome, either to the Sacred Congregation "de Propaganda Fide" or to the

Archivum Romanum Societatis Iesu, the latter being the central office of the society and home to the superior general. During the French and Indian War, the Holy See inquired as to who was in charge of the Catholics of English-speaking America. The vicars apostolic of London, Benjamin Petre (1672–1758) and Richard Challoner (1691–1781), who took Petre's place in 1758, confessed that in principle they should have been in charge, but that in practice they had never done anything in that regard.[3] After the Treaty of Paris, Challoner suggested that the Holy See appoint three vicars apostolic, one in Quebec City, one in Florida, and a third in Philadelphia. Nowhere else in the British Empire, he indicated, did Catholics enjoy more freedom for their religion than in Philadelphia.[4] Challoner also pointed out that the English Province of the Society of Jesus was doing its utmost to stop the appointment of a vicar apostolic for the British colonies. The Maryland Jesuits, he explained, had for so long enjoyed an exclusive mastery of those provinces that they would not suffer the arrival of a priest who did not belong to their society—and even less that of a bishop.[5]

In the event, no new arrangement was made until the American War of Independence. Well before the conclusion of the Treaty of Paris–Versailles (1783) and the arrival of the earliest petition from the United States in 1784, the Holy See had asked the nuncio in France, Archbishop Giuseppe Maria Doria Pamphili (1751–1816), to engage the French crown in ensuring that the treaty would contain a clause that would protect the Catholic Church in the United States.[6] In compliance with the long-established approach of Propaganda Fide, a body that traditionally favored the local ("national") clergy over "foreign" missionaries, the nuncio was instructed to seek the appointment of a superior chosen from among the American priests. In the end, Propaganda Fide succeeded in securing an American, John Carroll (1736–1815), as it had wished since the beginning.[7] Both the Holy See and the American clergy were well pleased with what they had achieved—and so was Benjamin Franklin (1706–90), the American negotiator, who privately boasted that Carroll's appointment had been achieved "on [his] Recommendation." Whatever Franklin's real influence, in the opinion of the Holy See officials, the Carroll choice was made in full agreement with the American representative.[8]

Carroll's 1789 appointment as bishop of Baltimore took place only a few months after the storming of the Bastille. The tragic events of the French Revolution turned some of the certainties of the Catholic world upside down. Protestant England became a haven for thousands of French émigrés, lay and religious, and the United States came to be regarded by some, even within the Holy See, as the promised land of a reborn Catholicism. In 1789 Antonio Dugnani (1748–1818), then nuncio in France, wrote that "the best solution is to go to America."[9] Napoleon Bonaparte (1769–1821) raised some enthusiasm at first, but his attitude toward the French church, let alone his imprisonment of the pope and the military *régime* that he imposed on Rome and the Papal States, transformed him into a "consummate brigand."[10] Seen from Carroll's view across the Atlantic, the French Revolution had tried to annihilate religion "through fire and sword," while Napoleon was trying to do the same through "the humiliation and the degradation" of a church "completely subjugated to the power of the state."[11]

The disruption caused by the French Revolution and the Napoleonic Wars made Atlantic communications often difficult and always unpredictable. Rome followed American events from afar and had few opportunities to influence its developments. Curiously enough, this was also the time of the appointment of the first United States consul to the Holy See. (Three earlier appointments had been made in Leghorn, Naples, and Genoa, in 1794, 1796, and 1797, respectively.) In 1797 Rome-born Giovanni Battista Sartori (1768–1854), who had lived in Philadelphia around 1793–95, won the coveted title, which he kept, fulfilling it by proxy, even after 1800, when he moved to Pennsylvania, where he was to live until 1832. (Sartori's correspondence is to be found in several Roman archives, and so is that of Felice Cicognani [fl.1814–48], a Roman lawyer who replaced him as US consul in 1823 and retained his title until 1836.)[12]

Meanwhile, the development of the Catholic Church in the United States proceeded along lines that were as difficult to plan as they had been impossible to foresee. One of the unexpected and yet somehow "providential" effects of the French Revolution was the arrival of about a hundred émigré priests in the United States. In 1793 Carroll remarked that the Illinois and Vincennes regions "in the past few months ha[d] been taking advantage of some excellent priests, provided by France."[13] Eventually the émigré priests replaced the generation, mainly consisting of former Jesuits, that had lived through the American War of Independence. Between 1789 and 1842 as many as fifteen out of thirty-seven appointments to US bishoprics went to French-speaking priests; twelve of them had been born in France.[14]

Given the dispersion of the French-speaking communities in the United States, their relatively small numbers, and the trickle of new arrivals from Europe, the power and influence of this French-speaking élite was astounding.[15] In conjunction with the clergy of Lower Canada (formerly the Province of Quebec), the émigré priests and their immediate successors managed to create a powerful international network, nourished by a common language, a shared culture, and a millenarian faith in the spiritual conquest of the American West, that lasted for at least two generations. Furthermore, these French-speaking priests shared another common feature, that is, a deep mistrust, if not a sheer loathing, of another group of Catholic immigrants: those of Irish origin. In the early nineteenth century, the Irish were certainly underrepresented in the United States hierarchy. Yet the French-speaking élite resented their alleged influence over the Holy See's top bureaucrats and despised them as representing the lowest orders of society. The Sulpician Ambroise Maréchal (1764–1828), archbishop of Baltimore from 1817 to 1828, was especially representative of this attitude. Meanwhile, the American church continued to grow and expand, even in the midst of internal conflicts and of the alleged threat represented by Evangelical revivalism.[16]

Although the United States was not among the Holy See's main preoccupations, after 1815 its existence slowly but surely made its way into the minds of Roman officials. Francesco Saverio Castiglioni (1761–1830) was created a cardinal in 1816 and died as Pius VIII in 1830, after a very short pontificate. In those fourteen years, the ecclesiastical map of North American Catholicism underwent profound changes. Four new bishoprics were added: Charleston and Richmond in the East (1820), Cincinnati in the West (1821), and Mobile in the South (1829).[17] Castiglioni's earliest acquaintance with the United States took place in 1822, when he was appointed to a special committee whose task was to broker an agreement between the Society of Jesus and the Archdiocese of Baltimore over the thorny question of the two-acre White Marsh estate in Maryland. Whether the propriety and the revenues of the estate should be reserved to the American province of the Society of Jesus was the contentious issue. Two years later, a memorandum containing Castiglioni's own reflections, among the most telling documents preserved in the Holy See's archives, shows that Propaganda Fide had a hidden agenda for the orderly development of the whole of North America. By placing all North American dioceses under two archbishoprics, Baltimore and Quebec City, "that noble idea of completing the Christian world on that side [of the world] would finally be implemented."[18] In 1829, during his short mandate as pope, Castiglioni had the opportunity to meet in Rome with a party of Osages from Saint Louis, Missouri. After two years spent touring the European capitals, the poor Osages found themselves so destitute that Pius VIII gave them permission to raise money by showing themselves in public, but then referred the issue to Propaganda Fide and avoided any further contact with them.[19]

Pius VIII's successor, Gregory XVI (1765–1846), who reigned from 1830 to 1846, also showed an unexpected interest in matters American. Before his election to the papacy, in his capacity as prefect of Propaganda Fide, Bartolomeo Alberto Cappellari (then known as Fra Mauro) had presided over delicate issues profoundly dividing the Catholic community in the United States. For US matters, Gregory XVI relied on Cicognani, who prior to his appointment as US consul in 1823 had been an English translator for Propaganda Fide and other Holy See departments. A self-taught admirer of the English-speaking world, Cicognani made sure that Gregory XVI honored American visitors with special audiences, showing them more attention than that granted to other nations.[20] Cicognani described the United States as home to an "essentially free and tollerating [sic]" government and suggested that the US federal mode of government could provide a solution to the convulsions of the Italian peninsula. Even Gregory XVI, Cicognani reported, appreciated American liberal institutions.[21] Dozens, if not hundreds, of American visitors flocked to Rome every year. The years from 1848 to 1850 alone witnessed over 850 American visitors, excluding permanent residents and the visitors' families.[22]

Aside from the popes' own interest—when this existed—more general reasons explain the sudden growth of documents of American interest in the Roman archives for the period after 1815, a true explosion that exponentially increased the number of letters, memoranda, proceedings, etc., relating to all sort of American issues. First of all, the 1808 erection of four new dioceses in the United States (Boston, New York, Philadelphia, and Bardstown), besides the elevation of Baltimore to the rank of archdiocese, increased the volume of institutional correspondence with the Holy See. (The first non-Spanish bishop of New Orleans was appointed in 1815.) Second, the earliest émigré priests and their successors proved to be keen and determined letter writers. They felt that their special role as political refugees, combined with a superior upbringing and learning, entitled them to special treatment on the part of the Holy See's bureaucrats. A third reason for this documentary explosion, and probably the most significant, was the growing conflict within the American church. Ethnic tensions, mainly between the French-speaking hierarchy and the growing immigrant community of Irish origin, together with the uneven restructuring of the Catholic Church along the lines of American democratic institutions, wrought havoc in many dioceses, parishes, churches, and communities. Those on opposite sides of these conflicts tended not to trust their hierarchical superiors; therefore, they directly petitioned Propaganda Fide and the Sacred Congregation of the Holy Office, the Holy See's department in charge of doctrinal issues. They also employed agents in Rome who actively lobbied for their cause. Often they also traveled to Rome in person to try to convince the pope and high-placed members of his entourage of the rectitude of their views.[23]

Finally, especially from the late 1820s onward, waves of a renewed European interest in the plight of the indigenous peoples of the American West reached Rome, both through visits by Native Americans and through European voices. The Perugia-born scoundrel priest Angelo Inglesi (ca. 1795–1825) embarked on a fundraising tour (1820–23) that elicited enthusiasm everywhere he went. In Rome he lectured the students of the Urban College, Propaganda Fide's elite school for prospective missionaries. He described "the needs of those savage peoples, ready to embrace our Holy Religion" and vividly pictured for these visionary youngsters a "vast field open to their zeal."[24] In 1832–34 the Urban College was home to two native students from L'Arbre Croche, Michigan, William Maccatebinessi or Maccodabinasse (d. 1833), also known as Blackbird, and Augustin Kiminitchagan (fl. 1834–40), also known as Augustin Hamelin. Unfortunately, the former died in Rome, and the latter soon returned home owing to health problems.[25] When Kiminitchagan became a chief in his own Ottawa Nation, the Holy See congratulated him and advised him to seek "the civilization, peace, and happiness" of his people by using "great moderation."[26] Almost at the same time, in 1834, another native student, the Californian Luiseño Pablo Tac (1822–41), joined the Urban College. Unfortunately, he too died in Rome before being able to return to his native land.[27]

PART 3

The early years of the pontificate of Pius IX (1792–1878), elected in 1846, did not result in further growing interest in the United States. Yet the European revolutions of 1848 and the experience of the Roman Republic (1849), short as it was, elicited a new awareness of Rome's position among Americans, Catholic as well as non-Catholic. Solicited by American Catholics, Pius IX even considered the option of transferring the Holy See to the other side of the Atlantic.[28] In consequence of the events of 1848–49, in 1852 Pius IX appointed Archbishop Gaetano Bedini (1806–64) nuncio in Brazil and apostolic delegate for Argentina, Uruguay, Paraguay, and Chile. Bedini was instructed to visit New York City and Washington, DC, on his way to South America. Bedini landed in New York City in 1853, but the strong opposition of Italian and German political exiles transformed his exploratory mission into a nightmare. In early 1854 he left the United States incognito and returned directly to Rome, not daring to show up in Brazil.[29]

Bedini's troubled journey shocked both Rome and American Catholics. The US hierarchy suggested that it was unwise to send Roman diplomats to a country, such as the United States, where such a fierce anti-Catholic movement existed.[30] Bedini himself rated his mission as important and successful. He had discovered to what extent the United States had improved economically, technologically, and politically. This was a country, he figured, that would soon lead the Americas. In his view, only huge Catholic immigration could prevent the United States from becoming a powerful anti-Catholic stronghold. On the other hand, if America were to become Catholic, the Catholic Church should protect the faith of the Catholic migrants to the New World.

In the instructions he received, Bedini had been asked to report on the situation of the existing Catholic immigrants.[31] In the report that he filed upon his return to Rome, addressed to cardinals Alessandro Barnabò (1801–74) and Giacomo Antonelli (1808–76), respectively prefect of Propaganda Fide and secretary of state, Bedini commented on the issue of the relationship between migration and the evident growth of Catholicism in North America. In his view, this growth had been an Irish victory. However, he warned against disregarding the other components of the new American Catholicism. If they felt abandoned, these groups could fall prey to any Protestant missionary, or even opt for an atheistic stand, as many participants in the revolutions of 1848 had done. Furthermore, Bedini disfavored the idea of replenishing a needy American Church through a call directed at Europe's clergy. The overabundance of European priests in the United States perpetuated old linguistic barriers; in doing so it pitted immigrant communities one against the other, thus dividing and weakening the American church. Instead, a shared language, English, ought to act as an element of cohesion. A new Pontifical North American College, Bedini finally suggested, ought to be erected in Rome to prepare American priests to deal with immigrant communities.[32]

At first, the 1854 Bedini report was not well received by the Roman bureaucracy. Several officials of the Holy See sided with the US bishops and blamed the nuncio for his disastrous journey to North America. They were also unconvinced that the future of Catholicism lay in the United States. Pius IX, however, who like Bedini was originally from Senigallia, stood firm in his support. When, in 1856, the former nuncio was appointed secretary of Propaganda Fide, he made a point of forcing everyone to read his report on the United States. Two years later, the Pontifical North American College was established in Rome.[33]

In the following decades, the Holy See showed a continuing interest in the flow of European immigrants to America.[34] In 1861 Cardinal Costantino Patrizi (1798–1876) reminded

Propaganda Fide of Bedini's opinions and blamed the US church for its poor assistance to Catholic immigrants.[35] In 1886 Germano Straniero (1839–1910), protonotary apostolic and domestic prelate of His Holiness, brought the cardinal's hat to James Gibbons (1834–1921), the archbishop of Baltimore. Straniero's lengthy report on his American journey echoes Patrizi's viewpoint on Bedini and the US church.[36] Meanwhile, the American prelates also worried about the immigrants' spiritual salvation. The issue was debated at the Third Plenary Council of Baltimore (November 9–December 7, 1884). Three years later, Propaganda Fide made a fateful decision in favor of "national" parishes, decreeing that American Catholics of German, Irish, French-Canadian, Italian, and Polish origin should be assisted by priests sharing the national origin of their parishioners.[37]

In 1885 Richard Gilmour (1824–91), bishop of Cleveland, Joseph Dwenger, bishop of Fort Wayne, and John Moore (1834–1901), bishop of Saint Augustine, the latter a former student of the Urban College, went to Rome to challenge the conclusions of the recent Third Plenary Council of Baltimore.[38] Upon arrival, they submitted to Propaganda Fide a fifteen-page printed memorandum on the "German question." In it they blamed American Catholics of German origin for asking for German priests even in places where Irish, French, or French-Canadians constituted the majority of parishioners. Gilmour and Moore explained that the "national" composition of American Catholicism had become more complex than ever. Newly arrived Bohemians and Poles, who had landed in the United States after the Civil War, had been joined in the 1880s by "Slavs," Hungarians, Italians, Swedes, and Russians. There was no need for German parishes, the bishops' memorandum concluded, because the second generations of all immigrant groups were melting into American society. In doing so, they abandoned their mother tongues and switched to English as their main language.[39]

Yet Moore's agenda included matters that went beyond the immigration issue. Together with other Urban College alumni, he exploited his Roman ties to lobby on a wide array of items. In fact, the German-Irish conflict had many facets whose outcomes often depended on the Vatican. For example, in the diocese of Newark, New Jersey, Patrick Corrigan (1835–94), an Irish-born priest who had arrived in the United States as a teenager, was involved in a lengthy conflict with his bishop, Winand M. Wigger (1841–1901), born in New York City of Westphalian parents. However, the issue at the heart of their struggle arose not from their different ethnic backgrounds but rather from their disagreement over whether bishops could be selected and presented by senior priests; as the issue at stake was the organization of an *American* Catholic Church, neither Corrigan nor Wigger emphasized his ethnic origin.[40]

The ethnic dimension was then only one aspect of a more complex dispute about the future of American Catholicism.[41] What concerns us here, however, is the fact that this dispute was argued before Roman officials, and these bureaucrats perceived only the ethnic aspect of this debate, or at best viewed it as the most significant issue at play. The historian must avoid blaming them altogether. After all, in the same fashion as these faraway bureaucrats learned the geography of North America in the seventeenth and eighteenth centuries, so they spent the nineteenth and twentieth centuries trying to comprehend the inner workings of American society. In this effort they were assisted by a number of mediators. These people—for example, Urban College alumni such as Moore, Corrigan, and Wigger—provided basic information on the United States but also interpreted it for the Vatican's use through the lenses of their own backgrounds and commitments.

In preparation for the Third Plenary Council of Baltimore, Propaganda Fide officials met in Rome with a number of American bishops on November 13, 1883. Two of them were Francis Silas Chatard (1834–1918), bishop of Indianapolis, and Charles J. Seghers (1839–86), archbishop of Oregon City. The former was an alumnus of the Urban College and from 1868 to 1876 had been rector of the Pontifical North American College; the latter, a Belgian by birth, was a former student of the American College in Louvain. In their opinion, labor organizations such as the Knights of Labor were in effect secret societies, by definition verboten for Catholics. For their part, Archbishop James Gibbons of Baltimore and Patrick A. Feehan (1829–1902), archbishop of Chicago, shared the opposite opinion. They justified their position with the need to establish a relationship with the working class and to integrate immigrants into the Church.[42]

The history of the struggle that shook the American church over the issue of the Knights of Labor is well known.[43] Of interest to American historians using Roman archives, however, is how the opposing sides attempted to convince the Vatican to share their views. On the one hand, Chatard asked for a straightforward condemnation of labor organizations. In his opinion, political, ethnic, and social (i.e., mutual aid) organizations were one and the same thing. He was especially negative about Irish associations, which he deemed all too inclined to resort to violent means. On February 5, 1885, for example, Chatard warned Cardinal Giovanni Simeoni (1816–92), the prefect of Propaganda Fide, that the Ancient Order of Hibernians was in fact a cover organization for former members of the "Molly Maguires," an antiestablishment secret society active in Ireland and in the eastern United States.[44]

On the other hand, Gibbons largely favored labor organizations and did not assume that they had an inherently violent character. A few days after Chatard sent his letter, Gibbons, too, wrote to Simeoni describing the Knights of Labor and asking that they be the object of a careful assessment. Their organization, which was fully legal under American law, boasted hundreds of thousands of members. While it was unfair to accuse them of violence, their political weight could indeed influence at least 500,000 votes in a federal election. Furthermore, many members of the Knights of Labor were Catholic immigrants. To alienate these men to please two or three bishops, Gibbons emphasized, would be unwise. It was true that Catholic members of the Knights of Labor were exposed to the negative influence of anarchists, socialists, and communists. Yet this was a danger that all Catholic workers had to endure in their workplaces. To condemn such a large organization, and hence to lose touch with its members, Gibbons concluded, would be a major error that would expose the American church to a new nativist threat similar to that of the Know-Nothings of a generation earlier.[45]

The conflict between the two positions represented by Chatard and Gibbons did not subside. On the contrary, it continued until World War I, and even later.[46] Over and over, Propaganda Fide and the Holy Office were requested to give their opinion on the Knights of Labor and other associations such as the Ancient Order of Hibernians, the Chosen Friends, the Independent Order of Foresters, the Knights of Pythias, the Machabees, the Odd Fellows, the Sons of England, the Sons of Temperance, or the United Workingmen.[47] Unable to act on their own, Vatican officials asked for the advice of foreign experts including David Fleming (1851–1915), an Irish Franciscan. Fleming came down in Gibbons's favor and explained his position through a number of reports on labor organizations in the United States, Canada, the United Kingdom, Australia, and Scandinavia.[48] In 1887 Gibbons found another warm supporter in Patrick G. Riordan (1841–1914), the archbishop of San Francisco. Riordan maintained workers' right to join unions and emphasized that nothing about the Knights of Labor could be construed as offensive to Catholics.[49] This prolonged debate was instrumental in convincing the Vatican of the significance of the social issue. One could stretch this argument a bit further and see Gibbons's influence behind the celebrated encyclical *Rerum novarum*, issued by Leo XIII (1810–1903) on May 15, 1891.[50]

Vatican files dealing with the US church show how and to what extent Vatican officials gathered information on American Catholicism in the 1880s. These files constantly grew in number, richness, and complexity. In 1887 Denis J. O'Connell (1849–1927), then rector of the Pontifical North American College in Rome, remarked that every American file in the Propaganda Fide archives was inextricably linked to others. Disputes between bishops and their clergy, diverse attitudes toward labor organization, ethnic grievances—they all represented facets of the same issue.[51] While they learned of and assessed the issues facing American Catholicism, Roman bureaucrats also wondered which Vatican department should take charge. Would Propaganda Fide keep its primacy, since the United States was still a missionary domain? Or should the Holy Office take charge, due to its responsibility for doctrinal issues? Or should not the secretary of state, on behalf of the pope, be in direct control, as he commonly managed international issues?[52] The decision to be made was of the utmost significance. In fact, according to Propaganda Fide's files on the Pontifical North American College of some years earlier, the American church was already reputed to be one of the most important and vigorous in the entire world.[53] Eventually, with the publication of the apostolic constitution *Sapienti consilio* in 1908, Pius X (1835–1914) removed most of the present-day United States and Canada, together with Britain, Ireland, the Netherlands, and Luxembourg, from the jurisdiction of Propaganda Fide and placed them under the Sacred Congregation of the Consistory.[54]

The establishment of an apostolic delegation in Washington, DC, in 1893 had already signaled a shift in the status of US Catholicism. Apostolic delegates were meant to examine and sort out significant issues and forward the appropriate files to Rome. Therefore, their ability to select their material and to explain its relevance had a strong and direct influence on Vatican knowledge and understanding of American Catholicism. The first apostolic delegate to the United States was Francesco Satolli (1839–1910), a former professor of dogmatic theology at the Urban College. Satolli went twice to the United States, first in 1889 and then in 1892.[55] On the eve of his second departure, the secretary of state, Mariano Rampolla del Tindaro (1843–1913), outlined the main issues on which he expected to be briefed: Catholic schools, ecclesiastical discipline and dissension within the US hierarchy, and conflict involving the immigrant clergy and faithful of French-Canadian, German, and Irish origin.[56] Satolli's official appointment as apostolic delegate came a few months after his arrival in the United States in 1892. On this occasion, his responsibilities were confirmed.[57] However, as is clear from his letters and even clearer from the files he sent to Rome, Satolli did not fully succeed in the tasks that Rampolla del Tindaro had entrusted to him. While he managed to defuse the Catholic schools issue, he failed to appease opposing immigrant communities and to stop dissension within the hierarchy. Therefore, when Satolli was replaced in 1896, the bulk of his instructions was reiterated to his successor, Sebastiano Martinelli (1848–1918). He was to appease immigrant communities and to enforce ecclesiastical discipline. At the end of his mandate (1901), however, Martinelli had hardly been more successful than his predecessor in fulfilling these tasks.[58]

In 1902 Archbishop Diomede Falconio (1842–1917), a Reformed Franciscan who had been apostolic delegate to Canada since 1899, was reassigned to the United States.[59] Falconio had a good firsthand knowledge of North America. He had arrived there for the first time in 1865, and from 1866 to 1871, and again in 1882–83, he had been on the faculty of the Franciscan Saint Bonaventure College in Alleghany, New York. In between, he had been secretary to Enrico Carfagnini (1823–1904), the bishop of Harbour Grace, in Newfoundland, a fellow Franciscan who had been born in the Kingdom of the Two Sicilies. Upon his return to Italy, Falconio became procurator general of the Order of Friars Minor (1889) and in 1892 was appointed bishop of Lacedonia. During his nine years in Washington, DC (1902–11), Falconio's strategy with regard to immigrant communities was rather consistent. He supported every community that asked for "national" priests. He imposed "ethnic" bishops or coadjutors wherever immigrant communities were particularly strong, as was the case for Chicago's Poles and the French Americans of Manchester, New Hampshire. When the appointment of an Irish or American bishop could not be avoided, he required that the candidate know the language of his prospective flock. Finally, he convinced Propaganda Fide that his secretary should be an English-speaking priest with a good grasp of current American affairs— although this required a ten-month epistolary exchange (April 1903–January 1904).[60]

Although Falconio, in turn, was not fully successful in fulfilling the Holy See's mandate, especially concerning ecclesiastical discipline, he was instrumental in persuading the Vatican to adopt his strategy regarding American affairs. This is evident from the 1912 instructions that Cardinal Gaetano De Lai (1853–1928), secretary of the Sacred Congregation of the Consistory, handed to Falconio's successor as apostolic delegate, Giovanni Bonzano (1867–1927). Bonzano's main task was to appease immigrant communities. De Lai warned Bonzano that the Church was running the risk of losing "millions" of souls because ethnic tensions now involved not only old immigrants of Irish, German, and French-Canadian origin but also new immigrants arriving from Poland, Italy, and Ukraine. Bonzano was not to neglect any immigrant community, old or new. They were all to be provided with priests and schools. In dioceses where the majority of the faithful were not Irish, Bonzano was instructed to support non-Irish episcopal candidates.[61] Bonzano led the apostolic delegation until 1922. He did his best to accomplish his mission even through the difficult years of World War I. He reported to the Vatican, to the American bishops, and to US federal authorities on the plight of German-speaking immigrants during the war. In Bonzano's view, they were unjustly accused of being enemies of the very country they had chosen for themselves.[62]

Appointed in 1922, Apostolic Delegate Pietro Fumasoni Biondi (1872–1960) continued the visitation of each diocese of the United States that his predecessor Bonzano had begun toward the end of his mandate. Fumasoni Biondi served until 1933, and the Vatican assessed the report of his nine-year visitation in 1932–33. He had amassed and organized reams of data about immigrant groups, together with data about Catholics belonging to the African American, Mexican American, and Native American communities. Overall, Fumasoni Biondi was particularly skilled in evaluating the linguistic struggle ongoing in American Catholicism. In the end, however, he favored a policy of gradual Americanization.[63] Many of these documents ended up in the archives of the Sacred Congregation of the Consistory, which after World War I took control of the American issue. Consequently, the number of documents of interest for the United States grew consistently, including those related to the apostolic visitation of the American dioceses in 1922–31.[64] In the 1920s, other Vatican departments, or congregations, also began to take an interest in the Catholic Church of the United States. In 1923 the Sacred Congregation of the Council (renamed the Congregation for the Clergy in 1967) was charged with overseeing discipline and the teaching of catechism in all American dioceses. In 1929 it was also charged with overseeing the administration of the American dioceses, so disputes of an ethnic nature fell within its new responsibilities, at least as far as local parishes and schools were concerned.[65]

Personal interests in North American matters on the part of the Vatican's top bureaucrats could indeed make a difference. For example, from 1919 to 1930 the prefect of the Congregation of the Council was Cardinal Donato Sbarretti (1856–1939), a highly influential member of the Roman Curia. He had been a member of the apostolic delegation in Washington, DC, and from 1902 to 1910 he was the apostolic delegate to Canada.[66] Together with Fumasoni Biondi, Sbarretti took a keen interest in the financial administration of the American dioceses, even before the crash of 1929. Given that interest, documents preserved in the archives of the Congregation of the Council offer precise information on interwar diocesan assets, including churches, schools, hospitals, and missions.[67] As far as discipline was concerned, the mandate of the Congregation of the Council granted it jurisdiction over a number of disputes involving bishops and immigrant communities. A most telling example is the fierce clash between the bishop of Providence, Rhode Island, William A. Hickey (1869–1933), and a group of Franco Americans of the diocese, known as La Sentinelle, that took place in 1924–29.[68]

When the Sentinelle affair ended, Vatican diplomats discovered that it was also the end of old-style ethnic disputes within the American Catholic Church. Ethnic conflicts did not stop abruptly following the Immigration Act of 1924 and the subsequent great reduction in Catholic immigration, but they were gradually superseded by other questions: How should the Vatican position itself with regard to the administration of President Franklin D. Roosevelt (1882–1945)?[69] How could the apostolic delegate convince the American government of the danger represented by communism, in both the Soviet Union and the rest of the world?[70] What should be the apostolic delegate's stand on Nazism? As was well known, the archbishop of Chicago, George Mundelein (1872–1939), was vehemently opposed to Adolf Hitler; the Vatican, for its part, wondered whether communism, Nazism, racism, and eugenics could be regarded as different, yet related, facets of totalitarianism.[71] Could diplomatic relations between the Vatican and the United States be improved, in spite of the political and social turmoil of the 1930s?[72] The unexpected death of Pius XI (1857–1939) left a number of these questions hanging for the duration of World War II. The danger of totalitarianism for Western democracies continued to be one of the Vatican's main preoccupations. Because racism had been a major aspect of totalitarianism in Europe, the Vatican was again confronted with the African American issue in the United States.[73]

PART 4

Having reached the end of this selective survey of the relationship between the Vatican and the United States between 1763 and 1939, the curious reader must undoubtedly have noticed that this introduction draws mainly on major archival repositories whose existence is generally well known, such as the Vatican Secret Archives, the Holy Office, Propaganda Fide, etc. (The countless documents they store are, of course, far from having been fully exploited or even known.) These institutional archives make it possible to study, often in astonishing detail, the many facets of the relationship between Rome and the United States over the course of the last two and a half centuries. Matteo Binasco's *Roman Sources* describes these archives and tells their potential users about their organization as well as the availability of appropriate finding aids and the present state of the historiographical literature. This is already a major asset that any new or seasoned researcher in Rome cannot fail to appreciate. But there is more. Simply by reading the names of the fifty-nine Roman repositories surveyed by Binasco and perusing their related "descriptions of holdings," one is impressed by their variety, a variety that mirrors the complexity of the relations between the United States (itself a rather mixed bag, to say the least) and that most complex galaxy that was—and to a certain extent still is—Rome's Catholic Church: the pope, the curia, the sacred congregations, the bureaucracy, the colleges, the resident foreign clergy, the lobbyists, the occasional visitors, the secular clergy, the regular clergy, and the women's communities and congregations. Let us then conclude this introduction by emphasizing some fresh insights that one gathers by reading—and using—Binasco's *Roman Sources*, with some examples drawn from documentary evidence discovered by its compiler during his pilgrimages from one Roman repository to another.[74]

The first distinction that one must make is between open and closed archives. For a variety of reasons, some archives and libraries are, in fact, closed to researchers. For example, the archives of the Venerable English College (founded in 1579), the Urban College of Propaganda Fide (1627), and the Pontifical Irish College (1628) were closed at the time of this writing. That is a pity. Many North American bishops (Francis Kenrick [1797–1863], archbishop of Philadelphia, for one) studied at the Urban College. Given the number of Irish priests and bishops who passed through the Irish College before serving in the United States, this archive contains a wealth of information on New York, Pittsburgh, Charleston, Chicago, Detroit, and other American locations. Meanwhile, in the first half of the nineteenth century Robert Gradwell (1777–1833) and Cardinal Nicholas P. S. Wiseman (1802–65), while rectors of the English College, constantly lobbied on behalf of their American associates. Also closed are the archives of the Society of the Catholic Apostolate, whose members are better known as the Pallottines. In 1884 they established the church of Our Lady of Mount Carmel in New York, a key institution for the local Italian and Italian American community. The Archives of the Maestre Pie Filippini and the General Archives of the Missionary Sisters of the Sacred Heart of Jesus are unavailable as well. These congregations provided significant assistance to the newly arrived Italian community; Mother Francesca (Frances) Saverio Cabrini (1850–1917), canonized in 1946, founded the Sacred Heart of Jesus community. Lack of staff seems to be the main reason for the unavailability of many of these archives; for example, at the Urban College the archives were open to researchers in the 1990s, whereas today they are closed. (Still, researchers are advised to check from time to time. The English College, for example, is simply reorganizing its holdings under the capable supervision of Schwarzenbach Research Fellow Maurice Whitehead, who was in charge of its archives at the time this book went to press.)

Among the open repositories, it is useful to distinguish between libraries and archives. Libraries store books, whereas archives preserve documents accumulated as a result of some institutional activity. In Rome, however, such a distinction must be used with care. Since most of the libraries are centuries old, they often also include a manuscript section. Take the Biblioteca Apostolica Vaticana (Vatican Library). Established around the fourth century—a thousand years before the invention of the printing press—the library holds some eighty thousand manuscripts in addition to drawings, paintings, and maps. A report on the Jesuits in Maryland in the 1630s, forwarded by the nuncio in Flanders, Giorgio Bolognetti (1595–1686), is there, as are the reports on New Orleans, Philadelphia, and Boston written between 1906 and 1910 by Italian journalist and vice consul Luigi Villari (1876–1959). Outside Vatican City proper, but still part of the Holy See's heritage, other libraries—such as the Casanatense, Vallicelliana, Angelica, and Corsiniana—hold unexpected treasures, such as the 1816–18 letters of Louisiana Vincentian Felice De Andreis (1778–1820) and the early twentieth-century correspondence of three renowned American and Italian scientists, Griffith C. Evans (1887–1973), George E. Hale (1868–1938), and Vito Volterra (1860–1940). Another library, that of the Waldensian Faculty of Theology, holds documentary material on the life of Alessandro Gavazzi (1809–89), a former Cleric Regular of Saint Paul (Barnabite) who became a Protestant chaplain in the army of Italian military leader Giuseppe Garibaldi (1807–82); his 1853–54 promotional tour in New York, Montreal, and Quebec City almost got him lynched.

As for archives proper, their variety is mindboggling. Institutional archives such as those of the Vatican Secret Archives, the Holy Office, or Propaganda Fide closely follow the daily routines of the Roman Church. It was the Holy Office (now the Congregation for the Doctrine of the Faith), for example, that had the last word on a prospective marriage between a Native American woman and a European settler, granting proper dispensations, or making their union null and void. Documents of American interest may also be found in unlikely institutional repositories, such as the Archivio Storico Generale della Fabbrica di San Pietro (the body overseeing the building of Saint Peter's Basilica). The Fabbrica features the correspondence of prominent members of the American hierarchy such as Bishop William H. O'Connell (1859–1944) of Boston and Archbishop Michael Joseph Curley (1879–1947) of Baltimore, who expressed their wish to purchase copies of the Saint Peter's mosaics. In the Archivio Storico della Congregazione per le Chiese Orientali, Binasco bumped into a politically incorrect opinion given in 1916 by the bishop of Columbus, James J. Hartley (1858–1944). The local Slovakian community of Byesville, Ohio, had petitioned Pope Benedict XV (1854–1922) for a priest who spoke their language. Bishop Hartley, who was against such a request, explained his position: "In the next world the Slovaks will not be able to speak to God in the Slovak tongue anyway."

Other Roman institutions remained quite separate from the Holy See proper, and their archives tend to reflect the life of each community. To the Irish College and the Basilica of San Paolo fuori le Mura (Saint Paul Outside the Walls), the Scots College and the Pontifical Institute of Santa Maria dell'Anima (a church traditionally linked to the German-speaking community) must be added. The institute's archives preserve, for example, the correspondence of Alois Hudal (1885–1963), who was its rector from 1923 to 1952 and played a key role in the migratory network that allowed many Nazi German and Croatian families to take refuge in the United States or South America after World War II. Other archives came into being after the Kingdom of Italy's 1870 conquest and annexation of Rome. It is in the Archivio di Stato di Roma and in Italy's Archivio Centrale dello Stato that researchers must look for the personal files of the *zuavi pontifici* (normally of Irish or Quebec origin) who fought for the pope against Garibaldi or for the records that Fascist Italy kept of its political exiles who had fled to the United States.

We have left for last any mention of the archives of the regular orders. But here is Elizabeth Galitzine (1797–1844), the assistant general of the Society of the Sacred Heart of Jesus, who in the early 1840s recommended that her sisters not let their disappointment show when dealing with the American public: "Avoid any air of repulsion and of boredom for the country, its customs, and its laws. Avoid any comparison with other countries that might be detrimental to America. Americans shy away from those who hurt their national pride." This document, and the archives of the order (not to be confused with Saint Frances Xavier Cabrini's community, mentioned above), are found in Rome, and so are those of several other women's orders, among them the Daughters of Saint Mary of Providence, who in 1913 established their first US mission in Chicago.

As for the men's orders, the significance for the study of US history of archives such as those of the Jesuits, the Franciscans, the Capuchins, the Carmelites and Discalced Carmelites, the Servants of Mary, the Dominicans, the Redemptorists, the Oblates, the Brothers of the Christian Schools (or Christian Brothers), and the Congregation of the Mission (or Vincentians) is also well known. In a 1917 letter discovered by Binasco, an American Capuchin explained to his superior why he and his confrères were never invited to social occasions. Could it be, he wondered, that "the appendages on our face, which people refer to as hairy entanglements, are repulsive to the American idea of appearance"? In fact, he added, "Catholics as well as non-Catholics are so accustomed to see priests clean-shaven," that the fathers had difficulty explaining that the Capuchins were priests, in spite of their whiskers and beards. This very practical preoccupation reminded us of other documents that we had found in Roman archives, such as a letter from a parish priest who wondered whether he could employ a Protestant organist in his church or a bishop who asked whether he could accept an oath taken on a Protestant Bible.

Seasoned Roman archive visitors all have their own special documents that they have encountered in the course of their research, and students and scholars visiting Rome for the first time can look forward to their own thrilling moments of discovery. This new book will whet their appetite for research in Rome and ease their entry into the maze of archives there. With time, patience, and the help of Binasco's *Roman Sources for the History of American Catholicism, 1763–1939*, the fog that obscures the view of those new to Roman archives will dissolve, leaving many great opportunities for fruitful research.

NOTES

1. Although this introduction was conceived and written collaboratively, Luca Codignola is the main author of Part 2, while Matteo Sanfilippo is the main author of Part 3.

2. Carl Russell Fish, *Guide to the Materials for American History in Roman and Other Italian Archives*, 7 vols. and index (Washington, DC: Carnegie Institution, 1911); Finbar Kenneally, OFM, ed., *United States Documents in the Propaganda Fide Archives: A Calendar. First Series* (Washington, DC: Academy of American Franciscan History, 1966–81); Anton Debevec, Mathias C. Kiemen, OFM, Alexander Wyse, OFM, James McManamon, OFM, William J. Short, OFM, and Giovanna Piscini, eds., *United States Documents in the Propaganda Fide Archives: A Calendar. Second Series*, 6 vols. to date (Washington, DC: Academy of American Franciscan History, 1980–2006).

3. [Christopher Stonor] to [Propaganda Fide], [February 1753], fols. 529rv–530rv, *Congressi, America Antille*, vol. 1, Archives of the Sacred Congregation "de Propaganda Fide" (Archivio Storico de Propaganda Fide, or APF); Stonor to Propaganda Fide, [December 1756], fols. 273rv–276rv, vol. 767, Scritture Originali riferite nelle Congregazioni Generali (SOCG), APF. On Stonor and, more broadly, on the vicars apostolic, see Thomas M. McCoog, SJ, "'Libera nos Domine?' The Vicars Apostolic and the Suppressed/Restored English Province of the Society of Jesus," in *Early Modern English Catholicism: Identity, Memory and Counter-Reformation*, ed. James E. Kelly and Susan Royal (Leiden: Brill, 2016), 81–101.

4. [Stonor] to [Propaganda Fide], [ca. August 2, 1763] (vicar apostolic in Philadelphia, Freedom), ser. B, vol. 137, S*tonor's Roman Agency*, 417–23, Westminster Diocesan Archives, or WDA; Richard Challoner to Stonor, September 6, 1763 (vicars apostolic in Quebec City, Florida), fols. 1rv–2rv, vol. 46, no. 67, WDA.

5. Challoner to Stonor, February 15, 1765, fols. 1rv–2rv, vol. 46, no. 81, WDA; Challoner to Stonor, June 4, 1771, fols. 543rv–544rv, vol. 1, *Congressi, America Centrale*, APF.

6. John Lewis, Bernard Diderick, Ignatius Matthews, James Walton, and John Carroll to Pius VI, November 10, 1783 (petition), fols. 349rv–350rv, vol. 2, *Congressi, America Centrale*, APF; [Leonardo Antonelli] to Giuseppe Maria Doria Pamphili, January 15, 1783 (treaty), fols. 58rv–59rv, vol. 242, *Lettere*, APF.

7. [Antonelli] to Carroll, June 9, 1784, fols. 492v–495rv, vol. 244, *Lettere*, APF; [Antonelli] to Carroll, July 23, 1785, fols. 437v–441rv, vol. 246, *Lettere*, APF; [Antonelli] to Carroll, Robert Molyneux, and John Ashton, July 12, 1788, fols. 491v–493r, vol. 252, *Lettere*, APF. The higher appointment was deferred due to the unclear financial implications of an American diocese and the uncertainty over Congress's attitude toward such an appointment.

8. [Antonelli] to Carroll, June 9, 1784, fols. 492v–495rv, vol. 244: *Lettere*, APF; [Antonelli] to Doria Pamphili, July 31, 1785, fols. 624rv–625rv, vol. 244, *Lettere*, APF. Quotation in Franklin's diary, July 1, 1784, in *The Writings of Benjamin Franklin, Collected and Edited with a Life and Introduction*, ed. Albert Henry Smyth (New York: Macmillan, 1905–10), 10:350.

9. Antonio Dugnani to [Francesco Savero Zelada], November 2, 1789, fols. 97v–98r, vol. 580: *Segreteria di Stato, Francia*, Vatican Secret Archives (Archivio Segreto Vaticano, or ASV). Quotation in fol. 98r: "il miglior partito è quello di andare in America."

10. Louis-Charles-Marie de Lombard de Bouvens to Joseph-Octave Plessis, August 12, 1810, ser. 90 CM, vol. 1, no. 94, Archives of the Archdiocese of Quebec (Archives de l'Archevêché de Québec or AAQ): "brigand consommé."

11. Carroll to [Plessis], July 28, 1806, in Thomas O'Brien Hanley, ed., *The John Carroll Papers* (Notre Dame, IN: University of Notre Dame Press, 1976), 2:524.

12. *Journal of the Executive Proceedings of the Senate of the United States of America*, vol. 5, 1797–99, 247 (Giovanni Battista Sartori); vol. 17, 1821–23, 337 (Felice Cicognani) (Washington, DC: US Government Printing Office, 1828–75).

13. [Carroll] to [Jean-François Hubert], May 12, 1793, vol. 1, no. 5, 7 CM, AAQ.

14. Here are the fifteen appointments: Jean-Louis-Anne-Madeleine Lefèbvre de Cheverus (1810), Benoît-Joseph Flaget (1810), Louis-Guillaume-Valentin Dubourg (1815), Ambroise Maréchal (1817), Jean-Baptiste David (1819), Jean Dubois (1826), Michel Portier (1826), Léo-Raymond DeNeckère (1830), Guy-Ignace Chabrat (1834), Simon-Guillaume Bruté de Remur

(1834), Antoine Blanc (1835), Jean-Mathieu-Pierre Loras (1837), Celestin-René-Laurent Guynemer de La Hailandière (1839), Pierre-Paul Lefevère (1841), and Jean-Marie Odin (1842). In the same period, episcopal appointments were made that concerned candidates of Irish origin (eleven) born in the United States (eight) and in England, the German states, and the Kingdom of the Two Sicilies (one each).

15. For the new arrivals, see Marcel Fournier, *Les Français au Québec 1765–1865: Un mouvement migratoire méconnu* (Sillery: Septentrion, and Paris: Éditions Christian, 1995).

16. On the anti-Irish attitude, see Luca Codignola, "Conflict or Consensus? Catholics in Canada and in the United States, 1780–1820," Canadian Catholic Historical Association, *Historical Studies* 55 (1988): 43–59.

17. For the history of Catholicism in the United States, see the syntheses by Robert T. Handy, *A History of the Churches in the United States and Canada* (Oxford: Clarendon, 1976); James J. Hennessey, SJ, *American Catholics: A History of the Roman Catholic Community in the United States* (New York: Oxford University Press, 1981); Jay P. Dolan, *The American Catholic Experience: A History from Colonial Times to the Present* (Garden City, NY: Doubleday, 1985); Mark A. Noll, *A History of Christianity in the United States and Canada* (Grand Rapids, MI: William B. Eerdmans, 1992) and Noll, *The Old Religion in a New World: The History of North American Christianity* (Grand Rapids, MI: William B. Eerdmans, 2002); Patrick Carey, *The Roman Catholics in America* (Westport, CT: Praeger, 1996); and the pertinent chapters in Stephen J. Stein, ed., *The Cambridge History of Religions in America* (Cambridge: Cambridge University Press, 2012). For the chronology of episcopal appointments, see Joseph Bernard Cole, *Dictionary of the American Hierarchy* (New York: J. F. Wagner, 1964); and Charles N. Bransom Jr., *Ordination of US Catholic Bishops, 1790–1989: A Chronological List* (Washington, DC: National Conference of Catholic Bishops and US Catholic Conference, 1990). See also the website of the *Official Catholic Directory* at http://www.officialcatholicdirectory.com/OCD/home.

18. Memorandum [prepared by Francesco Saverio Castiglioni in January 1823 for the general congregation of February 17, 1823, postponed until February 24, 1824], fols. 76rv–82rv, vol. 186, *Acta*, APF: "per così mettere in pratica quella nobile idea di completare il mondo cristiano in quella parte [North America] con l'arcivescovo di Québec e i suoi vescovi suffraganei."

19. Louis-Pierre-Vincent-Gaston-Gabriel Bellocq to Giovanni Soglia Cerroni, Rome, July 1, 1829 (permission), fols. 303[a]rv–303[b]rv, vol. 192, *Acta*, APF. At what time Pius VIII granted his permission for the Osages to be shown in public is unclear; still, that permission might have been granted on Pius VIII's behalf by a member of his bureaucracy. On Pius VIII, see Codignola, "Pius VIII and North America, 1816–1830," *Annali Accademici Canadesi* 10–11 (1995): 3–35.

20. Felice Cicognani to Tommaso Bernetti, February 20, 1832 (scheduling Americans' audiences), [unfoliated], fasc. 2, 1832, busta 663, rubr. 298, *Segreteria di Stato, Esteri*, 1831–58, ASV.

21. Cicognani to John Quincy Adams, December 31, 1824, in Leo Francis Stock, ed., *Consular Relations between the United States and the Papal States: Instructions and Despatches* (Washington, DC: American Catholic Historical Association, 1945), 12: "free and tolerating"; Cicognani to Martin Van Buren, February 21, 1831, in ibid., 33: "prevent jealousies"; Cicognani to John Forsyth, February 14, 1835, in ibid., 45 (Gregory XVI).

22. Howard Rosario Marraro, "American Travellers in Rome, 1848–1850," *Catholic Historical Review* 29, no. 4 (January 1944): 470–509 (882 visitors); Marraro, "Viaggiatori americani a

Roma," *Rassegna storica del Risorgimento* 51, no. 2 (aprile–giugno 1964): 237–56 (overall figure downsized to 858).

23. See Luca Codignola, "Roman Catholic Conservatism in a New North Atlantic World, 1760–1829," in *William and Mary Quarterly*, 3rd ser., 64, no. 4 (October 2007): 717–56, republished in Marguerite Ragnow and William D. Phillips Jr., eds., *Religious Conflict and Accommodation in the Early Modern World* (Minneapolis: University of Minnesota, Center for Early Modern History, 2011), 153–206. See also Catherine O'Donnell, "John Carroll and the Origins of an American Catholic Church, 1783–1815," *William and Mary Quarterly*, 3rd ser., 58, no. 1 (January 2011): 101–26.

24. Giovanni Giuseppe Vincenzo Argenti to John Thomas Troy, May 19, 1821, fol. 170rv, ser. Roman Correspondence, Troy, AB2/28/1, no. 135, Archives of the Archdiocese of Dublin: "rappresenta i bisogni di quei Popoli Selvaggi pronti ad abbracciare la nostra S. Religione." On Inglesi, see Luca Codignola, "Angelo Inglesi, from Rome with Love: The Ultimate Scoundrel Priest in North America, 1814–25," in *Itineraria* 15 (2016): 151–203.

25. For the most recent literature, see Giovanni Pizzorusso, "Indiani del Nordamerica a Roma (1826–1841)," *Archivio della Società Romana di Storia Patria* 116 (1993): 395–411, esp. 403–8; Roger Antonio Fortin, *Faith and Action: A History of the Archdiocese of Cincinnati, 1821–1996* (Columbus: Ohio State University Press, 2002), 29–30, 408n13; and Gregory Evans Dowd, *War under Heaven: Pontiac, the Indian Nations, and the British Empire* (Baltimore: Johns Hopkins University Press, 2002), 21.

26. [Angelo Mai] to Augustin Wummelin [recte Augustin Hamelin], August 20, 1836, fols. 704rv–705r, vol. 317, *Lettere*, APF: "civilizzazione, pace, e felicità," "molta moderazione." Two years later, more room was made available for prospective native students from Nova Scotia in spite of the college's being full, "given the special importance of the matter." Assurances were to be given, however, that they would not suffer with the Roman climate. See [Giacomo Filippo Fransoni] to Colin Francis MacKinnon, March 17, 1838, fols. 260rv–263r, vol. 318, *Lettere*, APF: "attesa la particolare importanza della cosa."

27. José Ildefonso de La Peña, SJ, to Carlo Maria Pedicini, September 18, 1834 (Pablo Tac's arrival), fols. 652rv–653rv, vol. 16, *Congressi, Collegio Urbano*, APF. On Tac, see Lisbeth Haas, ed., *Pablo Tac, Indigenous Scholar: Writing on Luiseño Language and Colonial History, c. 1840* (Berkeley: University of California Press, 2011).

28. Matteo Sanfilippo, *L'affermazione del cattolicesimo nel Nord America: Élite, emigranti e chiesa cattolica negli Stati Uniti e in Canada, 1750–1920* (Viterbo: Sette Città, 2003), 17, and Frank J. Coppa, *The Modern Papacy since 1789* (London and New York: Routledge, 2016). See also Coppa, *Pius IX: Crusader in a Secular Age* (Boston: Twayne, 1979), and Coppa, *Cardinal Giacomo Antonelli and Papal Politics in European Affairs* (Albany: State University of New York Press, 1990).

29. Matteo Sanfilippo, "Tra antipapismo e cattolicesimo: Gli echi della Repubblica romana e i viaggi in Nord America di Gaetano Bedini e Alessandro Gavazzi (1853–1854)," in *Gli Americani e la Repubblica Romana nel 1849* (Rome: Gangemi, 2000), 159–87, and Sanfilippo, "Alessandro Gavazzi: oltre l'Italia, l'America," *Barnabiti studi* 28 (2011): 245–67; David J. Endres, "Know-Nothings, Nationhood, and the Nuncio: Reassessing the Visit of Archbishop Bedini," *US Catholic Historian* 21, no. 4 (Fall 2003): 1–16.

30. See James F. Connelly, *The Visit of Archbishop Gaetano Bedini to the United States of America (June 1853–February 1854)* (Rome: Università Gregoriana Editrice, 1960), 160–64. For fifty years, American bishops continued to use the negative example of the Bedini riots to gain more freedom from Rome. See, for example, fols. 17rv–20rv, fasc. 3, rubr. 283, *Segreteria di Stato*, ASV. See also John Tracy Ellis, *The Life of James Cardinal Gibbons, Archbishop of Baltimore, 1834–1921* (Milwaukee: Bruce, 1952), 1:595–600, and Gerald P. Fogarty, SJ, *The Vatican and the Americanist Crisis: Denis J. O'Connell, American Agent in Rome, 1885–1903* (Rome: Università Gregoriana Editrice, 1974), 25, 219, 226.

31. Propaganda Fide's instructions to Gaetano Bedini (April 5, 1853), fols. 315v–317r, vol. 343: *Lettere*, APF.

32. Final report of Gaetano Bedini to Cardinal Giacomo Antonelli, [1854], fols. 9rv–50rv, fasc. 1, rubr. 251, *Segreteria di Stato, 1854*, ASV. See Robert F. MacNamara, *The American College in Rome, 1855–1955* (Rochester, NY: Christopher Press, 1956). On the North American College, see also Stephen M. DiGiovanni, *The Second Founder: Martin J. O'Connor and the Pontifical North American College* (Bloomington, IN: Trafford Publishing, 2013), and DiGiovanni, *Aggiornamento on the Hill of Janus: The American College in Rome, 1955–1979* (Downers Grove, IL: Midwest Theological Forum, 2016).

33. Bedini's report circulated as an appendix to the *ponenza* of 1856 on the Provincial Councils of Baltimore, Cincinnati, Saint Louis, and New Orleans (fols. 373rv–532rv, esp. 488rv–532rv, vol. 220, *Acta*, APF). For the Pontifical North American College, see the *ponenza* on its establishment in fols. 1rv–54rv, vol. 225, APF. A *ponenza* was a file assembling several documents on a certain issue scheduled for discussion.

34. Although the two words are often used as synonyms, we have elected to use "Holy See" for the years until 1871 and "Vatican" from 1871 onward. In 1870 the Kingdom of Italy conquered Rome and the Vatican became a very, very small state confined within its current borders. See David Kertzer, *Prisoner of the Vatican: The Pope's Secret Plot to Capture Rome from the New Italian State* (Boston: Houghton Mifflin Company, 2005), chap. 5.

35. Costantino Patrizi, *ponenza* on the Catholic Church in the United States, 1861, fols. 1rv–9rv, especially fol. 7r, vol. 225, *Acta*, APF.

36. Germano Straniero's report, 1886, fasc. 10, rubr. 280, 1902, *Segreteria di Stato*, ASV. The Germano Straniero Papers are now housed in the University of Notre Dame Archives.

37. *Rapporto sull'emigrazione italiana con Sommario*, November 1887, fols. 186rv–217rv, vol. 257, *Acta*, APF.

38. The Vatican delayed its approval of the council's proceedings, which were published one year later as *Acta et Decreta Concilii Plenarii Baltimorensis Tertii* (Baltimore: John Murphy, 1886).

39. Richard Gilmour and John Moore, *Memoriale sulla questione dei tedeschi nella chiesa di America*, Rome, October 2, 1885 (a printed report on the German issue in the United States), fol. 480rv, vol. 43/2, *Congressi, America Centrale*, APF.

40. Patrick Corrigan sent to Propaganda Fide his pamphlet *The Bishop and the Priest* (New York: American News Company, 1884), now to be found in fols. 37rv–78rv, vol. 43/1: *Congressi, America Centrale*. A contemporary view of Corrigan is in "Father Patrick Corrigan Dead: The Celebrated Hoboken Priest Died Last Evening of Pneumonia," *New York Times*, January 10, 1894, 1. A recent appraisal is in Kevin E. McKenna, *The Battle for Rights in the United States*

Catholic Church (New York: Paulist Press, 2007), 127–44. See also Colman Barry, *The Catholic Church and the German Americans* (Washington, DC: Catholic University of America Press, 1953), and Philip Gleason, *The Conservative Reformers: German-American Catholics and the Social Order* (Notre Dame, IN: University of Notre Dame Press, 1968).

41. See John T. McGreevy, *Catholicism and American Freedom: A History* (New York: W.W. Norton, 2003), 91–165.

42. Ellis, *Life of Gibbons*, 1:210–18 (James Gibbons and Patrick A. Feehan), 1:439–546 (Francis Silas Chatard and Charles J. Seghers). See also Kevin Codd, "A Favored Portion of the Vineyard: A Study of American Catholic Missionaries on the North Pacific Coast," PhD diss., Catholic University of Louvain, Louvain, 2007.

43. Henry Vincent Browne, *The Catholic Church and the Knights of Labor* (Washington, DC: Catholic University of America Press, 1949); Vincent J. Falzone, *Terence V. Powderly: Middle Class Reformer* (Washington, DC: University Press of America, 1978); and Robert E. Weir, *Beyond Labor's Veil: The Culture of the Knights of Labor* (University Park: University of Pennsylvania Press, 1996). See also "The Catholic Church and the Knights of Labour," in *The American Catholic History Classroom*, http://cuomeka.wrlc.org/exhibits/show/knights/kol-intro/church-kol, last consulted August 19, 2016.

44. Chatard to Giovanni Simeoni, February 5, 1885, fols. 156rv, 158rv, vol. 42/1: *Congressi, America Centrale*, APF. On the American Catholic Church, the Molly Maguires, and the Ancient Order of Hibernians, see Kevin Kenny, "The Molly Maguires and the Catholic Church," *Labor History* 36, no. 3 (1995): 345–76, and Kenny, *Making Sense of the Molly Maguires* (New York: Oxford University Press, 1998).

45. James Gibbons to Giovanni Simeoni, February 20, 1885, vol. 42/1, *Congressi, America Centrale*, APF.

46. See the related file in fasc. 51, sezione XII (Società Segrete), Archivio della Delegazione Apostolica degli Stati Uniti (ADASU), ASV. Documents assembled in this file cover the years 1892, 1894–96, 1907–10, 1950, and 1961. Documents pertaining to 1950 and 1961 are not open to researchers.

47. See nos. 1 (*Sulle Società dell'America del Nord*), 70 (*Stati Uniti: Sulle società segrete*), 1894, *Rerum Variarum*, Archives of the Congregation for the Doctrine of the Faith (ACDF).

48. See no. 2, [David Fleming], De Societate Secreta, "Ordo Independens Bonorum Templariorum" (Independent Order of the Good Templars), *Relatio et Votum*, May 1909, 1915, *Rerum Variarum*, ACDF, and [Fleming], *Brevis Relatio et Votum eiusdem Cons.ris*, November 1914, *Rerum Variarum*, ACDF. The latter includes all reports compiled by Fleming.

49. See the letters written by several American bishops in 1894: Québec e Vincennes—Baltimore: Intorno ad un dubbio dell'arcivescovo di Québec (Canada) sopra alcune associazioni operaie dell'America Settentrionale, *Rerum Variarum*, ACDF. See also James P. Gaffey, *Citizen of No Mean City: Archbishop Patrick Riordan of San Francisco (1841–1914)* (Wilmington, NC: Consortium Books, 1976).

50. *Rerum Novarum: Écriture, contenu et réception d'une encyclique. Actes du colloque international* (Rome: École Française de Rome, 1997), and Sabine Schratz, *Das Gift des alten Europa und die Arbeiter der Neuen Welt: Zum amerikanischen Hintergrund der Enzyklika Rerum Novarum (1891)* (Padernborn: Schoening, 2010).

51. Denis J. O'Connell to Propaganda Fide, September 10, 1887, fols. 245rv–246rv, vol. 47/2: *Congressi, America Centrale*, APF.

52. In early 1898 the Holy Office started to gather a very large file on so-called American-ism (pt. II, no. 5, 1900, *Rerum Variarum*, ACDF). On June 16, 1898, however, Leo XIII informed the Holy Office that he was taking personal charge of the issue (June 15, 1898, *Decreta*, ACDF). Eventually the pope repudiated "Americanism" in the apostolic letter *Testem benevolentiae nostrae*, dated January 22, 1899, and addressed to Gibbons. See *Leonis XIII pontificis maximi acta* (Rome: Ex Typographia Vaticana, 1899), 19:5–7.

53. See the file on the canonical construction of the college in *ponenza*, September 1, 1884, fols. 521rv–536v, esp. 522rv, vol. 253: *Acta*, APF.

54. On the Vatican and the national churches, see Péter Tusor and Matteo Sanfilippo, eds., *Il papato e le chiese locali: Studi/The Papacy and the Local Churches; Studies* (Viterbo: Sette Città, 2014). For the text of the apostolic constitution *Sapienti consilio*, see *Acta Apostolicae Sedis* (Rome: Typis Polyglottis Vaticanis, 1909), 1:7–108. On Propaganda Fide and the coming of age of national Catholic churches in Europe (England, Scotland, Ireland, and the Netherlands) and in North America (Canada, Newfoundland, and the United States), see ibid., 12–13. The *Acta Apostolicae Sedis* are also available online at http://www.vatican.va/archive/aas/index_it.htm.

55. On Francesco Satolli's first American visit, see fasc. unico, rubr. 241, *Segreteria di Stato, 1892*, ASV.

56. Mariano Rampolla del Tindaro to Francesco Satolli, [Vaticano 1892] (instructions), fols. 12rv–27rv, fasc. 3, sezione I (*Delegazione Apostolica*), ADASU, ASV.

57. For the establishment of the apostolic delegation, see fasc.1–4, rubr. 280, *Segreteria di Stato, 1897*, ASV. See also Robert J. Wister, *The Establishment of the Apostolic Delegation in the USA, 1892–1896* (Rome: Università Gregoriana, 1980), and Wister, "The First Apostolic Delegation," *US Catholic Historian* 12, no. 2 (Spring 1994): 27–45. For Satolli's faculties and authority, see the file in fols. 1rv–11rv, fasc. 20, posizione 74, *America*, II Periodo, *America*, Archives of the Secretariat of State, Relations with States Section (Archivio degli Affari Ecclesiastici Straordinari or AAES), Archivio Storico della Seconda Sezione della Segreteria di Stato. For the new instructions after the 1892 official appointment, see the file in ASV, ADASU, I, fasc. 4–5.

58. The instructions given to Satolli were summarized in Segreteria di Stato to Sebastiano Martinelli, [1896], fols. 22rv–25rv, fasc. 6, sezione I, ADASU, ASV.

59. File on Diomede Falconio's appointment, [1899], fasc. 25a, sezione I, ADASU, ASV. The Reformed Franciscans was a branch of the Franciscan order that was likely founded in 1519. In 1532 Pope Clement VIII granted permission to all friars who desired to strictly observe the rule of Saint Francis of Assisi to withdraw into the convents of Reformed communities. In 1897 Pope Leo XIII decided to bring together the Reformed Franciscans with the Recollects and the Observant branch of the Franciscan order.

60. On Falconio, see Matteo Sanfilippo, "Diomede Falconio, le Canada et les États-Unis," in Luca Codignola, Giovanni Pizzorusso, and Sanfilippo, *Le Saint-Siège, le Canada et le Québec: Recherches dans les archives romaines* (Viterbo: Sette Città, 2011), 101–7.

61. See file on Giovanni Bonzano's appointment, [1912], fasc. 91, sezione I, ADASU, ASV.

62. See Bonzano's letters in the following files: fasc. 115, *Stati Uniti: Cleveland-Boston 1918*, posizione 225, *America*, III Periodo, *America*, AAES; ibid., posizione 230, fasc. 115, *Stati Uniti:*

Washington 1918: Guerra e tedesco-statunitensi, fasc. 115, posizione 230, III Periodo, *America*, AAES; fasc. 118, *Stati Uniti: Washington 1919*: Mons. Bonzano si difende da alcune accuse, posizione 247, III Periodo, *America*, AAES.

63. See the file in fasc. 29, [1927–29], posizione 194, IV Periodo, *Inghilterra*, AAES.

64. See the reports, diocese by diocese, in ASV, ser. *Concistoriale*, sub-ser. *Visita Apostolica*, vols. 77–78: *Stati Uniti d'America visite apostoliche*. On the European immigrants and their clergy, Italians and Poles in particular, see the related files in fasc. 98, *Condizioni religiose degli immigrati europei*, November 23, 1922, *1922, Concistoriale, Ponenze*, ASV; and fasc. 17, *Degli scalabriniani*, February 21, 1924, *1924, Concistoriale, Ponenze*, ASV.

65. See Alejandro Mario Dieguez, "La sollecitudine pastorale della Chiesa nelle plenarie della Congregazione del Concilio durante il pontificato di Pio XI (1922–1939)," in *Studi in onore del Cardinal Raffaele Farina*, ed. Ambrogio Maria Piazzoni (Vatican City: Biblioteca Apostolica Vaticana, 2013), 1:497–522.

66. On Donato Sbarretti's Canadian mandate, see Giovanni Pizzorusso, "Donato Sbarretti, deuxième délégué apostolique du Canada," in Codignola, Pizzorusso, and Sanfilippo, *Le Saint-Siège*, 127–59.

67. Reports by American bishops on the economic assets of their dioceses in 1928 are to be found in 3 (*Stati Uniti*): Baltimora et al., *Relazione circa i beni ecclesiastici, 1928* (several files), *Stati Patrimoniali Esteri, Congregazione del Concilio, Sezione Amministrativa*, ASV. Other reports by American bishops for the years 1929–39 are in 4 (*Stati Uniti*) (several files), *Positiones Diocesi esteri, Congregazione del Concilio, Sezione Amministrativa*, ASV.

68. On the Sentinelle affair, see 933–34 (an enormous file, in two vols.), *Sezione Disciplinare, Congregazione del Concilio*, ASV. This issue was also examined by the Sacred Congregation "degli Affari Ecclesiastici Straordinari" in 1927. See the related file in fasc. 47, *Franco canadesi*, posizione 216, IV Periodo, *America*, AAES.

69. Fasc. 44–46, *Stati Uniti 1927–1932: Elezione presidenziale* (files on Herbert Hoover [1874–1964] and Franklin Delano Roosevelt), posizione 214, IV Periodo, *America*, AAES. See also fasc. 66–73, *Stati Uniti 1934–1944: Sac. Coughlin e i suoi discorsi alla radio*. There are also several files on Father Charles Coughlin (1891–1979), posizione 238, IV Periodo, *America*, AAES.

70. Fasc. 56–58, *Riconoscimento del Governo Sovietico di Russia*, posizione 32, IV Periodo, *America*, AAES; fasc. 84–86, *Stati Uniti 1936–1947: Comunismo*, posizione 246, IV Periodo, *America*, AAES; fasc. 91, *Stati Uniti 1938–1939: The World Problem*, posizione 251, IV Periodo, *America*, AAES.

71. Fasc. 87–90, *Chicago Germania 1936–1938: Protesta del Card. Mundelein contro il nazismo tedesco*, posizione 251, IV Periodo, *America*, AAES; no. 8: *Stati Uniti d'America—Il Segretario dell'Associazione Eugenia America chiede una spiegazione (da pubblicarsi nell'organo ufficiale dell'Associazione) circa la condanna dell'Eugenetica, 1931, Rerum Variarum*, ACDF.

72. Fasc. 65, *Stati Uniti 1937–1938: Trattative per le relazioni diplomatiche tra la S. Sede e gli Stati Uniti*, posizione 237 (1), IV Periodo, *America*, AAES.

73. Vols. 77–78: *Stati Uniti d'America visite apostoliche* (see the reports on the Southern dioceses), *Concistoriale, Visita Apostolica*, ASV. See also fasc. 41, *Stati Uniti 1926–1937: Assistenza religiosa ai negri*, posizione 207, IV Periodo, *America*, AAES.

74. For the references and quotations in Part 4, see the appropriate entries in this guide.

Roman Sources for the History of American Catholicism

A Different Perspective

MATTEO BINASCO

The use of Roman archives in studying the history of American Catholicism is not new to North American scholars. The potential offered by Roman archives has been recognized by a number of American and Canadian historians since the second half of the nineteenth century.[1] In 1911, American historian Carl Russell Fish set the agenda by publishing his *Guide to the Materials for American History in Roman and Other Italian Archives.*[2]

Fish's *Guide* opened a research path that from the mid-1960s expanded into four different projects. The first started in 1966, when the Academy of American Franciscan History began to catalogue all the documents of American interest in the archives of the Sacred Congregation de Propaganda Fide, the dicastery founded in 1622 to oversee missionary activity in Protestant and non-Christian regions. This project led to the publication of fourteen volumes that covered the period from 1622 to 1879.[3] However, these focused exclusively on documents of US interest, thus neglecting the fact that the borders between the United States and British North America were not clearly defined until the early nineteenth century.[4]

The second relevant research project involved Jesuit sources. This began in 1967 with the publication of the first volume of the *Monumenta Novae Franciae*, edited by the Canadian Jesuit Lucien Campeau.[5] This project, which ended in 2003 after Campeau's death and the publication of the last of the nine volumes, collected and edited all the sources on Jesuit activities in North America from the early seventeenth to the late eighteenth century. It revised substantially the pioneering work by Reuben Gold Thwaites under the overall title *Jesuit Relations and Allied Documents.*[6]

The third project was the three-volume collection edited by Josef Metzler, archivist of Propaganda Fide from 1966 to 1984, which was published between 1971 and 1976 to celebrate the 350th anniversary of the dicastery.[7] This collection of essays sought to illustrate the global outlook and engagement of Propaganda Fide, but the articles devoted to North

America were few in number: three on French America and only two on the United States, one focused on Louisiana and Maryland during the colonial period and one on the development of the US Catholic Church during the nineteenth century.[8]

The fourth research project was launched in 1977 by the National Archives of Canada and the Université Saint-Paul. Its initial aim was to prepare a calendar of all documents of British and French North America, that is, what later became the United States and Canada, from 1622 to 1799; its chronological focus was then extended to 1922, the year in which Benedict XV died (at the time, researchers at the Vatican archives were permitted access only to documents dated up to the end of his pontificate; in 2006, researchers were permitted to access documents dated through 1939, the year in which the pontificate of Pius XI ended). As mentioned earlier, the reason for this restriction of access is that the chronological limits for consultation are set by the popes. Each pope decides whether or not to extend the chronological limits. However, the project's geographical focus was increasingly limited to Canada. This project brought about the writing of a series of comprehensive guides and inventories, prepared by Luca Codignola, Giovanni Pizzorusso, and Matteo Sanfilippo, on all the documents of North American interest at Propaganda Fide.[9] It also paved the way for extending research in the Vatican archives and other Roman archives.[10]

A research guide titled *L'Amérique du Nord française dans les archives religieuses de Rome*, published in 1999, represents a major landmark in these painstaking efforts.[11] This impressive guide, covering 1600–1922, provides the best overview to date of Roman sources for the history of the Catholic Church in Canada and includes a number of items of US interest.

All these efforts have provided a much better understanding of the complex relationship that existed between the Holy See and the North American church by offering new insights on issues such as Americanism, rivalries between ethnic communities, European migrations, and the development of clerical networks between Rome and the North Atlantic world, to mention just a few.[12]

So far, the extensive studies carried out at Propaganda Fide and in other Roman archives on the history of the Catholic Church in Canada have not prompted similar projects on the church in the United States. The only relevant exception has been *Vatican Archives: An Inventory and Guide to Historical Documents of the Holy See*, edited by Francis Blouin and published in 1998. This imposing guide provides a comprehensive overview of the Holy See's extant historical documents dating back to the ninth century without focusing on a specific period or geographical area. Furthermore, the description of Propaganda Fide's holdings does not take into account the major archival reform implemented by the dicastery at the end of the nineteenth century.[13]

The rising interest of a number of US and Italian scholars in Roman sources has suggested the need to reframe American Catholicism in a new context informed by the perspectives of Atlantic and global history.[14] This need to adopt new, multidisciplinary approaches paved the way for a new initiative led by Notre Dame's Cushwa Center for the Study of American Catholicism, undertaken from mid-September 2014 to mid-September

2016.[15] The key aim of the project was to investigate the Roman archives to prepare a guide to sources related to the history of American Catholicism for the period from 1763 to 1939, corresponding to the end of the French and Indian War (1756–63) and the date after which the majority of holdings within the religious archives in Rome are closed for consultation.

Research focused on the major archives of the Holy See, namely those of Propaganda Fide, the Vatican Secret Archives, and the Jesuit archives, and on some minor archives. The latter have provided new documents that further demonstrate how Roman sources can broaden scholarship on American Catholicism.

Given the fact that it is difficult to emphasize the importance of one repository over another, this essay provides examples to highlight newfound material in less-known archives such as that of the Abbey of San Paolo fuori le Mura. In fact, American material proved to be particularly rich there in the collections related to Dom Bernard Smith (1812–92), an Irish Benedictine who acted as a Roman agent for many North American bishops from the early 1840s onward. His letters deal with a variety of issues, including complaints by John Hughes (1797–1864), the Irish-born Catholic bishop of New York from 1842 to 1864, that "the Italians could not build a church in New York; and if they could they would not. They would rather give the money to [Giuseppe] Mazzini."[16] Giuseppe Mazzini (1805–1872) was one of the most prominent leaders of the Italian Risorgimento. Smith's correspondence also highlighted problems faced by clergy in dioceses where there were few priests, and priests of poor quality at that. This problem surfaces in a letter from William George McCloskey (1823–1909), bishop of Louisville from 1868 to 1909, who in late August 1878 lamented: "Drunkenness . . . the curse of the priesthood in this country, has deprived me of the service of no less than four priests, since last November."[17]

Smith was also in contact with a number of prominent lay Americans, including some members of the Seton family. One of them was Henry Seton (1839–1927), second son of William and Emily Seton and captain of the Union Army, who in mid-June 1862 wrote to update Smith on the progress of the Civil War in Virginia and the harsh political divisions between the two sides. Indeed, Smith explicitly stated: "This is a war to the death—no compromise—the South as it has existed must be blotted out like Carthage and the proud southerner will be an extinct animal, only to be seen stuffed in Barnum's Museum!"[18]

The richness of the American material contained in the so-called minor repositories sheds new light on the activity of the regular orders that operated in the United States. For example, the documents contained in the archives of the Curia Generalizia of the Franciscan order enhance our understanding of the difficulties facing the first friars who arrived in the United States during the 1820s. Here it is worth mentioning a letter addressed to Cirilo de Alameda y Brea (1781–1872), minister general from 1817 to 1824, from Charles Bonaventure Maguire (1768–1833), an Irish Franciscan who lectured at Saint Isidore's in Rome from the late 1790s through the early 1810s. Maguire reported that "each Sunday I have to preach twice: the crowd of heretics who come to listen to me, each time that I preach, is immense. For God's grace, they often convert to the Holy See. I wrote to the provincial of

Ireland for sending me one or two other priests; but I fear that there are none to spare who come to this mission; a priest in these countries who is not able to preach well is despised and seen as useless."[19]

Roman sources are extremely useful in the case of women's congregations. Indeed, the correspondence between superiors in Rome and members active in the United States provides a clear picture of how these congregations had to establish and develop their ministries with limited personnel and resources. Noteworthy here is a letter that Rosa Bertolini, an Italian member of the Daughters of Saint Mary of Providence, wrote from Chicago in 1919 to her superior, Marcellina Bosatta. Speaking about the difficulty in finding new novices, Bertolini openly stated: "In America it is almost a miracle to have some. Nuns almost steal the girls, for they are so scarce."[20]

The archives of women's congregations as well as those of male regular orders all contain untapped material that might broaden our knowledge of Italian immigrants who arrived in the United States between the late nineteenth century and the first three decades of the twentieth. In particular, the letters and lengthy reports written by Italian missionaries active amid their fellow countrymen convey a vivid picture of the conditions in which their communities lived. For example, an anonymous account from 1912 on the Philadelphia mission of the Missionary Sisters of the Sacred Heart of Jesus, the women's congregation founded in 1880 by Saint Francesca Saverio Cabrini (1850–1917), details Protestant efforts to convert Italian immigrants from Catholicism. The report states: "Before leaving Philadelphia Reverend Mother [Cabrini] entrusted us with the mission to go, at least two or three times a week, to visit the families who for years and years had been far from their holy church, lured by the Protestants, and we put many on the right track: they returned to the practice of their religion, they approached the sacraments, and removed their children from the Protestant schools, sent them to our own. The Protestant minister sees us with an evil eye, because his church is emptying."[21]

We must take into account that these reports were not all written in the same way but were influenced by the specific contexts and periods in which they were compiled. For example, Agostino Morini (1826–1909), a missionary of the Servants of Mary who was active between Chicago and Green Bay, Wisconsin, from 1870 to 1888, sent a report to Rome in mid-January 1887 providing a dismal picture of the initial phase of Italian migration to the United States. Writing about his fellow countrymen, Morini stated:

> There is . . . a large number of Italians who are scattered in small groups and, together with Norwegians, Swedes, Germans, and Irish, work to build railways, to dig canals, and to dig in mines, especially coal. A dozen of them are probably living in a small town, about forty in a place a few hundred miles from any urban center, and in winter, perhaps thirty here and sixty there in the forests, where they cut trees. They arrive from Italy filthy and ignorant; they do not even know the principal mysteries of the Holy Faith, or are Garibaldine militants who speak nothing but obscenities and stuff of hell against priests and against the pope. Their swearing is out of this world.[22]

By contrast, the diary of the Dominican Antonino Maria D'Achille, which is preserved in the archives of the Dominican Roman province of Saint Caterina da Siena, offers a very different view of the Italian community in New York during the early 1920s. D'Achille, who lived in the United States from January to November 1924, was likely influenced by the Fascist propaganda of that period.[23] This emerges in his description of the celebration of Mass in the church of Madonna del Carmine in New York in mid-July 1924, in which he emphatically affirmed that "we are in New York! There is so much fervor and affection in these Italian people towards the Virgin Mary. Everywhere a waving of American and Italian flags; say what you like, no other people in the world is able to have a show like this. And a people that has such energy in the depth of the soul cannot perish."[24]

Since most of the lesser-known archives have been recently reopened or are scarcely explored, there are still no detailed inventories that precisely describe their material pertaining to US Catholicism. Moreover, it is necessary to combine these new sources with those found in the Vatican Secret Archives, the archives of Propaganda Fide, and the Vatican Library. This combination of "old" sources with new will improve scholarship on the relations between the United States and the Holy See, further demonstrating the truly global dimension of American Catholicism.

In this volume the reader will find repository-specific bibliographies at the end of each profile of an archive or library, as well as a select bibliography at the back. The repository-specific bibliographies contain two types of references: (1) works that provide a detailed and (where possible) up-to-date description of the material held in the archive or library in question and (2) scholarly books or articles that use materials pertaining to American Catholicism contained in that repository. The volume's select bibliography is meant to direct researchers to further practical aids. It lists a selection of other guides and inventories for key Roman repositories, descriptions of relevant archives and libraries in and beyond Rome, and published documentary sources for US Catholic history. Works in the repository-specific bibliographies whose entries are not complete (they usually have just author last names and short versions of titles) are found in their full forms in the select bibliography at the back of the book.

NOTES

1. John Dawson Gilmary Shea, *The Catholic Church in Colonial Days: The Thirteen Colonies–The Ottawa and Illinois Country–Louisiana–Florida–Texas–New Mexico and Arizona* (New York: Edward Jenkins' Son, 1886); Shea, *Life and Times of the Most Rev. John Carroll, Bishop and First Archbishop of Baltimore: Embracing the History of the Catholic Church in the United States, 1763–1815* (New York: Edward Jenkins' Son, 1888); and Shea, *History of the Catholic Church in the United States from the Division of the Diocese of Baltimore, 1808, and Death of*

Archbishop Carroll, 1815, to the Fifth Provincial Council of Baltimore, 1843 (Rahway, NJ: Mershon, 1890). We must take into account that Shea did not visit the archives of Propaganda, but he had copies made by Michael Corrigan, archbishop of New York. Those copies are now preserved at Georgetown College Archives. The quotations and citations in the footnotes that appear in his 1886 book are imprecise. I thank Professor Luca Codignola for this reference. On Archbishop Corrigan, see Robert Emmet Curran, *Michael Augustine Corrigan and the Shaping of Conservative Catholicism in America, 1878–1902* (New York: Arno, 1978).

2. For a more detailed discussion of the errors present in Fish's *Guide*, see Luca Codignola, "L'Amérique du Nord et la Sacrée Congregation 'de Propaganda Fide,' 1622–1799: Études," *Bulletin du Centre de recherche en civilisation canadienne-française* 21 (1980): 1–12.

3. Finbar Kenneally, ed., *United States Documents in the Propaganda Fide Archives: A Calendar, First Series*, vols. 1–7 and index (Washington, DC: Academy of American Franciscan History, 1966–81); Anton Debeveč et al., eds., *United States Documents in the Propaganda Archives: A Calendar, Second Series*, vols. 8–13 (Washington DC: Academy of American Franciscan History, 1980–2006).

4. Luca Codignola, "Des Canadiens à Rome à la recherche de leurs racines?" in *Little Do We Know: History and Historians of the North Atlantic World, 1492–2010*, ed. Matteo Binasco (Cagliari: Istituto di Storia dell'Europa-Consiglio Nazionale delle Ricerche, 2011), 189–90.

5. Lucien Campeau, SJ, ed., *Monumenta Novae Franciae*, 9 vols. (Montreal-Quebec-Rome: Apud Monumenta Hist. Soc. Iesu-Les Éditions Bellarmin-Les Presses de l'Université Laval, 1967–2003).

6. Reuben G. Thwaites, ed., *The Jesuit Relations and Allied Documents: Travels and Explorations of the Jesuit Missionaries in New France, 1610–1791*, 73 vols. (Cleveland: Burrows Brothers, 1896–1901). For a discussion and comparison of Campeau's and Thwaites's editions, see Luca Codignola, "Jesuit Writings according to R. G. Thwaites and Lucien Campeau, SJ: How Do They Differ?" in *Little Do We Know*, 219–40.

7. Josef Metzler, OMI, ed., *Sacrae Congregationis de Propaganda Fide Memoria Rerum: 350 anni a servizio delle missioni, 1622–1972* (hereafter *Memoria Rerum*), 3 vols., (Freiburg: Herder, 1971–76).

8. Lucien Campeau, SJ, "Les initiatives de la S. Congrégation en faveur de la Nouvelle-France," in *Memoria Rerum*, vol. 1, part 2, 727–95; Lucien Lemieux, "Provision pour l'Église canadienne, A: La Congrégation de la Propagande, modératrice et promotrice d'une Église canadienne en expansion (1760–1840)," in ibid., vol. 3, part 1, 729–48; Alexander Baran, "Provision pour l'Église Canadienne, B: Further Development after 1840," in ibid., vol. 3, part 1, 749–57; Charles Edwards O'Neill, SJ, "North American Beginnings in Maryland and Louisiana," in ibid., vol. 1, part 1, 713–26; O'Neill, "The United States of America," in ibid. 2:1162–84. See also O'Neill, *Church and State in French Colonial Louisiana: Policy and Politics to 1732* (New Haven, CT: Yale University Press, 1966).

9. Luca Codignola, *Guide to Documents Relating to French and British North America in the Archives of the Sacred Congregation "de Propaganda Fide," 1622–1799* (Ottawa: National Archives of Canada, 1991); Codignola, *Vatican: Archives of the Sacred Congregation "de Propaganda Fide"; Calendar of Documents Relating to French and British North America in the Archives of the Sacred Congregation "de Propaganda Fide,"* and *Guide to Documents Relating to French and*

British North America in the Archives of the Sacred Congregation "de Propaganda Fide" in Rome, 1622–1799, in *ArchiVIA 4: Colonial Archives; Findings Aids on CD-ROM/Archives coloniales; Instruments de recherche sur CD-ROM* (Ottawa: National Archives of Canada/Archives Nationales du Canada, 1996); Codignola, *Calendar of Documents Relating to North America (Canada and the United States) in the Archives of the Sacred Congregation "de Propaganda Fide" in Rome, 1622–1846,* 6 vols. (Ottawa: Library and Archives Canada and the Research Centre for Religious History in Canada of Saint Paul University, 2012); Giovanni Pizzorusso, "La 'Nuova Serie' dell'Archivio di Propaganda Fide e la storia degli italiani in Nord America," *Il Veltro* 34, no. 1–2 (1990): 67–85; Pizzorusso, "Archives du Collège Urbain de Propaganda Fide," *Annali Accademici Canadesi* 7 (1991): 93–98; Pizzorusso, *Inventaire des documents d'intérêt canadien dans les Archives de la Congrégation "de Propaganda Fide," 1904–1914* (Ottawa-Rome: Archives nationales du Canada-Centre Académique Canadien en Italie, 1993); Pizzorusso and Matteo Sanfilippo, *Inventaire des documents d'intérêt canadien dans les Archives de la Congrégation 'de Propaganda Fide' sous le pontificat de Pie IX (1846–1877)* (Rome-Ottawa: Centre Académique Canadien en Italie-Université St-Paul, 2001). Researchers must also take into account that the archives of both the University of Notre Dame and Saint Louis University have a number of microfilms of some of the key series of Propaganda.

10. Monique Benoit, *Inventaire des principales séries de documents intéressant le Canada, sous le pontificat de Léon XIII (1878–1902), dans les archives de la Sacrée Congrégation "de Propaganda Fide" à Rome* (Ottawa: Archives Nationales du Canada, 1986); Giovanni Pizzorusso and Matteo Sanfilippo, "Inventario delle fonti vaticane per la storia dell'emigrazione e dei gruppi etnici nel Nord America: Il Canada (1878–1922)," *Studi Emigrazione,* monografic issue 31 (1994): 607–745; Sanfilippo, "Fonti ecclesiastiche per la storia dell'emigrazione e dei gruppi etnici nel Nord America: Gli Stati Uniti (1893–1922)," *Studi Emigrazione,* monographic issue 32 (1995): 605–768; Pizzorusso and Sanfilippo, *Inventaire des documents concernant le Canada dans les Archives Secrètes et la Bibliothèque Apostolique du Vatican, ainsi que dans les Archives de la Congrégation des Affaires Ecclésiastiques Extraordinaires, les Archives du Saint-Office et les Archives d'État de Rome: Pontificat de Pie IX (1846–1877)* (Rome-Ottawa: Centre Académique Canadien en Italie-Université St-Paul, 2001).

11. Pierre Hurtubise, Luca Codignola, and Fernand Harvey, eds., *L'Amérique du Nord française dans les archives religieuses de Rome, 1600–1922* (Quebec: Les Éditions de l'IQRC, 1999).

12. For a full list of the works, see the select bibliography at the end of the book.

13. Francis X. Blouin, ed., *Vatican Archives: An Inventory and Guide to Historical Documents of the Holy See* (New York: Oxford University Press, 1998); see also Blouin, ed., *Supplement #1: The Archives of the Congregation for the Doctrine of the Faith; Including the Archives of the Former Congregation of the Holy Office and the Archives of the Former Congregation for Forbidden Books* (Ann Arbor: Bentley Historical Library, University of Michigan, 2003); Blouin, Elizabeth Yakel, and Leonard A. Coombs, "Vatican Archives: An Inventory and Guide to Historical Documents of the Holy See; A Ten-Year Retrospective," *The American Archivist* 71 (2008): 433–55. For a critical review of this guide, see Sergio Pagano, B, "Una discutibile 'guida' degli Archivi Vaticani," *Archivum Historiae Pontificiae* 37 (1999): 191–201.

14. For an overview of the concept of global Catholicism, see Vincent Viaene, "International History, Religious History, Catholic History: Perspectives for Cross-Fertilization (1830–1914),"

European History Quarterly 38 (2008): 578–607; Ian Linden, *Global Catholicism: Diversity and Change since Vatican II* (London: Hurst, 2009); Linden, *Global Catholicism: Pluralism and Renewal in a World Church* (New York: Columbia University Press, 2011); Joseph P. Chinnici, OFM, "The Cold War, the Council and American Catholicism in a Global World," *US Catholic Historian* 30, no. 2 (Spring 2012): 1–24.

15. The project was supervised by Kathleen Sprows Cummings, Luca Codignola, and Matteo Sanfilippo.

16. John Hughes to Bernard Smith, September 25, 1861, ser. *Monaci dell'Ottocento*, shelf no. 27, palchetto c, *Smith 1*, 1840–1861: *America, Canada*, dossier no. 15, not foliated or paginated, Archives of the Abbey of San Paolo fuori le Mura (Archivio Storico di San Paolo fuori le Mura or ASSP).

17. William George McCloskey to Bernard Smith, August 22, 1878, unfoliated and unpaginated, ser. *Monaci dell'Ottocento*, shelf no. 27, palchetto c, *Smith III*, 1877–1884: *America*, dossier no. 33, ASSP.

18. Captain Henry Seton to Bernard Smith, July 17, 1862, unfoliated and unpaginated, ser. *Monaci dell'Ottocento*, shelf no. 27, palchetto c, *Smith 2*, 1862–1876: *America*, dossier no. 16, ASSP.

19. Charles Bonaventure Maguire to [Cirilo Alameda y Brea], March 20, 1822, fols. 3–4, *America Settentrionale, Buffalo, Imm. Conc. U.S.A., 1848–1869*, M119, General Archives of the Franciscan Order (Archivio Storico Generale dell'Ordine dei Frati Minori or AGOFM-Storico): "ogni Domenica devo predicare due volte: la folla di eretici, che vengono ascoltarmi, ogni volta che predico è immensa. Per la grazia di Dio si convertono assai spesso alla Santa Sede; ho scritto al M. Provinciale d'Irlanda di mandarmi uno o due altri preti; ma temo molto che non ce ne sono da sparmiare chi convengono a questa missione; un prete in questi paesi che non sa ben predicare, è sprezzato, e riguardato come inutile."

20. Rosa Bertolini to Marcellina Bosatta, April 3, 1919, *Raccolta di lettere delle prime suore d'America, anni 1913–1935*, vol. 8, 1919, General Archives of the Daughters of Saint Mary of Providence (Archivio Curia Generale Figlie di Santa Maria della Provvidenza): "In America è quasi un miracolo ad avere qualcuna. Tutte le suore quasi se le rubano le ragazze, tanto sono scarse."

21. Box no. 2, San Donato Philadelphia, 1912, no. 60, pp. 1–2, General Archives of the Missionary Sisters of the Sacred Heart of Jesus: "Prima di lasciar Philadelphia la Venerata Madre ci affidò anche la missione di andare, non meno di due o tre volte la settimana, a visitare le famiglie che da anni ed anni erano lontane dallo loro Santa Chiesa, adescate dai Protestanti e molti e molti ne rimettemmo sulla buona strada: ritornarono alla pratica della loro religione, si accostarono ai sacramenti, e levati i propri bambini dalle scuole protestanti, li mandano alle nostre. Il ministro protestante ci vede di mal occhio, perché la sua chiesa si va vuotando."

22. Agostino Morino to general of the Servites, January 19, 1887, p. 3, *Epistula Priorum Generalium II*, 77, General Archives of the Servants of Mary: "Ci è poi un gran numero d'Italiani che si spargono in piccoli gruppi, e insieme con Norvegi, Svedesi, Tedeschi e Irlandesi lavorano a fare le stradeferrate, a scavar canali, a scavare nelle mine specialmente del carbone. Ce ne sarà una dozzina in un paesetto, una quarantina in un posto lontano qualche centinaio di miglia da ogni paese, forse in inverno un 30 qua e un 60 là nelle foreste a tagliare gli alberi. Vengono dell'Italia sudici, ignoranti che non sanno neppure i misteri principali della Santa Fede, oppure garibaldini che non parlano altro che oscenità e roba d'inferno contro i preti e contro il papa, e bestemmie di fare oscurare il sole."

23. Peter D'Agostino, "'Fascist Transmission Belts' or Episcopal Advisors? Italian Consuls and American Catholicism in the 1930s," *Cushwa Center for the Study of American Catholicism: Working Paper Series* 24 (Spring 1997): 1–39.

24. Diary of Antonino Maria D'Achille, July 16, 1924, *Fondi Personali* CM II19 (6), Archives of the Dominican Roman Province of Saint Catherine of Siena: "siamo a New York! Quanto fervore di affetto di questo popolo italiano verso la Madonna. Dovunque sventolio di bandiere italiane e americane. Si dica quello che si vuole; ma nessun altro popolo del mondo è capace di presentare uno spettacolo simile. E' un popolo che ha questa energia in fondo all'anima non può perire."

CHAPTER 1

Archives of the Holy See

This chapter contains profiles of archives that are located in Vatican City or that are under the jurisdiction of the Holy See. It includes the Historical Archives of the Congregation for the Evangelization of Peoples, or "de Propaganda Fide," and the Vatican Secret Archives, the two religious repositories in Rome that contain the largest number of documents on the history of the Catholic Church in the United States. This chapter also includes information on the Vatican Library, which, given its unique nature, has a number of manuscript collections containing notable documents on American Catholicism from the colonial period up until the early decades of the twentieth century.

Archivio Storico della Congregazione per la Dottrina della Fede/
Archives of the Congregation for the Doctrine of the Faith
Address
    Palazzo del Sant'Uffizio, Vatican City, 00120 Rome
Contact Details
    Phone: 39-0669884778
    Fax: 39-0669883409
    Email: archivio2@cfaith.va

STATUS
Open to researchers Monday–Saturday, 8:30 a.m.–1:00 p.m. The archives close for Italian national holidays and from mid-July until the end of September. An appointment with the archivist is required to reserve a seat in the study room; a seat reservation is valid for two weeks and may be renewed. In the study room, researchers can consult the Shades program, an online inventory of the collections. Most documents are written in Italian or Latin. Material post-1939 cannot be consulted.

HISTORY

The Congregation for the Doctrine of the Faith was officially established on July 21, 1542, with the bull *Licet ab initio*, issued by Pope Paul III (1468–1549). Initially its name was "the Sacred Congregation of the Roman and Universal Inquisition," and it sought to defend the Catholic Church from heresies and condemn false theological doctrines. In 1908 Pope Pius X (1835–1914) changed its name to "the Supreme Sacred Congregation of the Holy Office." In 1917, Benedict XV (1854–1922) abolished the Congregation of the Index (founded in 1571) and merged it with the Holy Office. In 1965 Pope Paul VI (1897–1978) changed its name to the "Sacred Congregation for the Doctrine of the Faith." After 1985, every dicastery in the Roman Curia removed the adjective "Sacred" from its official title, so the Sacred Congregation for the Doctrine of the Faith became the Congregation for the Doctrine of the Faith.

DESCRIPTION OF HOLDINGS

Given its crucial role of the Holy Office in fighting heresy and supervising theological disputes, its archives hold vast documentation concerning many different parts of the world from the first half of the sixteenth century to the twentieth century. The holdings include three broader collections: (1) material directly related to the Congregation for the Doctrine of the Faith, (2) collections of the suppressed Congregation of the Index, and (3) a collection of the suppressed Inquisition of Siena. Material of American interest is particularly abundant in the first collection. The Congregation of the Index was suppressed as part of the reform of the papal curia carried out by Benedict XV. The Inquisition of Siena was closed in 1782 by Grand Duke Pietro Leopoldo (1747–92) as part of his political reform program in Tuscany.

The types of documents preserved in the archives of the Holy Office are as follows: decisions made by the congregation (*Decreta*), doctrinal issues (*Res doctrinales*), disciplinary issues (*Res disciplinares*), marriage issues (*Res matrimoniales*), various doubts (*Dubia varia*), various dossiers dealing with a variety of unsolved issues (*Materiae diversae, Rerum Variarum*), and miscellaneous documents from different parts of the world (*Stanza Storica*). This latter collection follows a geographical and thematic classification. For example, vol. D4a7, which is devoted to the missionary faculties of the English province of the Society of Jesus, includes a dossier titled *Circa Missionem ad Provincia Marilandiae in America Septentrionali* (fols. 727r–748v) on the Jesuit mission in Maryland in the seventeenth century.

One good example of the diverse material in these archives is a letter, dated August 19, 1923, from Pietro Fumasoni Biondi (1872–1960), apostolic delegate in the United States from 1922 to 1933, to Cardinal Rafael Merry del Val (1865–1930), secretary of the Congregation of the Faith from 1914 to 1930. In it Fumasoni Biondi described the death and memorial service of the American president Warren G. Harding (1865–1923), adding that "there have been public and unanimous expressions of sympathy from the citizens of every party and every creed."[1]

The Holy Office dealt with many interesting problems; one instance may be seen in the dossier submitted in 1876 by Marcolino Cicognani, an Italian Dominican, in which he described secret societies in California. In the dossier, Cicognani warned against the Society of

Saint Patrick and its members, who "organized dances and not without danger of sin, abandoned themselves to other public amusements especially on public holidays, neglecting to participate in the Holy Mass and to attend the sacred functions."[2]

The Holy Office archives contain further evidence of the doctrinal issues American clergy contended with. One example is an 1816 letter forwarded by Carlo Maria Pedicini (1769–1843), Propaganda's secretary from 1816 to 1823, to Fabrizio Turriozzi (1755–1826), assessor of the Holy Office. The letter summarized some doubts raised by Benoît-Joseph Flaget (1763–1850), bishop of Bardstown from 1808 to 1841 (and subsequently of Louisville after the see was transferred there), such as whether it was legitimate for Catholics to swear oaths on Protestant Bibles.[3]

BIBLIOGRAPHY

Del Col, Andrea. *Inquisizione in Italia: Dal XII al XXI secolo*. Milan: Mondadori, 2006.

Lavenia, Vincenzo, Adriano Prosperi, and John A. Tedeschi, eds. *Dizionario storico dell'Inquisizione*. 4 vols. Pisa: Edizioni della Normale, 2010.

Pizzorusso, Giovanni. "Le fonti del Sant'Uffizio per la storia delle missioni e dei rapporti con Propaganda Fide." In *A dieci anni dall'apertura dell'archivio della Congregazione per la Dottrina della Fede: Storia e archivi dell'Inquisizione (Roma, 21–23 febbraio 2008)*, 393–423. Rome: Accademia dei Lincei Scienze e Lettere, 2011.

Sanfilippo, Matteo. "America settentrionale e americanismo." In *Dizionario storico dell'Inquisizione*, ed. Adriano Prosperi, Vincenzo Lavenia, and John A. Tedeschi, 55–57. Pisa: Edizioni della Normale, 2010.

———. "Gli ordini religiosi nell'Archivio della Congregazione per la Dottrina della Fede." In *Gli archivi per la storia degli ordini religiosi*. Vol. 1: *Fonti e problemi (secoli XVI–XIX)*, ed. Massimo Carlo Giannini and Matteo Sanfilippo, 63–76. Viterbo: Edizioni Sette Città, 2007.

Tedeschi, John A. "The Dispersed Archives of the Roman Inquisition." In *The Inquisition in Early Modern Europe: Studies on Sources and Methods*, ed. G. Hennigsen, John Tedeschi, and Charles Amiel, 13–32. DeKalb: Northern Illinois University Press, 1986.

———. "The Organization and Procedures of the Roman Inquisition: A Sketch." In *The Prosecution of Heresy: Collected Studies on the Inquisition in Early Modern Italy*, ed. John Tedeschi, 47–88. Binghamton, NY: Medieval and Renaissance Texts and Studies, 1991.

Wolf, Hubert. *Storia dell'Indice: Il Vaticano e i libri proibiti*. Rome: Donzelli, 2006.

Archivio Storico della Penitenzieria Apostolica/

Archives of the Apostolic Penitentiary

Address

Piazza della Cancelleria 1, 00186 Rome

Contact Details

Phone: 39-0669887643

Fax: 39-0669887557

Email: archivio@penitenzieria.va

Website: www.penitenzieria.va/content/penitenzieriaapostolica/it/archivio-storico.html

STATUS

Open to researchers Monday–Friday, 9:00 a.m.–1:00 p.m. On Monday, Tuesday, and Thursday the archives are also open from 3:00 p.m. to 5:30 p.m. The archives close for Italian national holidays and from July 15 until September 16. A reference letter, advance appointment, and completed request form are required to gain access to the material. Documents are written in Latin. Material post-1939 cannot be consulted.

HISTORY

The Penitenzieria Apostolica is the highest-ranking tribunal of the Holy See and has jurisdiction over absolutions, dispensations, graces, and indulgences. Its origins go back to the end of the twelfth century, but it was with the bull *In apostolice dignitatis*, issued by Pope Eugene IV (1383–1447) in 1438, that the Penitenzieria was officially established.

DESCRIPTION OF HOLDINGS

The first indication of the existence of the archives of the Penitenzieria comes from the *Acta Cardinalium*, which says that in 1583 these holdings were transferred from the rooms "in Belvedere" to the place where the meetings of the Apostolic Chamber were held. At present, the archives comprise forty sections, of which thirteen are open for consultation. These open sections cover a period from the early fifteenth century to the late nineteenth.

Material of American interest may be present in the sections *Matrimoniali* and *Suppliche*. The *Matrimoniali* section consists of 1,881 volumes that contain material related to the requests for matrimonial dispensations addressed to the Penitenzieria by poor people from 1701 to 1884. In each volume the requests are arranged in alphabetical order according to the diocese of origin. Researchers should note that the names of the dioceses are in Latin and do not always correspond to modern names. The *Suppliche* section consists of 413 volumes of dispensation requests made during the nineteenth century. Although initial exploration of these sections has not yet yielded any material of American interest, it remains probable that some such material is present.

BIBLIOGRAPHY

Saraco, Alessandro, ed. *La Penitenzieria Apostolica ed il suo Archivio*. Rome: Edizioni Paoline, 2012.

Tamburini, Filippo. "Archivio della Sacra Penitenzieria Apostolica." In *Guida delle fonti per la storia dell'America Latina negli archivi della Santa Sede e negli archivi ecclesiastici d'Italia*, ed. Lajos Pásztor, 349–52. Vatican City: Tipografia Poliglotta Vaticana, 1970.

———. "Sacra Penitenzieria Apostolica." In *Dizionario degli Istituti di Perfezione*, 8:169–81. Rome: Edizioni Paoline, 1988.

Archivio Storico della Pontificia Università Lateranense/

Archives of the Pontifical Lateran University

Address

   Piazza San Giovanni in Laterano 4, 00184 Vatican City

Contact Details

   Phone: 39-0669895603/39-3404651219

   Fax: 39-0669886107

   Email: m.onorati@pul.it

   Website: www.pul.it/it/biblioteca/archivio-storico-pul/

STATUS

Open on Tuesday and Friday, 10:00 a.m.–5:00 p.m. It is necessary to contact the archivist in advance to make an appointment and to gain access to the material. Most of the material is in Italian or Latin. It is possible to consult the material written after 1939 with the archivist's permission.

HISTORY

Following the official suppression of the Society of Jesus in 1773, Pope Clement XIV (1705–74) entrusted the faculties of philosophy and theology of the Collegio Romano, the Jesuit University of Rome, to the secular clergy of Rome. This laid the foundations of the Lateran University, to which Pope Leo XII (1760–1829) granted the Sant'Apollinare palace in 1824. In 1853 Pope Pius IX (1792–1878) established the schools of canon law and civil law, and from that moment onward the university was named Ateneo del Pontificio Seminario Romano. In 1959 Pope John XXIII (1881–1963) transformed the institute into a pontifical university known from then on as the Pontifical Lateran University.

DESCRIPTION OF HOLDINGS

The Archives of the Pontifical Lateran University mainly contain details pertaining to the students, the teaching staff, and the administration of this institution. Material of American interest pre-1939 is mainly found in the matriculation registers relating to students who attended courses at the Sant'Apollinare palace. The matriculation registers are found in volumes 409–31. The volumes are in alphabetical order. In each there are individual dossiers on the students enrolled. Researchers must take into account that the information in the dossiers is not uniform, as some dossiers are complete, while others provide only a few details, such as a student's name and his year of matriculation. At present the names of seventeen American students have been identified. However, given the importance of this institution, it is likely that more names would be found in the post-1939 material.

BIBLIOGRAPHY

La Pontificia Università Lateranense: Profilo della sua storia, dei suoi maestri e dei suoi discepoli.
   Rome: Libreria editrice della Pontificia Università Lateranense, 1963.

Archivio del Pontificio Istituto Orientale/
Archives of the Pontifical Oriental Institute
Address
>   Piazza Santa Maria Maggiore 7, 00185 Rome
Contact Details
>   Phone: 39-064474170
>   Email: biblioteca@pontificio-orientale.it

STATUS
Closed at the time of this writing. The archives are being reorganized.

HISTORY
The Pontifical Oriental Institute was officially established in 1917 by Benedict XV (1854–1922) with the key aim of enabling patrons to study Eastern Christianity. In 1922 it was entrusted to the Jesuits.

DESCRIPTION OF HOLDINGS
The Archives of the Pontifical Oriental Institute contain heterogeneous material that covers the period from 1911 to 1993. It mainly consists of correspondence exchanged by the various rectors, matriculation registers, account books, teaching material, and pictures. At present the names of twelve American students have been identified in the matriculation registers for the period from 1917 to 1939. However, given the importance of this institution, it is likely that more names would be found in the post-1939 material.

BIBLIOGRAPHY
Poggi, Vincenzo. *Per la storia del Pontificio Istituto Orientale: Saggi sull'istituzione, i suoi uomini e l'Oriente Cristiano.* Rome: Pontificio Istituto Orientale, 2000.

Archivio Storico della Congregazione per l'Evangelizzazione dei Popoli, o "de Propaganda Fide"/
Historical Archives of the Congregation for the Evangelization of Peoples, or "de Propaganda Fide"
Historical Archives of the Congregation "de Propaganda Fide"
Address
>   Via Urbano VIII 16, 00120 Vatican City
Contact Details
>   Phone: 39-0669871523
>   Fax: 39-0669885633
>   Email: arch.storico@propagandafide.va
>   Website: www.archiviostoricopropaganda.va

STATUS

Open Monday–Thursday, 8:30 a.m.–5:30 p.m., and Friday, 8:30 a.m.–1:30 p.m. The archives close for Italian national holidays and from mid-July until mid-September. A reference letter and an application form are required to gain access to the material. Most material is in English, French, Italian, or Latin, though there are also documents in German, Polish, and in some cases Native American languages. Material post-1939 cannot be consulted.

HISTORY

The earliest attempts to establish the Congregation of Propaganda were made during the sixteenth century by Pope Saint Pius V (1504–72) and Pope Clement VIII (1536–1605). The former tried to found a permanent congregation of cardinals devoted to the spiritual welfare of the Catholic missions, following a suggestion made by Saint Francis Borgia (1510–72), Jesuit general from 1565 to 1572. His plan, however, failed to materialize due to opposition from Philip II (1527–98), king of Spain from 1556 to 1598, who rejected papal interference in missionary matters. In 1599 Clement VIII, backed and encouraged by Cardinal Giulio Antonio Sartori (1532–1602), founded the congregation of cardinals "*super negotiis Sanctae Fidei et Religionis Catholicae*," commonly known as "de Propagatione Fidei" or "de Propaganda Fide." Because of its conflict with the Spanish Crown's royal patronage, by which Spanish kings exercised control over the Church in the Spanish colonies of South America, this congregation was suppressed in 1604.

Pope Gregory XIII (1554–1623) officially established the Sacred Congregation "de Propaganda Fide" with the bull *Inscrutabili divinae providentiae*, dated June 22, 1622.[4] The new congregation had three key aims: (1) to spread the Catholic faith among non-Catholics, (2) to defend Catholicism in areas where Catholics and non-Catholics lived in close proximity, and (3) to achieve the union of the Orthodox and Protestant churches with the Catholic Church. As such, Propaganda had to supervise and coordinate missionary activity in all Protestant and non-Christian regions. In 1982 the name of the congregation was changed to the Congregation for the Evangelization of Peoples.

From Propaganda's founding, it had jurisdiction over North America. Not until 1908, when Pope Pius X (1835–1914) issued the bull *Sapienti consilio*, were the United States and Canada, with the exception of some apostolic vicariates in the north, removed from Propaganda's control. Given Propaganda's supervision of missionary activity in Protestant and non-Christian countries worldwide, Propaganda's archives are the most important repository for the history of the Catholic Church in the United States and, more broadly, in North America, between the early seventeenth century and the early decades of the twentieth.

DESCRIPTION OF HOLDINGS

Researchers should note that material in the archives of Propaganda is organized according to two different systems based on time period: The first filing system applies to material from the congregation's founding until 1892, whereas the second applies to material from 1893 until 1939.

The following description of the archives' holdings, therefore, has two parts: The first provides details about series filed according to the old classification system, and the second part describes material filed according to the new classification system. A bibliography follows the description.

The Old Filing System (1622–1892)

The material received and collected by Propaganda followed the same filing pattern until 1892; this pattern mirrored the way in which the cardinals of Propaganda worked. The following descriptions provide details on the series that contain material of American interest. Researchers should note that what follows is not a complete inventory of all the series of the Propaganda archives. Such a thorough treatment may be found in the writings of Nikolaus Kowalsky and Josef Metzler, two former Propaganda archivists.

1. Acta

The *Acta* series may be considered the most important of all the series of Propaganda. Its 345 volumes contain the proceedings of the general congregations (*congregazioni generali*) held by the cardinals with the congregation's secretary. The names of Propaganda members (marked either as in attendance or absent) were listed at the beginning of each of the proceedings, followed by the date and location of the meeting. Items for discussion were numbered and were typically introduced by the cardinal who had jurisdiction over the geographical territory concerned. Each item was summarized, usually, in five to ten lines; marginal notes provide additional insights into the geographical locations or the issues discussed. Each of the proceedings ends with the final decision of the general congregation.

From 1622 until May–June 1657, Latin was used. After this, the organization of the *Acta* changed radically, as Italian became the official language, with Latin remaining only in the introductory remarks and the concluding account of the decision made (*rescriptum*).

An additional change was introduced toward the end of the eighteenth century. Each item under discussion became a file in itself (*ponenza*), drafted and introduced by a cardinal (*cardinal ponente*). This system was used regularly from 1810 onward. Each *ponenza* consisted of a report by the *cardinal ponente*, along with copies or abstracts of the original documents that he had consulted in preparing the file. This compilation was known as a *Sommario*. Researchers should note that until 1668, *ad hoc* congregations, known as *congregazioni particolari*, were filed within the *Acta* series. From 1669 onward, though, proceedings of *ad hoc* congregations were filed separately in the series *Congregazioni Particolari* (see below).

A major problem of the *Acta* series is that, in theory, the proceedings of the general congregations should find their corresponding original documents in the series titled *Scritture Originali riferite nelle Congregazioni Generali* (*SOCG*). This is true for the proceedings from 1669 onward, for which the *SOCG* series is organized chronologically. From 1622 to 1668, however, the *SOCG* series was arranged by geographical region. This makes it much more difficult to locate the original documents that correspond to those in the *Acta* series.

Given the great number of documents of American interest in this series, it will be of no use to indicate specific volume numbers or items of special significance. Researchers can avail themselves of the inventories compiled or edited by Luca Codignola, Carl Russell Fish, Finbar Kenneally, Giovanni Pizzorusso, and Matteo Sanfilippo.

2. *SOCG*

This series consists of 1,044 volumes covering the years from 1622 to 1892. It contains the material that the cardinals of Propaganda used for their discussions during general congregations, namely letters, memoranda, petitions, and reports that the various nuncios, bishops, and missionaries addressed to the Roman ministry from all over the world. The series *SOCG* was once divided into two parts. Part One, sometimes referred to as *Lettere Antiche*, consists of 417 volumes for the period from 1622 to 1668. Part Two, sometimes referred to as *Scritture corrispondenti agli Atti*, consists of 627 volumes covering the period from 1669 to 1892.

Part One of the *SOCG* series employs a geographical filing system and is difficult to use. During the seventeenth century, cardinals had a limited knowledge of the areas administered by Propaganda, especially those outside Europe; therefore, they often indicated as Maryland or Virginia areas that do not correspond to their modern locations. An even more significant problem of Part One is that documents from multiple countries were sometimes filed in the same volume. A typical case in point is vol. 106, which, although filed under the heading of "England," also contains documents on Georgia, Ireland, Persia, Scotland, Spain, and Tartary. Another issue to keep in mind is the circuitous international network that Propaganda used. Reports on the Maryland mission, for instance, were sent to Rome through the nuncio in Brussels because the latter was in charge of England and its colonies.

Part Two of the *SOCG* series is much easier to use due to the chronological filing system adopted in 1669 by Federico Baldeschi Colonna (1625–81), Propaganda's secretary from 1668 until 1673 and later a cardinal. The filing system used in Part Two favors the cross-referencing of original documents received by Propaganda (*SOCG*) and the related proceedings (*Acta*). Material of American interest is available in many volumes of the *SOCG* series; therefore, researchers should refer to the inventories mentioned above for the *Acta* series.

3. *Fondo Vienna*

The *Fondo Vienna* series consists of seventy-four volumes. Interestingly, this series did not stem from the administrative work of Propaganda but was created in 1925 when the Austrian government returned the volumes then referred to as "Fondo Vienna" to the Roman ministry. Those volumes had been taken to France by the troops of Napoleon Bonaparte

(1769–1821) during the French occupation of Rome. This new series, then, consists of volumes originally taken from other series, mainly from *SOCG*, *Congregazioni Particolari*, and *Decreti*. Because these volumes were returned only after the other collections had been numbered, the volumes of the Fondo Vienna were kept together and organized into eight subseries.

Below are listed the series held by the Propaganda archives. As shown, some subseries are identical to their original series of provenance; others require brief explanations.

I. *SOCG*, vols. 1–20
    Congregazioni Particolari, vols. 21–24
    Congressi, vols. 25–38
    Decreti, vols. 39–50

II. *Collectio Decretorum*, vols. 51–55, which contains the decrees, decisions, and instructions issued by Propaganda and subsequently collected in four volumes by the order of Pope Benedict XIV (1675–1758); vol. 55 is the index to this subseries.

III. *Dubia et resolutiones*, vols. 56–61, which contains material relating to cases discussed by the Sacred Congregations of the Council, the Holy Office, and the Rites. It comprises seven volumes, of which volume 1 is missing.

IV. *Registro dei Brevi*, vols. 62–70, which is a list of briefs issued between 1701 and 1809, collected in twelve volumes; vols. 1, 2, and 4 are missing; vol. 70 is an alphabetical index of the briefs by country.

V. *Varia*, vols. 71–74, which contains four volumes of miscellaneous origin. Material of American interest is to be found in vols. 30, 37, 39, 41, 43–44, 47–48, 58, 61, 66, and 68–69.

4. *Informazioni*

This series of seventeen volumes, covering the years 1696–1730, is divided into two parts. Part One consists of fourteen volumes (vols. 118, 120, 134–36, 156–58, and 162–67), possibly once kept in the Archives of the Society of Jesus. With the exception of vols. 135 and 136, which deal, respectively, with Ethiopia, Southeast Asia, and various missions (vol. 135 deals with the missions in Ethiopia and Southeast Asia, vol. 136 with various missions), all the other volumes concern China. Part Two comprises three volumes, numbered I–III, which contain information that was possibly collected and sent to Rome by Saverio Marini (1728–1813), bishop of Rieti from 1779 to 1813, regarding Propaganda's financial state. Material of American interest is in vol. 136 only.

5. *Istruzioni*

This series consists of seven volumes covering the years from 1623 to 1808; given that there are only seven volumes for such a long period, it is more than likely that some volumes are missing. This series, one of the most important in Propaganda's archives, contains instructions sent by the Roman ministry to missions' superiors, bishops, vicars apostolic, and nuncios on various issues pertaining to discipline. The first two volumes, unnumbered, deal with the period from 1623 to 1648. The subsequent three volumes are marked as 1–3, with two more as B and C. Each of these five volumes contains instructions dating from the second half of the eighteenth century to the beginning of the nineteenth century. Material of American interest is to be found in vols. 1, 3, and C.

6. *Miscellanee*

This series consists of 126 volumes that cover a period from the last decades of the sixteenth century until the end of the nineteenth. Because documents of this series were once stored on three different sets of shelves of Propaganda, the *Miscellanee* are now divided into three similar subseries: (1) *Miscellanee Varie*, with 51 volumes, (2) *Miscellanee Generali*, with 35 volumes, and (3) *Miscellanee Diverse* with 35 volumes. Documents of American interest are to be found in vols. I, III, VI, XI, XIII, XIVa, and XLVII of *Miscellanee Varie*; vol. XIV of *Miscellanee Generali*; and vols. 6, 20, and 22 of *Miscellanee Diverse*.

7. *Udienze*

This series contains 252 volumes covering the period from 1666 to 1895, with vols. 1–37 covering the period prior to 1800. The *Udienze* series originated in 1666, when general congregations ceased to be held in the presence of the pope, who had attended them from 1622 to 1665. When this custom ceased in 1666, it became the duty of Propaganda's secretary to refer to the pope the matters that required his approval. These meetings between the secretary and the pope, called *udienze*, were usually held on prearranged and fixed days.

This series mainly contains documents on matters of a personal and private nature, such as requests for favors, indulgences, or marriage dispensations. The organization of the *Udienze* series follows no regular pattern. In the early stage, all matters dealt with in the audiences were recorded in the form of a register. Later a separate sheet began to be used for each item, and at the end of the *udienza* the secretary noted the pope's decision. From the third volume onward, the original documents containing the core of each matter were also included in the volume.

Because the number of questions dealt with in the *udienze* increased over time, a system of registers was created, initially called *Ricordi per Mons. Segretario* (memos for the secretary), later *Foglio di Udienza* (audience sheets). Six registers were compiled for Propaganda's internal use. These are divided as follows: (1) deputations and ordinary faculties, eight volumes for the years 1699–1856; (2) extraordinary faculties, nine volumes for the years 1760–1850; (3) register of audiences, twenty-three volumes for the years 1764–1832; (4) minutes of audiences, six volumes for the years 1764–1803; and (5) audiences, three volumes for the years 1810–48. In addition to these, there is also a general index of twenty-eight volumes covering the period from 1666 to 1897, as well as four special indices. Material of American interest is to be found in vols. 177–82.

8. *Decreti*

This series contains thirteen volumes possibly compiled for Propaganda's internal use. It includes the decrees of the general congregations, which do not differ from the *rescripta* found in the *Acta* series. Vols. 1–8 cover the years from 1622 to 1819, although there is a gap between 1675 and 1791; vol. 9 contains drafts of decrees, while vols. 12 and 13 deal with Propaganda's temporal state and Asia, respectively.

9. *Brevi e Bolle*

This series consists of thirteen volumes containing the most solemn and important pontifical decision pertaining to the territories under the jurisdiction of Propaganda. Vol. 1 deals with the period prior to 1800, while vols. 12 and 13 are a collection of faculties (i.e., spiritual powers) and of *professiones fidei*, respectively. Material of American interest is to be found in vols. 1–6.

10. *Congregazioni Particolari*

This series contains sixteen volumes and two miscellanea covering the years from 1622 to 1864. The *Congregazioni Particolari* series includes the proceedings of the meetings of ad hoc commissions (*congregazione particolare*) of cardinals specifically chosen by the pope to consider matters of particular relevance to the Holy See.

It must be noted that for the years 1622–68 the proceedings of the congregazioni particolari are scattered amid the minutes of the *Acta* series; the original documents pertaining to this series are consequently filed in the *SOCG* series. While vols. 1–10 of the *Congregazioni Particolari* series are arranged according to the matters discussed, vols. 11–161 are arranged instead according to their countries of origin or the matters treated and tend to follow a roughly chronological order.

For vols. 11–161, there are three volumes of indices organized by location and the matters treated. Material of American interest is to be found in vols. 3, 6–7, 20–21, 105, 116, 137, 145–46, and 154. Of these volumes, vols. 20 and 137 have "America" clearly indicated in their titles, while vols. 145 and 154 are both marked with the heading *America Settentrionale*. In vols. 158–59, this series also contains material pertaining to the Pontifical North American College of Rome for the years 1851–60.

11. *Lettere*

This series contains 388 volumes covering the period from 1622 to 1892. The *Lettere* series is a collection of copies of the letters written by Propaganda and sent to its correspondents around the world; it should therefore contain copies of all the congregation's letters. The *Lettere* series is, then, key to understanding the strategies and the reasons behind the decisions made by the Roman ministry.

From 1622 to 1657, most outgoing letters were written in Italian, less commonly in French. These documents were bound together in volumes titled *Lettere volgari* (vols. 2–8 and 10–32). During the same period, other letters were written in Latin and were bound together in volumes titled *Lettere latine* (vols. 1 and 9). From 1658 to 1669 (vols. 33–54), outgoing letters were filed according the country interested in the issue at stake. From 1670 to 1679 (vols. 55–68) and from 1721 to 1807 (vols. 110–293), Propaganda opted for a chronological arrangement. Outgoing letters were collected each year in two volumes, one with letters written by Propaganda's secretary, the other with letters written by other members of the congregation, normally its prefect. From 1680 to 1720 (vols. 69–109), outgoing letters continued to be chronologically arranged, but all material (the correspondence of both Propaganda's secretary and that of the other members of the congregation) was included in a single volume. All outgoing letters from 1808 to 1819 were also collected in a single volume. During the years from 1820 to 1892, decrees were also included in the *Lettere* series, which then took on the definitive title of *Lettere e Decreti della Sacra Congregazione e Biglietti di Monsignor Segretario (LDB)*.

Until 1804, each volume of the *Lettere* series had an index or summary of contents at the end of the volume itself. There is also a general volume (vol. A) of indices for the years from 1750 to 1755. Material of American interest is scattered across many volumes of this series; for further specifications, researchers should consult the inventories mentioned in the bibliography.

12. *Congressi*

The *Congressi* series consists of 1,451 volumes that preserve letters, memoranda, and petitions addressed to the congregation. These documents do not substantially differ in nature from the documents filed in the *SOCG* series; the two series are separate only because the documents filed in the *Congressi* series were considered less important at the time. The *Congressi* series was not created at the beginning of Propaganda but was formed around 1668, when the series *SOCG* was reorganized according to a chronological filing system.

The *Congressi* series is divided into two main parts and many subseries. Part One contains letters from missionary areas and therefore follows a geographical distribution. Part Two consists of material related to the more local institutional activities of the congregation or of the institutions that depended on it, like the Propaganda Fide Printing Press or the Pontifical Urban College "de Propaganda Fide."

Material of American interest is plentiful in both parts of the *Congressi* series. In Part One, the subseries *America Antille* (eleven volumes, 1634–1892) and *America Centrale* (fifty-nine volumes and two miscellanea, 1673–1892) contain a vast amount of information on the United States. Three other subseries of particular importance are *Anglia* (twenty-nine volumes and six miscellanea, 1627–1892); *Irlanda* (forty-five volumes, 1625–1892); and *Scozia* (nine volumes, 1623–1892).

In Part Two, relevant subseries containing American material are *Collegio Urbano* (twenty-two vols. and eleven miscellanea, 1677–1892); *Collegi Vari* (sixty-six vols., 1424–1892); *Ministri* (eleven vols. and one miscellanea, 1623–1892); *Missioni* (twenty-eight vols. and twenty-two miscellanea, 1646–1892); and *Sacra Congregazione* (two volumes, 1622–1892).

Of particular interest in the subsection *Collegi Vari* are vols. 1 (*Americano del Nord a Roma, 1856–1892*); 17 (*Collegi Esteri*, section 7, *Americano in Lovanio, 1858–1892*); 18 (*Collegi Esteri*, section 8, *Irlandese di Tutti i Santi in Dublino, 1842–1892*); 34 (*Ibernese di Roma, 1635–1842*); 37 (*Inglese di Roma, 1624–1845*); 38 (*Inglese di Roma, 1846–1885*); 41 (*Irlandese in Roma, 1846–1892*); 43 (section 3, *Brignole Sale-Negroni in Genova, 1846–1891*); 43 (section 5, *Piacenza per gli Emigrati Italiani in America, 1887–1892*); 50 (*PP. Agostiniani Irlandesi in S. Maria in Posterula, 1850–1888*); 51 (*PP. Minori Riformati di S. Isidoro, 1625–1909*); 58 (*S. Clemente, 1809–1832*); 63 (*Scozzese di Roma, 1600–1842*); and 64 (*Scozzese di Roma, 1851–1892*).

13. *Sinodi Diocesani*

This series of nineteen volumes and two miscellanea covers the period from the beginning of the nineteenth century until the first decade of the twentieth; it contains the progressively numbered proceedings of the diocesan synods held in the territories under Propaganda's jurisdiction. It has a lot of material on countries like Canada and the United States, which were removed from the congregation's jurisdiction after the issue of the bull *Sapienti consilio* in 1908.

14. *Collezioni d'Istruzioni, Circolari e Decreti a Stampa*

This series contains three volumes that cover a period from the mid-seventeenth century until 1903. The volumes are not arranged in chronological order, nor are the three volumes paginated. Documents within each volume are itemized and numbered. This series contains the copies of many printed Propaganda documents of general interest, such as circular letters, decrees, and instructions. Material of American interest is to be found in vol. 1, which includes, for instance, instructions pertaining to the appointment of bishops in the United States in 1834.

15. *Biglietti del S. Offizio–Biglietti e Risoluzioni del S. Offizio*

The first series consists of twelve volumes covering the years 1671–1892. In addition to these, there is a five-volume table of contents organized according to the geographical framework of the missions. The second series consists of three volumes. Both series contain material on the correspondence with the Sacred Congregation of the Holy Office. The origin of neither series is known; they were discovered by the Italian historian Giovanni Pizzorusso some years ago. Several volumes concern issues of mixed marriages, baptisms, and the administration of other sacraments in Canada before and after the 1760 Conquest, with additional documents pertaining to other parts of North America.

The New Filing System (1893–1938)

In 1893 a new filing system was implemented in the Propaganda archives, a system that used *rubriche* (code numbers corresponding to contents) and *protocollo* (entry numbers assigned to incoming documents by date of reception). This new Italian filing system, called *Nuova Serie*, applied to every series except the *Acta* series, which remained as it was. The new system responded to the widening scope of the congregation's activity and the corresponding different needs of missionary administration and organization.

For the years from 1893 until 1922, code numbers and related contents are fully listed in the Kowalsky-Metzler inventory.[5] With regard to the rubriche, nos. 1–62 file material thematically; no. 100 contains various material; and nos. 101–62 are organized by geographical areas. In 1923 the rubriche system was revised, and *sottorubriche*, or subfolders, were created to provide further detail.

A continuous sequence of entry numbers (protocollo) applies to the years 1893–1908. For 1909 onward, the numbering sequence starts anew at the beginning of each year. At present, documents of the *Nuova Serie* can be consulted up to 1938.

Material of American interest is particularly rich for the years 1893–1908. Of special significance for this period is rubrica 153 (*America, Stati Uniti*), which contains reports written by bishops after visiting their dioceses. These extremely useful reports provide first-hand descriptions of the ethnic composition of the dioceses. Further material of American interest is to be found in the following rubriche: 5 (secular clergy), 6 (Urban College), 7 (letters written by the former students of the Urban College), 8 (other colleges and seminaries), 9 (universities, academies, and schools), 12–13 (female and male religious orders), 15–16 (Catholic confraternities and secret societies prohibited by the church), 32 (ecclesiastical goods); 33–39 (sacraments; rubrica 39 includes marriage dispensations), 44 (indulgences), 52 (honorific titles), and 62 (vows and dispensations).

After the bull *Sapienti consilio* (1908) removed the United States from Propaganda's jurisdiction, the material of American interest was considerably reduced. Rubrica 153, concerning the Church in the United States, was simply abolished. From 1910 onward, all material of American interest is filed in rubrica 151, which regrouped documents relating to North and South America.

Material of American interest from 1908 to 1938 is dispersed in various rubriche and sottorubriche. Most items of interest deal with issues relating to the apostolic vicariates. For example, a 1924 report describes the apostolic vicariate of North Carolina, which included under its jurisdiction a colony of Italian Waldensians.[6] Material available in rubriche and sottorubriche from 1908 onward also provides information on the activity of the American clergy outside the United States. One good example is provided by a 1928 report from Pietro Fumasoni Biondi (1872–1960), apostolic delegate in the United States, to Cardinal Gugliemo Van Rossum, Propaganda's prefect. Fumasoni Biondi reported on the mission that the American Benedictines had established in 1891 in the Bahamas, an area then under the jurisdiction of the bishop of New York, despite the fact that the Bahamas were at that time a territory of the British Empire.[7]

Further material of American interest for the 1920s and 1930s is mainly to be found in rubrica 69 (*Località non dipendenti da Propaganda Fide*), sottorubrica 4 (*America Settentrionale*); rubrica 72 (*Congregazione di Propaganda Fide*), sottorubrica 4 (*Alunni-Ammissioni-Rimpatrio-Varie*); rubrica 81 (*Società missionarie senza voti dipendenti da Propaganda*), and sottorubrica 9 (*Società delle missioni estere di Maryknoll*).

BIBLIOGRAPHY

Codd, Kevin. "The American College of Louvain." *Catholic Historical Review* 93, no. 1 (January 2007): 47–83.

Codignola, Luca. *Guide to Documents Relating to French and British North America in the Archives of the Sacred Congregation "de Propaganda Fide," 1622–1799.* Ottawa: National Archives of Canada, 1991.

Debevec, Anton, Mathias C. Kiemen, and Alexander Wyse, eds. *United States Documents in the Propaganda Fide Archives: A Calendar. Second Series.* Vols. 8–10. Washington, DC: Academy of American Franciscan History, 1980–83.

DiGiovanni, Stephen M. "Archbishop Ambrose Maréchal: Recently Discovered Documents." *US Catholic Historian* 20, no. 2 (2002): 45–52.

Doorley, Michael. "Irish Catholics and French Creoles: Ethnic Struggles within the Catholic Church in New Orleans, 1835–1920." *Catholic Historical Review* 97, no. 1 (January 2001): 34–54.

Fish, Carl Russell. *Guide to the Materials for American History in Roman and Other Italian Archives.* Washington, DC: Carnegie Institution, 1911.

Guilday, Peter Keenan. *The Life and Times of John Carroll, Archbishop of Baltimore (1735–1815).* New York: Encyclopedia Press, 1922.

———. *The Life and Times of John England, First Bishop of Charleston, 1786–1842.* New York: America Press, 1927.

———. "The Sacred Congregation de Propaganda Fide (1622–1922)." *Catholic Historical Review* 6, no. 4 (January 1921): 478–94.

Hanley, Thomas O'Brien, SJ, ed. *The John Carroll Papers.* 3 vols. Notre Dame, IN: University of Notre Dame Press, 1976.

Hennesey, James, SJ. *American Catholics: A History of the Roman Catholic Community in the United States.* New York: Oxford University Press, 1981.

Hill, Harvey. "American Catholicism? John England and the Republic in Danger." *Catholic Historical Review* 89, no. 2 (April 2003): 240–53.

Kenneally, Finbar, OFM, ed. *United States Documents in the Propaganda Fide Archives: A Calendar. First Series.* Vols. 1–7. Washington, DC: Academy of American Franciscan History, 1966–81.

Kowalsky, Nikolaus, OMI, and Josef Metzler, OMI. *Inventory of the Historical Archives of the Congregation for the Evangelization of Peoples or "de Propaganda Fide."* 3rd ed. Rome: Pontificia Universitas Urbaniana, 1988.

McKevitt, Gerald. "Northwest Indian Evangelization by European Jesuits, 1841–1909." *Catholic Historical Review* 91, no. 4 (October 2005): 688–713.

Metzler, Josef Metzler, OMI. "Indici dell'Archivio Storico della S. C. 'de Propaganda Fide.'" *Euntes Docete: Commentaria Urbaniana* 21 (1968): 109–30.

O'Neill, Charles Edwards, SJ. "North American Beginnings in Maryland and Louisiana." In *Sacrae Congregationis de Propaganda Fide Memoria Rerum: 350 anni a servizio delle missioni, 1622–1972,* ed. Josef Metzler, OMI, vol. 1, Part 2, 713–26. Freiburg: Herder, 1971.

———. "The United States of America." In *Sacrae Congregationis de Propaganda Fide Memoria Rerum: 350 anni a servizio delle missioni, 1622–1972,* ed. Josef Metzler, OMI, 2:1162–184. Freiburg: Herder, 1972.

Pizzorusso, Giovanni. "Archives du Collège Urbain de Propaganda Fide." *Annali Accademici Canadesi* 7 (1991): 93–98.

———. "Archives of the Sacred Congregation 'de Propaganda Fide.' Calendar of Volume I (1634–1760) of the Series Congressi America Antille." *Storia Nordamericana* 3, no. 2 (1986): 117–64.

———. "Archivio della Congregazione 'de Propaganda Fide,' 1788–1918." *Fonti ecclesiastiche romane per lo studio dell'emigrazione italiana in Nord America (1642–1922),* monographic issue of *Studi Emigrazione/Migration Studies* 33, no. 124 (December 1996): 617–71.

———. "Archivio della Congregazione 'de Propaganda Fide.'" *Fonti ecclesiastiche per la storia dell'emigrazione e dei gruppi etnici nel Nord America: Gli Stati Uniti (1893–1922).* Monographic issue of *Studi Emigrazione/Migration Studies* 32, no. 120 (December 1995): 690–721.

———. "Tre lettere di Giovanni Battisti Scalabrini (1889–1892) sull'assistenza spirituale agli italiani negli Stati Uniti nel fondo 'Udienze' dell'Archivio storico della Congregazione 'de Propaganda Fide.'" *Archivio Storico dell'Emigrazione Italiana* 6 (2010): 151–57.

Pizzorusso, Giovanni, and Matteo Sanfilippo. *Inventaire des documents d'intérêt canadien dans les Archives de la Congrégation 'de Propaganda Fide' sous le pontficat de Pie IX (1846–1877).* Rome-Ottawa: Centre Académique Canadien en Italie-Université St-Paul, 2001.

Quinn, John F. "'Three Cheers for the Abolitionist Pope!' American Reaction to Gregory XVI's Condemnation of the Slave Trade, 1840–1860." *Catholic Historical Review* 90, no. 1 (January 2004): 67–93.

Sanfilippo, Matteo. "Roman Sources for the History of American Catholicism." *American Catholic Studies Newsletter* 37, no. 1 (2010): 1–22.

———, ed. *Fonti ecclesiastiche per la storia dell'emigrazione e dei gruppi etnici nel Nord America: Gli Stati Uniti (1893–1922).* Monographic issue of *Studi Emigrazione/Migration Studies* 32, no. 120 (December 1995).

Sanfilippo, Matteo, and Giovanni Pizzorusso, eds. *Gli archivi della Santa Sede come fonte per la storia moderna e contemporanea.* Viterbo: Edizioni Sette Città, 2001.

Trisco, Robert F. *Bishops and Their Priests in the United States.* New York, London: Garland, 1988.

———. "An Extra-Canonical Institution: The Annual Meeting of American Archbishops, 1890–1917." *Jurist* 68, no. 1 (2008): 53–91.

———. *The Holy See and the Nascent Church in the Middle Western United States, 1826–1850.* Rome: Gregorian University Press, 1962.

Archivio Storico del Vicariato di Roma/

Archives of the Vicariate of Rome

Address

   Via dell'Amba Aradam 3, 00186 Rome

Contact Details

   Phone: 39-0669886323/39-0669886322

   Fax: 39-0669886322

   Email 1: Domenico. Rocciolo@VicariatusUrbis.org

   Email 2: ArchivioStoricoDiocesano@VicariatusUrbis.org

STATUS

Open to researchers Monday–Friday, 8:30 a.m.–1:00 p.m.; on Tuesdays they are also open from 2:30 p.m. until 5:00 p.m., and on Thursdays they close at 11:00 a.m. The archives close for Italian national holidays from mid-July until mid-September. It is necessary to contact the head in advance to access the material; a reference letter is required. Applications to consult particular documents are due before 10:00 a.m. on the research day. The material is in English, French, Italian, or Latin. Material post-1939 cannot be consulted.

HISTORY

The Vicariate of Rome is the administrative body supervising the Diocese of Rome, of which the pope is the bishop and the cardinal vicar acts as his delegate. The vicariate began to have a clear jurisdiction and specific duties in 1558.

DESCRIPTION OF HOLDINGS

The Archives of the Vicariate of Rome contain vast documentation spanning the twelfth century to the 1980s. At present, the material can be divided as follows: (1) *Parrocchie*, 7,500 volumes containing the registers of baptisms, weddings, and burials, as well as the status (the list of parishioners) for every parish in Rome for the years 1531–1920; (2) *Cresime*, 248 registers of confirmations for the years 1589–1980; (3) *Ordinazioni*, fifty-six registers that list priests ordained in the years 1512–1902; (4) *Segreteria del Vicariato*, eighty-seven volumes for the years 1571–1900 and 1,120 folders for the years 1646–1911; (5) *amministrazione del vicariato*, 460 folders for the years 1805–1965; (6) *confraternite*, with material on the twenty-one Roman confraternities from 1485 until 1940; (7) *Capitoli*, with material on nine church chapters of Rome; (8) *Altri fondi e documenti*, which is split into *Fondo Ottoboni*, which has 880 volumes for the years 1485–1901, and *Fondo Buon Governo e Bandi*, with ninety-three folders for the years 1606–1922; and (9) *Reliquie*, with ninety-nine folders for the years 1553–1964.

Material of American interest is scattered in different series. Of particular interest is the series *Reliquie*, which contains documents pertaining to bishops' requests for the vicariate to send relics to their dioceses. One example of this is an 1881 request from Léon Bouland, a French priest of the Notre Dame des Victoires parish in Boston, asking that relics be sent. In his application, he explained that "my French parish, the only one which exists in the city of Boston, is located in the heart of Protestantism."[8]

There is additional material in the ordination registers—particularly from vol. 42 to vol. 56—that provides details about the American priests ordained in Rome during the nineteenth century and the first decade of the twentieth. Further material is located in the section *Segreteria del Vicariato*, which contains the following items: (1) *Atti, corrispondenza*, palchetto 65, plico no. 193, and *Scuole, istituti, convitti*, with a dossier (no. 30) on the Pontifical North American College from 1935 to 1953; (2) *Atti, Segreteria*, palchetto 65, plico no. 194 II-*Raccolta corrispondenza Stati Esteri*, with a bundle of documents titled "*Stati Uniti d'America,*

1855–1860"; (3) *Atti, Segreteria*, palchetto 65, plico no. 217, with a dossier on the International Eucharistic Congress held in Chicago in 1926; and (4) *Atti, Segreteria*, palchetto 65, plico no. 63, with a dossier devoted to John Davis, a Philadelphia priest, dated 1875.

Given how much material there is in the archives of the vicariate, more material of American interest probably remains to be found.

BIBLIOGRAPHY

Del Re, Niccolò. *Il vicereggente del Vicariato di Roma*. Rome: Istituto di Studi Romani, 1976.

Rocciolo, Domenico. "La costruzione della città religiosa: Strutture ecclesiastiche a Roma tra la metà del Cinquecento e l'Ottocento." In *Storia d'Italia: Annali*, vol. 16: *Roma, la città del papa: Vita civile e religiosa dal giubileo di Bonifacio VIII al giubileo di papa Wojtyla*, ed. Luigi Fiorani and Adriano Prosperi, 367–93. Turin: Giulio Einaudi Editore, 2000.

———. "I documenti dell'Archivio Storico del Vicariato e le ricerche per la storia religiosa di Roma." In *Luigi Fiorani, storico di Roma religiosa e dei Caetani di Sermoneta*, ed. Caterina Fiorani and Domenico Rocciolo, 55–66. Rome: Edizioni di Storia e Letteratura, 2013.

Archivio del Collegio Urbano "de Propaganda Fide" /
Archives of the Urban College "de Propaganda Fide"

Address

Via Urbano VIII 16, 00165 Rome

Contact Details

Phone: 39-0669881024

Fax: 39-0669881332

Email: collegiourbano@collegiourbano.org

Website: www.collegiourbano.org

STATUS

Closed to researchers at the time of this writing.

HISTORY

The Urban College was officially established in 1627 by Pope Urban VIII (1568–1644), and in 1641 it was placed under the control of the Sacred Congregation "de Propaganda Fide." The college sought to educate the best students from regions where Catholicism was not the official religion and train them as secular missionaries. The Urban College was located in Propaganda's palace in Piazza di Spagna until 1926, when it was transferred to its current location on the Janiculum Hill (Gianicolo).

DESCRIPTION OF HOLDINGS

Because the archives of the Urban College have been closed to researchers for some time, a detailed inventory of the material of American interest cannot be provided. However, the biographical studies Giovanni Pizzorusso compiled about Canadian students shows that material of American interest probably does exist. Series *VI Elenco* and *VII Registro* contain the names of the students admitted to the college, with details about the origins, age, diocese of provenance, and date of admission and departure from the Urban College for each student. Two series that might contain additional material on American students are *II Liber Ordinationum* and *III Liber mortuorum*, which record, respectively, students' ordinations and deaths. Two further series of interest are *IV Diario*, which provides an overview on the college's daily activity, and *X Lettere*, which contains letters (known as *lettere di stato*) written by former students after returning to their countries. Researchers must note that most of the documents pertaining to the Urban College and its students are also preserved in the archives of Propaganda in the series *Congressi*, subseries *Collegio Urbano*.

BIBLIOGRAPHY

Codignola, Luca. "The Molding of a Roman Élite: Ralph Smith and Felix Theophilus Dougherty, The First American Students at Rome's Collegio Urbano, 1783–1824." *Itineraria* 13 (2014): 1–15.

Jezernik, M. "Il Collegio Urbano di Propaganda Fide." In *Sacrae Congregationis de Propaganda Fide Memoria Rerum*, ed. Josef Metzler, OMI, vol. 1, Part 1, 465–82. Freiburg: Herder, 1971.

Pizzorusso, Giovanni. "Archives du Collège Urbain de Propaganda Fide." *Annali Accademici Canadesi* 6 (1990): 93–98.

———. "Una presenza ecclesiastica cosmopolita a Roma: Gli allievi del Collegio Urbano di Propaganda Fide." *Bollettino di Demografia Storica* 22 (1995): 129–38.

Archivio Storico della Congregazione per le Chiese Orientali /
Historical Archives of the Congregation for the Oriental Churches
Address
    Via della Conciliazione 34, 00193 Rome
Contact Details
    Phone: 39-0669884282/39-0669884482
    Fax: 39-0668984300
    Email 1: cco@orientchurch.va
    Email 2: gianpaolo.rigotti@orientchurch.va
    Website: www.vatican.va/roman_curia/congregations/orientchurch/index_it.htm

STATUS
The archives are open Monday–Friday, 9 a.m.–1:00 p.m., and close for Italian national holidays and from the end of June until the end of September. Because seats in the study room are limited, researchers should make an advance appointment with the archivist to gain access to the material; only three volumes per day may be requested. Researchers should also send a letter of reference to His Eminence Leonardo Cardinal Sandri. Most material is in English, Italian, or Latin, although there are also documents written in Eastern European languages. Material post-1939 cannot be consulted.

HISTORY

The origins of the Congregazione per le Chiese Orientali can be traced back to 1573, when Pope Gregory XIII (1502–85) established the Congregatio de Rebus Graecorum. The congregation supervised matters pertaining to the Catholics of Byzantine and Greek rites and helped to spread the Catholic faith to other people of Eastern Europe and the Middle East. In 1599 Pope Clement VIII (1536–1605) renamed it Congregatio super negotiis sanctae Fidei et religionis catholicae. This congregation was responsible not only for Catholics of the Greek rite but also for promotion of the Catholic faith in Latin regions and, later, in pagan lands. By 1600 it was referred to as Propaganda Fide, a name it kept until 1622, when it was replaced by the Sacra Congregatio de Propaganda Fide, which incorporated its tasks. With the apostolic constitution *Romani Pontifices* of January 6, 1862, Pope Pius IX established the Congregatio de Propaganda Fide pro negotiis ritus orientalis (Congregation for the Propagation of the Faith for Affairs of the Oriental Rite).

With the May 1, 1917, motu proprio *Dei Providentis*, Pope Benedict XV (1854–1922) established an autonomous and independent congregation named Congregatio pro Ecclesia Orientali. With the apostolic constitution *Regimini Ecclesiae Universae* (August 15, 1967), Pope Paul VI (1897–1978) changed its name to Congregatio pro Ecclesiis Orientalibus. Paul VI, and subsequently Pope John Paul II (1920–2005), gave to the Congregazione per le Chiese Orientali the task of supervising matters pertaining to the Oriental Church, with jurisdiction over the following: Egypt and the Sinai Peninsula, Eritrea and northern Ethiopia, southern Albania and Bulgaria, Cyprus, Greece, Iran, Iraq, Lebanon, Palestine, Syria, Jordan, and Turkey.

DESCRIPTION OF HOLDINGS

The archives of the Congregazione per le Chiese Orientali are divided into three chronological sections: (1) material from 1862 to 1892, (2) material from 1893 to 1927, and (3) material from 1928 to 1962.

The first section contains the oldest documents, which were transferred from Propaganda to the Congregazione per le Chiese Orientali in 1929 and in 1961. It consists of the following series: (1) *Acta*, with 22 volumes; (2) *Scritture originali delle Congregazioni generali*, with 24 volumes; (3) *Udienze di Nostro Signore*, with 26 volumes; (4) *Scritture riferite nei Congressi*, with 94 volumes; and (5) *Lettere e decreti*, with 25 volumes.

The second section consists of the following series: (1) *Acta*, with 26 volumes; (2) *Udienze di Nostro Signore*, with 7 volumes; (3) *Titoli generali o "rubriche,"* with 212 files, each of which concerns a specific theme; (4) *Leone XIII*, with 12 files; (5) *Latini*, with 62 files; and (6) *Pontificia Commissione pro Russia*, with an unknown number of files.

The third section consists of two series: *Oriente (Affari generali)*, with 488 files, and *Chiese orientali e Liturgia*. The latter is further subdivided into the following subseries: (1) *Albanesi*, with 14 files; (2) *Armeni*, with 134 files; (3) *Bulgari*, with 29 files; (4) *Caldei*, with 80 files; (5) *Copti*, with 50 files; (6) *Etiopi*, with 47 files; (7) *Georgiani*, with 4 files; (8) *Greci*, with 50 files; (9) *Italo-albanesi*, with 39 files; (10) *Latini*, with 89 files; (11) *Liturgia*, with 51 files; (12) *Malabaresi*, with 100 files; (13) *Malankaresi*, with 18 files; (14) *Maroniti*, with 198 files; (15) *Melkiti*, with an unknown number of files; (16) *Romeni*, with 79 files; (17) *Russi*, with 102 files; (18) *Ruteni*, with 239 files; (19) *Siri*, with 48 files; and (20) *Ucraini*, with 21 files. Each of the above subseries contains different alphabetically arranged folders. A full description of all the series and a history of the archives are available in an essay written by Gianpaolo Rigotti.[9]

Material of American interest is scattered across all series of the three sections of the archives, especially the third section. Of particular importance is the series dealing with the Ruthenian communities established in the United States. For instance, this series contains a petition written in 1916 by a group of Slovak emigrants of Byesville, Ohio, to Pope Benedict XV. Their parish had been served by two Slovak priests and, subsequently, by an Irish priest who did not understand their language. Because of this they had asked James Joseph Hartley (1858–1944), bishop of Columbus from 1904 to 1944, to send another Slovak priest, but the bishop rejected their request, stating: "It is enough that a man go to church even if he does not understand the services, and prays by himself. In the next world the Slovaks will not be able to speak to God in the Slovak tongue anyway."[10]

BIBLIOGRAPHY

Ferencz, Nicholas. *American Orthodoxy and Parish Congregationalism*. Piscataway, NJ: Gorgias Press, 2006.

Kuckera, M. J. "The Juridical Rapport between the Oriental Churches in the Diaspora in North America: Experiences and Perspectives." In *Nuove terre nuove chiese: Le comunità di fedeli orientali in diaspora*, ed. Luis Okulik, 177–96. Venice: Marcianum, 2008.

Marti, Federico. *I Ruteni negli Stati Uniti: Santa Sede e mobilità umana tra Ottocento e Novecento*. Milan: Giuffrè Editore, 2009.

Rigotti, Gianpaolo. "L'archivio della Congregazione per le Chiese Orientali: Dalla Costituzione apostolica Romani Pontifices (1862) alla morte del card. Gabriele Acacio Coussa (1962)." In *Fede e martirio: Le chiese orientali cattoliche nell'Europa del Novecento; Atti del Convegno di storia ecclesiastica contemporanea, Città del Vaticano, 22–24 ottobre 1998*, ed. Aleksander Rebernik, Gianpaolo Rigotti, and Michel Van Parys, OSB, 247–95. Vatican City: Libreria Editrice Vaticana, 2003.

———. "Le comunità cattoliche orientali in diaspora nel Nord America: Il caso dei Ruteni e degli Ucraini." In *L'Europa e la sua espansione religiosa nel continente nordamericano*, ed. Luciano Vaccaro, 2:619–60. Milan: Centro Ambrosiano, 2012.

La Sacra Congregazione per le Chiese Orientali nel Cinquantesimo della fondazione. Rome: Tipografia Italo-Orientale "San Nilo," 1969.

Sanfilippo, Matteo. "I ruteni nelle Americhe: Emigrazione e viaggio." In *Da est ad ovest, da ovest ad est: Viaggiatori per le strade del mondo*, ed. Gaetano Platania, 397–429. Viterbo: Edizioni Sette Città, 2006.

———. *La Santa Sede e l'emigrazione dall'Europa Centro Orientale negli Stati Uniti fra Otto e Novecento*. Viterbo: Edizioni Sette Città, 2010.

Simon, Konstantin. "Alexis Toth and the Beginnings of the Orthodox Movement among the Ruthenians in America." *Orientalia Christiana Periodica* 54 (1998): 387–428.

———. "Before the Birth of Ecumenism: The Background Relating to the Mass 'Conversion' of

Oriental Rite Catholics to Russian Orthodoxy in the United States." *Diakonia* 20, no. 3 (1986): 128–51.

―――. "The First Years of Ruthenian Church Life in America." *Orientalia Christiana Periodica* 60 (1994): 187–232.

Archivio Storico della Segreteria di Stato, Sezione per i Rapporti con gli Stati (formerly known as Affari Ecclesiastici Straordinari) /

Archives of the Secretariat of State, Section for Relations with States

Address

Segreteria di Stato, Cortile del Belvedere, 00120 Vatican City

Contact Details

Phone: 39-0669883871/39-069881045

Email: asv@asv.va

Website: www.vatican.va/roman_curia/secretariat_state/sezione-rapporti-stati/archivio
-storico/contatti/contatti_it.html

STATUS

The archives are open Monday–Friday, 9:00 a.m.–1:00 p.m. The archives close from mid-July until mid-September. It is necessary to bring a reference letter and to send a request indicating the documents to be consulted to Archbishop Paul Gallagher. Researchers must take into account that the accreditation process may take weeks. Digital and printed indices can be consulted only at the archives themselves. The majority of the material is in English, Italian, or Latin. Material post-1939 cannot be consulted.

HISTORY

On July 19, 1814, Pope Pius VIII (1761–1830) transformed the congregation Super negotiis ecclesiasticis regni Galliarum, which had been established by Pope Pius VI (1717–99) in 1793, into the Congregatio extraordinaria praeposita negotiis ecclesiasticis orbis catholici. In 1824 Pope Leo XII (1760–1829) changed its name to Congregatio extraordinaria praeposita negotiis ecclesiasticis extraordinariis (Affari Ecclesiastici Straordinari in Italian), and entrusted it with the task of supporting the Segreteria di Stato in matters of particular difficulty. The close link with the segretario di Stato was confirmed by the fact that the latter supervised the congregation on behalf of the pope. During the nineteenth century, the Sacra Congregazione degli Affari Ecclesiastici Straordinari dealt with international issues, including relations with the newborn Kingdom of Italy, which became more thorny after the 1871 annexation of Rome.

In 1908 the Segreteria di Stato was reorganized into three sections: (1) one devoted to *affari straordinari*, thus incorporating the members of the former congregation; (2) another devoted to *affari ordinari*; and (3) another still devoted to the tasks of the Cancelleria dei Brevi Apostolici. This reorganization was ratified in 1917 by the new Code of Canon Law. Yet the reform of the papal curia, known as *Regimini Ecclesiae Universae*, implemented by

Pope Paul VI (1897–1978) in 1967, again detached *affari straordinari* from Segreteria di Stato, thus transforming the former into a distinct organism known as Consiglio per gli Affari Pubblici della Chiesa. In 1988 Pope John Paul II (1920–2005) returned the Consiglio per gli Affari Pubblici della Chiesa to the Segreteria di Stato. Since then, the consiglio has been organized into two sections: (1) *Affari Generali* and (2) *Rapporti con gli Stati*. *Affari Pubblici* was merged with the section *Rapporti con gli Stati*, supervised by an archbishop.

DESCRIPTION OF HOLDINGS

The institutional history of the Affari Ecclesiastici Straordinari, combined with the specific historical context in which it operated, is well mirrored by the complexity of its archives. At present these are subdivided into different periods that roughly correspond to the various phases of this congregation's history. Researchers can consult the material for the following periods: (1) for 1822 to 1878, including some documents for the years from 1814 to 1822; (2) for 1878 to 1903; (3) for 1903 to 1922; and (4) for 1922 to the period after World War II. Beyond these four periods, there are also some specific series, such as the papers of the cardinals who worked for the congregation. The papers of the cardinals are just beginning to be investigated, and, at present, they do not seem to contain material of American interest.

However, the documentation found for the above four periods does contain a large amount of material on the Catholic Church in the United States. This material is found in files dealing with specific matters and arranged in a geographical section, usually classified as United States of America. (In some instances there is material pertaining to specific dioceses, such as Boston or New York.) The files progressively increase in volume during the twentieth century. Files relating to the period between World War I and World War II are especially numerous and deal with a wide variety of matters, such as the religious conditions of the Polish and Slovak migrants (posizione 150, fascicoli 11–12; posizione 175, fascicolo 20); on the Catholic University of Washington (posizione 155, fascicolo 20); on the establishment and activity of the National Catholic Welfare Council during the 1920s (posizione 172, fascicoli 14–18); on several apostolic delegates (the papers of Pietro Fumasoni Biondi [1872–1960] during the years from 1922 to 1933 are contained in posizione 176, fascicolo 21); on assistance to the Catholic African American faithful (posizione 207, fascicolo 41); and on the anti-Catholic activities of the Ku Klux Klan (posizione 184, fascicolo 33).

BIBLIOGRAPHY

Pásztor, Lajos. "La Congregazione degli Affari Ecclesiastici Straordinari tra il 1814 e il 1850." *Archivum Historiae Pontificiae* 6 (1968): 191–318.

Regoli, Roberto. "Il ruolo della Sacra Congregazione degli Affari Ecclesiastici Straordinari durante il pontificato di Pio XI." In *La sollecitudine ecclesiale di Pio XI. Alla luce delle nuove fonti archivistiche*, ed. Cosimo Semeraro, 183–229. Vatican City: Editrice Vaticana, 2010.

Sanfilippo, Matteo. *La Sante Sede e l'emigrazione dall'Europa centro-orientale negli Stati Uniti tra Ottocento e Novecento*. Viterbo: Edizioni Sette Città, 2010.

Archivio Storico delle Celebrazioni Liturgiche del Sommo Pontefice /
Archives of the Liturgical Celebrations of the Supreme Pontiff

Address

Palazzo Apostolico, 00120 Vatican City

Contact Details

Phone: 39-0669883253

Fax: 39-0669885412

Email: ucepo@celebra.va

STATUS

Closed. Researchers are advised to contact the archives, indicate the nature of their research, and ask for an appointment. If access is granted, it is usually granted for between 9:00 a.m. and noon; a reference letter is required. Most documents are in Latin. Material post-1939 cannot be consulted.

HISTORY

The origins of the Office of Masters of the Apostolic Ceremonies, or Magistri Caerimoniarum Apostolicarum, can be traced back to the eighth century. From the fifteenth century onward, this office acquired a growing importance, as masters began to keep records of their activity. In 1563, Pope Pius IV (1499–1565) granted special rights to masters, and the 1917 reform implemented by Pope Benedict XV (1854–1922) made masters part of a college headed by a prefect. In 1970 the Prefecture of Pontifical Ceremonies changed its name to Ufficio per le Cerimonie Pontificie (Office of Papal Liturgical Celebrations).

The apostolic constitution *Pastor bonus* of June 28, 1988, changed the name of the Ufficio per le Cerimonie Pontificie to the Ufficio delle Celebrazioni Liturgiche del Sommo Pontefice (the Office for Liturgical Celebrations of the Supreme Pontiff), from then onwards a distinct office of the papal curia. Currently the office manages all liturgical celebrations and other sacred functions attended by the pope or by a cardinal acting on his behalf. It also oversees the celebrations of the consistory as well as the liturgical celebrations of the College of Cardinals during sede vacante periods. The archives of the Ufficio delle Celebrazioni Liturgiche del Sommo Pontefice mainly contain diaries and official documents written by masters of the apostolic ceremonies.

Material of American interest is mainly found in the section pertaining to the reports and oaths of cardinals, *Relazioni e giuramenti di cardinali.* An example of this American material is provided by box no. 32, dossier no. 28, which contains a report written in 1886 by papal delegate Msgr. Germano Straniero for Cardinal James Gibbons (1834–1921).

BIBLIOGRAPHY

Dante, Leonida Enrico, ed. *Catalogo dell'Archivio della Prefettura delle Cerimonie Apostoliche.* Rome, 1956.

Sanfilippo, Matteo. *L'affermazione del cattolicesimo nel Nord America.* Viterbo: Edizioni Sette Città, 2003.

Archivio Storico Generale della Fabbrica di San Pietro /

Archives of the Fabbrica di San Pietro

Address

    Vatican City, 00120 Rome

Contact Details

    Phone: 39-0669885470

    Fax: 39-0669885518

    Email: archiviofsp@fsp.va

    Website: www.vatican.va/various/basiliche/san_pietro/it/fabbrica/arc_storico/informa
       zioni.htm

STATUS

Open to researchers Monday–Saturday, 8:30 a.m.–12:30 p.m. The archive is closed on official Vatican holidays and from mid-July to the third week of September. A reference letter and an advance appointment with the archivists are required. Material is in English and Italian. Material post-1939 can be consulted with the archivist's permission.

HISTORY

The Archivio Storico Generale della Fabbrica di San Pietro holds material related to the Fabbrica di San Pietro. The establishment of the Fabbrica can be traced back to 1506, when Pope Julius II (1503–13) decided to build a new Vatican basilica to replace the old Constantinian basilica. To that end, the pope in 1509 established an administrative and legal body to supervise the building of the new basilica and collect alms from the faithful.

DESCRIPTION OF HOLDINGS

The archive was officially established on January 13, 1579. At present, the archive consists of nine thousand archival units organized into one hundred *armadi*. The archive is divided into the following sections: (1) *Fabbrica di San Pietro*, which covers the period from 1506 until recent times; (2) *Fondo della Piazza*, from the mid-fifteenth century to 1598; (3) *Fondo Quarantotti*, from the end of the seventeenth century to 1765; (4) *Fondo Galli*, from the end of the eighteenth century to 1859; (5) *Fondo Arciconfraternita SS.mo Sacramento*, from 1540 to 1976; and (6) *Fondo Accossato Margherita e Manto Roberta*, from the end of the eighteenth century to the beginnings of the nineteenth.

    Material of American interest can be found in two volumes: *Armadio* 84, D (4), no. 45 and *Armadio* 84, D (4), no. 51; both are in the section *Fabbrica di San Pietro*. These volumes cover the years 1936–51 and provide information about the activity of John Rossi, an Italian American who acted as general representative of the Vatican Mosaic Studio for the United States and Canada from the 1930s onward. The documentation mainly consists of requests for permission to study the paintings and mosaics preserved by Saint Peter's Basilica, along with a series of receipts, legal complaints, and extracts from various newspapers relating to the exhibitions organized in the United States of material coming from the Vatican Mosaic Studio.

The documents show the varied reception of this material among American Catholics. A clear example is provided by a letter that Rossi penned to Msgr. Ludwig Kass, secretary of the Sacred Congregation of Saint Peter's Basilica, on May 25, 1938. In it Rossi openly declared: "I am finding very little success in selling what I took with me, as times here are so bad and this especially for New York and New Jersey. They inform me that out-side of New York I will find it more better [*sic*]" and that "in the future I will not make mistakes on the American taste in art for they admire and appreciate the rough and not the polished mosaics."[11]

A further example of how this material raised interest among the North American Catholic clergy comes from an anonymous author's undated list of American and Canadian bishops and cardinals who were willing to buy copies from the Vatican Mosaic Studio. The list includes the most prominent members of the American and Canadian Catholic hierarchy, such as William Henry O'Connell (1859–1944), bishop of Boston; Michael Joseph Curley (1879–1947), bishop of Baltimore; and Jean-Marie-Rodrigue Villeneuve (1883–1947), archbishop of Quebec.[12] Additional material can be found elsewhere in the section *Fabbrica di San Pietro*, although, given its vast content, this requires in-depth research of all volumes from the nineteenth century to the twentieth.

BIBLIOGRAPHY

Di Sante, Assunta. "L'Archivio Storico Generale della Fabbrica di San Pietro in Vaticano e i suoi strumenti di corredo." In *La Casa di Dio: La fabbrica degli uomini; Gli archivi delle fabbricerie; Atti del convegno di Ravenna (26 settembre 2008)*, ed. Gilberto Zacchè, 49–59. Modena: Enrico Mucchi Editore, 2009.

Di Sante, Assunta, and Simona Turriziani. "L'Archivio Storico Generale della Fabbrica di San Pietro." In *Magnificenze Vaticane: Tesori inediti dalla Fabbrica di San Pietro*, ed. Alfredo Maria Pergolizzi, 189–97. Rome: De Luca Editori d'Arte, 2008.

Biblioteca Apostolica Vaticana /

Vatican Library

Address

Cortile del Belvedere, V-00120 Vatican City

Contact Details

Phone: 39-0669879411

Fax: 39-0669884795

Email: bavsegre@vatlib.it

Website: www.vatlib.it/home.php

STATUS

Open to researchers Monday–Friday, 8:45 a.m.–5:15 p.m., and closed from mid-July until mid-September. Contact the library in advance and provide a reference letter to gain access to the material. Researchers should also consult the online catalogs (at www.vatlib.it/home .php?pag=cataloghi_online) for the specific reference numbers of the material sought. With rare exceptions, undergraduate students are not admitted into the library. Due to the limited number of seats in the study room, graduate students are admitted with the following restrictions: (1) students enrolled in master's degree programs are admitted until the end of May, (2) PhD candidates are admitted until mid-June. The majority of the material is in English, Italian, or Latin. Material post-1939 cannot be consulted.

HISTORY

The earliest origins of the Vatican Library can be traced to the fourth century, when there is evidence of the existence of the Scrinium, which was both an archive and a library. At the end of the eighth century, some sort of professional librarian seems to have been at work, though the earliest archives and library disappeared in the first half of the thirteenth century. During the Avignon Papacy (1309–77), Pope John XXII (1244–1334) began to build a new library. After the papacy returned to Rome in 1377, Pope Nicholas V (1397–1455) made the growing body of Greek and Latin manuscripts available to scholars. It was, however, Pope Sixtus IV (1414–84) who, with the bull *Ad decorem militantis Ecclesiae*, dated June 15, 1475, officially established the Vatican Library. From then on, the library expanded its collections of archival material, manuscripts, and printed books. With the founding of the Vatican Secret Archives in 1612, a substantial part of the library's archival collection was transferred there.

DESCRIPTION OF HOLDINGS

Given its vast collections, which contain material dated from the early Middle Ages until the twentieth century, the Vatican Library is considered, together with the Vatican Secret Archives, the main repository of the documents of the Catholic Church. At present, the Vatican Library holds 180,000 manuscripts, 1,600,000 printed books, more than 8,600 *incunabula* (books printed [not handwritten] before 1501), 300,000 coins and medals, 150,000 prints and drawings, and over 150,000 pictures. Material of American interest is mainly to be found in the printed books section and in the collections of manuscripts.

Given the profusion of items contained in the printed books section, it is not possible to provide a detailed inventory. Researchers can use the online catalog of the printed books, at opac.vatlib.it/iguana/www.main.cls?searchProfile=PRINT&sUrl=search#mode=advanced. Researchers should note that collection no. 130 of the printed book section is entirely devoted to the United States.

As previously mentioned, the Vatican Library also contains a rich collection of manuscripts with material on the United States both for the colonial period and for the nineteenth and twentieth centuries. Given that the material in this section covers a vast period, its inventory is split into two parts: (1) collections for the period from the sixteenth century until the late eighteenth, and (2) collections for the period from the nineteenth to the twentieth century.

Manuscripts from the Sixteenth Century to the Late Eighteenth

One of the richest manuscript collections of the Vatican Library on the early period of the Americas is the *Barberiniani Latini*. This important collection derives from the private collection of the Barberini family, which played a seminal role in the papal curia during the seventeenth century, particularly with Pope Urban VIII (born Maffeo Barberini, 1568–1644) and his two nephews, Cardinals Antonio (1607–71) and Francesco (1597–1679) Barberini. This collection, though particularly rich in the history of the Spanish expansion in South America and the Caribbean, also contains material on the English and French settlements in North America. For example, MS no. 4605 provides information on the Capuchin mission at Port-Royal, in today's Province of Nova Scotia, and the plans for its expansion toward Virginia; MS no. 8620 contains a copy of the report on Maryland written by Carlo Rossetti (1615–81), nuncio in England from 1639 to 1642.

The collection *Borgiani Latini* derives from the private collection of Stefano Borgia (1731–1804), secretary and prefect of Propaganda Fide, 1770–89 and 1798–1804. Most of the *Borgiani Latini* collection is concerned with areas outside Europe, particularly Asia. The only relevant document of American interest is no. 291, fol. 266, which contains a brief on the establishment of the Catholic mission in North America dated November 17, 1779.

The collection *Ottoboniani Latini* was established by Pope Alexander VIII (born Pietro Vito Ottoboni, 1610–91) as his own private collection. Most of the material consists of diplomatic correspondence, mainly related to the French and Spanish settlements in North America. MS no. 2536 contains two reports from the archives of Propaganda Fide: The first, dated December 27, 1625, refers to the discovery of Newfoundland; the second, dated December 28, 1630, refers to the Puritans' settlement in New England.

The collection *Reginense Latino* contains part of the private library of Queen Christina of Sweden (1626–89), created during her residence in Rome from 1655 to 1689. This collection contains a report about the Americas (no. 651) written in 1627 by Leonardo Moro (1576–1627), a Venetian ambassador to Spain. Further material of American interest may be found in MS no. 2105, which contains many maps of North America.

The collection *Urbinati Latini* derives from the private library of the dukes of Urbino and was added to the Vatican Library in 1658. It mainly contains diplomatic material on the activity of the Spaniards in South America and the Caribbean. Material on North America is to be found in MSS 1048–49, 1053–54, 1075–83, 1085–87, 1113, and 1115–17. This material pertains to the raids carried out by Francis Drake (1540–96) and, more broadly, to the activities of the English along the coast of Virginia during the last two decades of the sixteenth century.

The collection *Vaticani Latini* is the original and main repository of the manuscripts of the Vatican Library. Like the collections described above, *Vaticani Latini* has some material concerning the early phase of European expansion in the Americas. For example, MS no. 6227 provides details on the expeditions led by Walter Raleigh (ca. 1554–1618) and his half-brother, Humphrey Gilbert (ca. 1539–83), in Guyana and North America at the end of the sixteenth century. Material on the status of the Catholic missions is in MSS 7220 and 12072. The former contains a report on the Catholic missions in Africa, America, and Asia, which Niccolò Forteguerri (1674–1735), secretary of Propaganda Fide from 1730 to 1735, wrote and sent to Pope Clement XI (1649–1721). The latter manuscript contains a copy of a description of the state of the worldwide missions under Propaganda Fide's control, which Urbano Cerri (1634–79), secretary of the Roman ministry from 1675 to 1678, wrote to Pope Innocent XI (1611–89) in 1678. There is additional material of American interest in MS 10364, titled *Gli ozi letterari*, Tomo I: *Differenze tra l'Inghilterra e le Colonie dell'America*. This consists of newspaper extracts and summaries concerning the United States during the revolutionary period. This material was collected by Andrea Lazzari (1754–1831), a secular priest and erudite appointed protonotary apostolic in 1797.

Manuscripts from the Nineteenth and Twentieth Centuries

Material of American interest on the nineteenth and twentieth centuries is in the collection *Vaticani Latini*, especially in MS no. 9565 (fols. 125–53), which provides statistical reports on the American dioceses under Propaganda Fide's control in 1839. Of particular interest for the history of the Italian migration to North America are the collections *Toniolo* and *Villari*.

The former contains the correspondence of Giuseppe Toniolo (1845–1918), economist, sociologist, and one of the most influential members of the Italian Catholic movement. The *Toniolo* collection consists of 41 boxes of 7,097 letters for the period from 1863 to 1918. Given his prominence, Toniolo communicated with numerous influential Catholics, lay and religious, including Archbishop Pietro Pisani (1871–1960), who from 1908 to 1910 traveled extensively among the Italian communities of Canada and the United States. The *Toniolo* collection contains an additional 21 boxes preserved in the section *Scriptorum Serie I: Manoscriptorum*; these may contain relevant material, but they cannot be consulted at present.

The *Villari* collection comprises 105 volumes of the correspondence of Pasquale Villari (1827–1917) and his son Luigi Villari (1876–1959). Their correspondence covers the period from the last three decades of the nineteenth century to the first two decades of the twentieth. Inventories 432/I and 432/II provide a summary and a chronology of the material contained in this collection. Pasquale Villari, a university professor and a member of the Italian parliament, was appointed minister of education in 1891. From 1896 to 1903, he also served as president of the Dante Alighieri Society, which was established in Italy in 1889 to promote Italian culture and language worldwide. As president of the Dante Alighieri Society, Pasquale Villari was granted prestigious positions in the United States. For example, in 1904 he was appointed external honorary member of the American Academy of Arts and Sciences.[13]

Luigi Villari's correspondence is more plentiful than his father's. He worked in the Italian Foreign Office and was later a newspaper correspondent. He also served as Italy's vice consul in three American cities: New Orleans in 1906, Philadelphia in 1907, and Boston from 1907 to 1910. Through his consular experience, Luigi Villari became increasingly attuned to the conditions of Italian immigrants in the United States. In a letter addressed to his father in early November 1909, he reported on a lecture offered in Boston by Leopoldo Franchetti (1847–1917), an Italian senator and expert on the problems of the *mezzogiorno*, or the Italian south. Luigi Villari was concerned, for he perceived that the speech "was very beautiful, and well received, but the trouble [was] that the people that [Franchetti] invited to assist the ignorant immigrants and to act as well-meaning intermediaries between them and the Americans [were] the very 'prominent citizens' who profit[ed] from the peasants' ignorance. The day when there is a good and complete educational system in the whole of Italy is the day when those people lose their jobs!"[14]

Beyond the items contained in the printed books and the manuscripts, additional material of American interest might be available in the collection *Indirizzi al Pontefice* (unavailable for consultation at the time of this writing). The collection contains the letters of petitions that the Catholic communities throughout the world addressed to the pope. Another collection of interest is titled *Raccolta fotografica*, and it is part of the broader section titled *Gabinetto della grafica*. This collection contains photographs and drawings of the celebrations, ceremonies, and travels of the popes from the pontificate of Pius IX (1792–1878) until that of John Paul II (1920–2005). Much of this collection is composed of pictures sent from dioceses and missions from all over the world; although the collection is closed at the time of this writing, these images provide great insight into the history of the Catholic Church for the nineteenth and twentieth centuries.

BIBLIOGRAPHY

De Nicolò, Paolo. "Profilo storico della Biblioteca Vaticana." In *Biblioteca Apostolica Vaticana*, ed. Leonard E. Boyle and Paolo de Nicolò, 17–36. Florence: Nardini, 1989.

Fish, Carl Russell. *Guide to the Material for American History in Roman and Other Italian Archives.* Washington DC: Carnegie Institution, 1911.

Manfredi, Antonio, ed. *Le Origini della Biblioteca Apostolica Vaticana tra Umanesimo e Rinascimento (1447–1534).* Vol. 1 of *Storia della Biblioteca Apostolica Vaticana.* Vatican City: Biblioteca Apostolica Vaticana, 2010.

Ostuni, Maria Rosaria. "Carteggi di Pasquale Villari." In *Fonti ecclesiastiche romane per lo studio dell'emigrazione italiana in Nord America (1642–1922).* Monographic issue of *Studi Emigrazione/Etudes Migrations* 33, no. 124 (December 1996): 615.

Piazzoni, Ambrogio M., Antonio Manfredi, and Dalma Frascarelli. *La Biblioteca Apostolica Vaticana.* Rome: Vatican Museums, 2012.

Pizzorusso, Giovanni, and Matteo Sanfilippo. *Dagli indiani agli emigranti: L'attenzione della Chiesa romana al Nuovo Mondo, 1492–1908.* Viterbo: Edizioni Sette Città, 2005.

Rossignani, Elena, and Giovanni Morello, eds. *Carteggi Villari: Inventario.* 2 vols. Vatican City: Biblioteca Apostolica Vaticana, 1975–76.

Sanfilippo, Matteo. *L'affermazione del cattolicesimo nel Nord America.* Viterbo: Sette Città, 2003.

———. "Carteggi di Giuseppe Toniolo." In *Fonti ecclesiastiche romane per lo studio dell'emigrazione italiana in Nord America (1642–1922).* Monographic issue of *Studi Emigrazione/Etudes Migrations* 33, no. 124 (December 1996): 614.

Vian, Paolo. "I carteggi di Giuseppe Toniolo alla Biblioteca Vaticana: Genesi, consistenza e fortuna del fondo." In *Giuseppe Toniolo: L'uomo come fine; Con saggi sulla storia dell'Istituto Giuseppe Toniolo di studi superiori*, ed. Aldo Carera, 273–301. Milan: Vita e Pensiero, 2014.

Archivio Segreto Vaticano /
Vatican Secret Archives
Address
    Cortile del Belvedere, 00120 Vatican City
Contact Details
    Phone: 39-0669883314
    Fax: 39-0669885574
    Email: asv@asv.ca
    Website: www.archiviosegretovaticano.va

STATUS

Open to researchers Monday–Thursday, 8:45 a.m.–4:45 p.m.; Friday, 8:45 a.m.–2:00 p.m.; and Saturday, 8:45 a.m.–12:45 p.m. The archives close for Italian national holidays, during specific Vatican celebrations, and from the end of June until the end of September. Researchers are advised to consult the Vatican Secret Archives calendar at www.archiviosegretovaticano.va /content/archiviosegretovaticano/en/consultazione/giorni-e-orari-di-apertura.html.

Researches are advised to consult the new admission procedure and complete the admission request form available at http://www.archiviosegretovaticano.va/content/archivo segretovaticano/en/consultazione/admission-request.html. From Monday to Thursday, researchers can request five volumes, three in the morning before noon and two between 12:30 p.m. and 1:00 p.m. On Friday, only three volumes may be requested before noon. On Saturday, no volumes can be requested, and only the catalogs may be consulted in the index room. Requests for material to be consulted on Saturday must be made on Friday between 12:30 p.m. and 1:00 p.m. Most material is in English, French, Italian, or Latin, though some documents are written in German or Eastern European languages. With the exception of the collections *Archivio del Concilio Vaticano II* and *Ufficio Informazioni Vaticano, Prigionieri di Guerra*, material post-1939 cannot be consulted.

HISTORY

The Vatican Secret Archives are the private archives of the Pope. The word "Secret" is used to indicate the private nature of these holdings. These archives have roots stretching back to the Middle Ages, at which time evidence suggests that the Scrinium existed; it was both archive and library. Most of this material, however, disappeared in the first half of the thirteenth century, and it was in 1612 that Pope Paul V (1552–1621) officially established the Vatican Secret Archives. In its early days, the archives contained material from the Middle Ages and, more especially, documents from the fifteenth and sixteenth centuries; during the seventeenth and eighteenth centuries, the collections were enriched by material from Avignon, papers from Liège pertaining to Pope Adrian VI (1459–1523), and the documents from Castel Sant'Angelo.

During the Napoleonic occupation of Rome, the material contained in the Vatican Archive (and in the archives of other Roman ministries) was transferred to Paris. When this material was returned to Rome, some series were permanently lost, while others reappeared in various archives. Pope Leo XIII (1810–1903) opened the Vatican Secret Archives to researchers in 1881.

DESCRIPTION OF HOLDINGS

At present, the Vatican Secret Archives contain six hundred collections that occupy 85 linear kilometers of space and span a period of time from the eighth century to the twentieth. Material available for consultation extends only to the end of the papacy of Pius XI (1857–1939), although there are several notable exceptions to this rule. For example, there are two different collections of interest to historians of American Catholicism that may be consulted, even though the content of both extends beyond the official limit. The first of these is *Archivio del Concilio Vaticano II* (index no. 1198, vols. I–XXI), which covers the years 1962–65; the second is *Ufficio Informazioni Vaticano, Prigionieri di Guerra* (1939–47), index *Stampati* 63 (1–2), which contains material on World War II prisoners.

The Vatican Secret Archives abound in material and continue to grow through continuous transfers of archival collections from other institutions, private families, and other Roman congregations. Therefore, some collections pertinent to American historical studies, currently unavailable, may become available over the next few years. One such collection is the *Pontificia Opera di Assistenza*, which Pope Pius XII (1876–1958) founded in 1944, largely through the generosity of prominent American Catholics. It sought to provide assistance to needy populations.

Given the myriad collections kept in the Vatican Secret Archives, researchers should consult the indexes available in the index room. The booklet provided to a researcher when obtaining or renewing an entry card lists all open and closed collections and contains an updated general bibliography. Some recently opened collections are listed without an index number; consult index room staff for assistance.

The following collections contain material of American interest. The title of each collection is indicated in Italian and followed, when possible, by related index numbers as available in the index room.

1. *Antille* (formerly *Delegazione Apostolica in Cuba e Portorico*)

This collection (index no. 1205) contains 106 folders that cover the period from 1905 until 1946. Material pertains to the apostolic nunciature of Cuba, Puerto Rico, and the Greater and Lesser Antilles. Material of American interest is very limited and is found in folder no. 59, in which there are a few documents on Placide Luis Chapelle (1842–1905), archbishop of New Orleans from 1897 to 1905, who served as the first apostolic delegate to Cuba and Puerto Rico from 1898 until the end of May 1905.

2. *Archivio Particolare di Pio IX*

This collection comprises three series: (1) *Commissione Speciale Immacolata Concezione*; (2) *Oggetti Vari*, index no. 1132; and (3) *Sovrani e particolari*, index no. 1131. The series *Oggetti Vari*, which contains 2,187 letters, includes a report (document no. 989) written by the bishop of Louisville, who claimed to have French-speaking faithful within his flock.

3. *Archivio Particolare di Gregorio XVI*

This collection (index no. 11175) holds part of the private archives of Pope Gregory XVI (1765–1846). It consists of 26 folders. Folder no. 2 (fols. 277–95) contains the correspondence of Giuseppe Bonfigli, vice consul of the Holy See in United States during Gregory XVI's pontificate.

4. *Carte Morelli*

Material in this collection (index Sala Indici, Stampati, no. 153) pertains to Domenico Morelli de Curtis (1792/93?), consul general of the Kingdom of the Two Sicilies in the United States from 1833 to 1838. The collection's 51 volumes cover the period from 1832 to 1861 and are further divided into the following series: (1) *A. Console delle Due Sicilie negli Stati Uniti d'America (1833–1838)*, (2) *B. Console delle Due Sicilie in Grecia (1839–1845)*, (3) *C. Console delle Due Sicilie in Tripoli (1845–1849)*, (4) *D. Console delle Due Sicilie a Genova (1850–1855)*, (5) *E. Console delle Due Sicile a Venezia (1855–1861)*, and (6) *F. Memorandum, ricordanze, scritti diversi e carte personali*. Documents of American interest are found in the series *A. Console delle Due Sicilie negli Stati Uniti d'America (1833–1838)*, which contains seven volumes on Morelli's activity as consul general in the United States.

5. *Concilio Vaticano I*

This collection (index no. 1172 [I–II]) contains material pertaining to the First Vatican Council (1869–interruption in 1870). Originally kept in the archives of the secretary of the council, the collection was transferred to the Vatican Secret Archives in 1937. This collection can be divided into four parts: (1) boxes no. 1–36 (manuscripts section) contain material on the acts of the synods, activities of the commission before the council, specific questions (about topics such as Jews, music in the churches, and socialism), the dogma of infallibility, correspondence during and after the council, and pastoral letters; (2) boxes no. 138–272 contain printed acts and works of the commissions; (3) boxes no. 273–331 contain observations, proceedings of the general congregations, and registers of attendance; and (4) boxes no. 332–847 contain books, pamphlets, newspapers, items, and autograph letters and memoranda of the conciliar fathers. In the first part of this collection are documents signed by the French-speaking bishops of Canada and the United States.

6. *Concilio Vaticano II*

Material in this collection concerns the Second Vatican Council (1962–65). The twenty-one-volume index (no. 1198), which is updated regularly, contains inventories of 2,001 envelopes. Here there is plentiful material of American Catholic interest. Each volume of the index begins with a description of the clergy members present at each conciliar session. For example, vol. 1, folder 4, records the names of Cardinal Francis Joseph Spellman (1889–1967), archbishop of New York (1939–67), and Egidio Vagnozzi (1906–80), archbishop of Myra and apostolic delegate to the United States (1958–68), both of whom attended the general session on October 22, 1962. The documents in vols. 1997–2000 deal with the reception of the Second Vatican Council by the American press from 1961 to 1965.

7. *Congregazione del Concilio*

This collection (index nos. 910–24, 1140, and 1173–1173A) of 3,386 archival units is divided into fifteen series as follows: (1) *Concilia*, (2) *Libri Decretorum*, (3) *Libri Litterarum*, (4) *Libri Litterarum Visitationum Sacrorum Liminum*, (5) *Miscellanea Codices de Immunitate*, (6) *Miscellanea Codices Externi*, (7) *Miscellanea Codices Varii*, (8) *Positiones*, (9) *Positiones Archivi Secreti*, (10) *Regesta Litterarum super Residenti*, (11) *Relationes Dioecesium*, (12) *Sezione Amministrativa*, (13) *Sezione Catechistica*, (14) *Sezione Disciplinare*, and (15) *Varia*.

Pope Pius IV (1499–1565) established the Congregation for the Clergy, originally called the Congregation of the Council (Congregazione del Concilio), in 1564 to ensure that the decrees issued by the Council of Trent (1545–63) were respected by all members of the Catholic clergy. In 1622 some responsibilities of the Congregation for the Clergy were given to the Sacred Congregation for the Propagation of the Faith (Sacra Congregatio de Propaganda Fide, now the Congregation for the Evangelization of Peoples). Since North America remained under the jurisdiction of Propaganda Fide until 1908, there is scant American material here from before the twentieth century.

The series *Positiones*, however, includes as a subseries *Stati patrimonaiali estero*, which lists properties of the Catholic Church in some European and extra-European dioceses as provided by apostolic nuncios at the request of the Congregation of the Council from 1927 onward. Folders 3 and 4 contain material about the United States.

8. *Congregazione Concistoriale*

Pope Sixtus V founded the Sacred Congregation of the Consistory (Congregazione Concistoriale), now the Congregation of Bishops, in 1588 to examine matters relating to the construction, suppression, union, or subdivision of dioceses and monasteries. As such, the congregation had both administrative and judiciary authority. From 1625 on, the secretary of the Consistorial Congregation was also the secretary of the College of Cardinals, so the archives of the Consistorial Congregation also contain material on the activity of the college and its consistories (these being regular meetings of cardinals with the pope to discuss issues of canonization, liturgical practice, diplomacy, patronage, policy, and protocol). The earliest records of the College of Cardinals date to the first half of the fourteenth century. Since 1722, the pope has supervised the congregation's activity. When Pope Pius X (1835–1914) issued the constitution *Sapienti consilio*, he entrusted supervision of American and Canadian dioceses to the Consistorial Congregation.

Material belonging to this congregation has been transferred to various sections of the Vatican Secret Archives in several stages. The material stored here, which covers a period dating from the fourteenth century until the late twentieth, is divided into two broad collections: (1) *Archivio Concistoriale*, the Consistorial Archives, and (2) *Congregazione Concistoriale*, the Consistorial Congregation (now named the Congregazione per i Vescovi or the Congregation of Bishops).

A. *Archivio Concistoriale*. This collection of material, dating from the fourteenth century until the early 1900s, is divided into 24 series: (1) *Acta Camerarii*, index Sala Indici, Stampati nos. 5 and 6, and Schedario Garampi; (2) *Acta Congregationis Concistorialis*, index Sala Indici, Stampati nos. 5 and 6; (3) *Acta Concistorialia*, index Sala Indici, Stampati no. 6; (4) *Acta Miscellanea*, index Sala Indici, Stampati nos. 5 and 6, Schedario Scarampi; (5) *Acta Vicecancellarii*, index Sala Indici, Stampati nos. 5 and 6, Schedario Scarampi; (6) *Affari pendenti*, index nos. 714–15; (7) *Carte Sciolte*; (8) *Cedularum et Rotolorum*, index no. 1121; (9) *Collegio dei Cardinali*; (10) *Collezioni*; (11) *Concistori (Propositiones)*; (12) *Conclavi*; (13) *Congregationes Concistoriales I*, index Sala Indici, Stampati no. 6; (14) *Congregationes Concistoriales II*, index Sala Indici, Stampati no. 6; (15) *Congregationis Concistorialis Acta*, index nos. 707–13, Sala Indici, Stampati no. 6; (16) *Congregationis Concistorialis Miscellanea*; (17) *Epistolae Regiae*, index no. 1197, Sala Indici, Stampati no. 6, Schedario Garampi; (18) *Iuramenta fidelitatis et Professiones fidei*, index no. 1295; (19) *Liber Mandatorum*; (20) *Positiones*; (21) *Praeconia et Propositiones*; (22) *Processus Concistoriales*; (23) *Rescripta*; and (24) *Risoluzioni*, index no. 707, Sala Indici, Stampati no. 6.

Most material of American interest may be found in the 61-volume series *Acta Camerarii*, which contains the official acts prepared for the consistories from 1489 to 1866; the 368-volume *Acta Congregationis Concistorialis*, with material on the Consistorial Congregation's activity, 1584–1908; the 299-volume *Processus Concistoriales*, with bureaucratic material concerning episcopal appointments from 1564 to 1906; and the 170-volume *Praeconia et Propositiones*, which contains memoirs compiled from canonical inquiries made between 1658 and 1907.

In the *Acta Miscellanea*, which comprises 100 volumes of material on the College of Cardinals from 1409 to 1809, vol. 11 mentions the 1565 Huguenot expedition to Florida. In general, though, there is little material of American interest in the above series because, following the French and Indian War (1756–63), Propaganda Fide had jurisdiction over American and Canadian dioceses. Material of American interest steadily increased for the years after 1909, when the Consistorial Congregation obtained control of the North American dioceses.

B. *Congregazioni Per i Vescovi.* This collection is divided into eight series: (1) *Cappellani Militari*, index no. 1169; (2) *Ponenze*, index no. 1277; (3) *Positiones*, index no. 1289; (4) *Relationes Dioecesium*, index no. 1169; (5) *Sedi e Vescovi titolari*, index no. 1176; (6) *Vescovo dell'esercito e dell'armata*, index no. 1169; (7) *Visita Apostolica*, index no. 1213; and (8) *Visita Apostolica dei Seminari d'Italia*, index no. 1267. Material of American interest is located mainly in the series *Ponenze, Positiones, Relationes Dioecesium*, and *Visita Apostolica.*

The series *Ponenze* contains documents pertaining to the selection and appointment of bishops and their assignments to particular dioceses. After the promulgation of *Sapienti consilio* on June 29, 1908, the congregation acquired greater importance within the papal curia, obtaining complete and personal jurisdiction over the bishops. Its duties included drafting acts of provision, selecting the candidates, and presenting those candidates to the pope for approbation and appointment. The Consistorial Congregation had jurisdiction over all decrees regarding the conservation or status of dioceses (as well as prelatures and abbeys nullius), including their establishment, unification, suppression, and alteration of borders, along with the constitution of cathedral chapters.

Volumes of material are arranged alphabetically by diocese, and each volume contains a series of chronologically ordered folders holding numbered protocols. *Ponenze* contains material dating from a 1910 deliberation over which of several candidates (Edmond Francis Prendergast, Thomas Francis Kennedy, John Walter Shanahan, or Eugene Augustine Garvey) ought to be appointed archbishop of Philadelphia.[15]

The series *Positiones* comprises 1,126 volumes of documents related to broader matters that the congregation discussed during its general meetings, 1909–48. At present, only material from 1939 or earlier may be consulted.

Material of American interest is found in the ninety-eight volumes pertaining to the US dioceses (from Albany to Winona). Additionally, there are five volumes, titled *Stati Uniti*, which are subdivided as follows: (1) *Stati Uniti I, 1909–1919*; (2) *Stati Uniti II, 1916–1921*; (3) *Stati Uniti II, 1916–1921*; (4) *Stati Uniti IV, 1919*; and (5) *Stati Uniti V, 1919–1921.* Among other material of American interest, this series includes a dossier on African and Native Americans in the United States in 1919.[16]

Material in the series *Relationes Dioecesium* pertains to the history and status of each Catholic diocese, 1909–89. This series contains surveys of dioceses that bishops were made to compile every ten years for their visits *ad limina* (the obligatory visits of bishops to Rome that were instituted in 1725). During the second half of the nineteenth century, American bishops began to write and send these surveys to Propaganda, but they generally did not respect the ten-year deadline. In 1909 Pius X entrusted to the Consistorial Congregation the task of evaluating these surveys. The congregation decided to prepare a 150-question survey to be answered by every bishop every five years; because this was poorly received by bishops around the world, the survey was reduced to 100 questions in 1918. Starting in the 1910s, American bishops began to complete and send the first of these surveys to the Consistorial Congregation.

The *Relationes Dioecesium* series sheds light on individual American dioceses, particularly the different ethnic groups in them. Material is arranged by diocese in numbered dossiers. One example of the kind of information found in this series comes from a 1921 report from the Diocese of Chicago, which stated that there were in the diocese 1,200,000 Catholics, compared with 30,000 Jews and 1,700,000 Protestants.[17]

The series *Visita Apostolica* contains material on the apostolic visits made to the dioceses. Material of American interest for the period 1922–31 is available in two volumes (no. 77 covers Dioceses Albany–Mobile, and no. 78 covers Dioceses Natchez–Winona), which together contain a huge amount of information about these dioceses, including the geographical territory, history, number of clergy, and educational system of each; the ethnic composition of the Catholic faithful (with particular emphasis placed on national parishes); and common problems certain dioceses experienced, such as alcoholism or clerical greed. One rather characteristic observation comes from the report that Pietro Fumasoni Biondi (1872–1960), apostolic delegate in the United States (1922–33), made of his 1928 visit to the New York diocese. In it Fumasoni Biondi stated: "The greatest foreign element in New York, and, at the same time, the one for which it is easier to be Americanized is the Italian element." He reckoned that there were almost half a million Italians in the Archdiocese of New York, which claimed fifty-two Italian parishes served by 132 priests.[18]

9. *Congregazione degli Studi* (now Educazione Cattolica)

When Pope Leo XII established the Congregazione degli Studi in 1824, it held ample power over the schools and universities under the control of the Holy See. After 1870 its jurisdiction was limited to Catholic universities founded and run by ecclesiastical authorities. The reform of 1908 removed seminaries from the hands of the Congregazione degli Studi and put them under the jurisdiction of the Consistorial Congregation. In 1915 Pope Benedict XV established the Congregazione dei Seminari e delle Università degli Studi, which merged the Congregazione degli Studi with the Consistorial Congregation. At present this collection (index no. 1268) consists of 67 folders that cover the period from 1870 to 1915. An example of the type of American material present is that found in folder no. 59, position no. 4503, which contains documents pertaining to the degree cum laude in sacred theology obtained by the priest Francis Hughes of New York in 1908.

10. *Congregazione dei Riti*

Pope Sixtus V (1521–90) officially established the Congregazione dei Riti (Congregation of the Rites) in 1588 to ensure that liturgical and sacramental decrees were respected and to oversee beatification and canonization processes. In 1969 the Congregation of the Rites became two distinct congregations: the Congregazione per il Culto Divino e la Disciplina dei Sacramenti (the Congregation for Divine Worship and the Discipline of the Sacraments), which supervises divine worship and correct observance of the sacraments, and the Congregazione delle Cause dei Santi (Congregation for the Causes of Saints), which oversees beatification and canonization processes.

Each of the two congregations maintains its own archives with different collections. The collection *Congregazione per il Culto Divino e la Disciplina dei Sacramenti* contains more than 3,200 archival units that cover the period from 1873 to the late 1980s. It is presently divided into four series: *Officium I, Officium II, Officium III,* and *Ufficio Vigilanza.* The different sections of these series are described in index no. 1304.

The collection *Congregazione delle Cause dei Santi-Processus* contains 13,283 archival units cataloged under the following index numbers: 1047, 1147, and 1147A. Material of American interest is found mainly in this collection, which contains twenty-four volumes (from no. 6057 to no. 6080) on the process of canonization of Saint Elizabeth Ann Bayley Seton (1774–1821).

Another volume of interest is no. 3716, which contains all the documents pertaining to the cause for Mary Wilson, an American novice of the Sacred Heart who, it is believed, was healed in 1867 by the appearance of Saint John Berchmans (1599–1621).

11. *Congregazione Disciplina Regolare*

This congregation was established by Pope Innocent XII (1615–1700) primarily to carry out disciplinary reforms in Italian convents; the new congregation additionally held jurisdiction over matters of discipline involving male and female regular orders of the whole Catholic Church. At present, this collection is divided into ten series: (1) *Audientiae*; (2) *Carte Varie*; (3) *Decreta*, index no. 1105; (4) *Ordini Religiosi Diversi*; (5) *Pendenze*; (6) *Registra*; (7) *Rescritti*; (8) *Risposte*; (9) *Rubricellae*; and (10) *Segreteria.* One example of the material of American interest in this series is a request that Honorius Schneider, a Franciscan active in the United States, sent to Pope Pius X in late December 1904 in which he asked to be laicized.[19]

12. *Dataria Apostolica*

The collection Dataria Apostolica originated in the fourteenth century, when an officer of the Papal Chancellery was tasked with dating petitions submitted to the pope, dispatching papal correspondence, and drafting official acts. In the fifteenth century this officer was named the datarius and given financial responsibilities. In the early seventeenth century, the Dataria Apostolica was chiefly concerned with the concession of certain matrimonial dispensations and the collation of specific benefices. Starting in 1622, however, the dataria also supervised the processes of inquiry for candidates for bishoprics outside Italy. From 1754 onward, the dataria also set up and carried out canonical processes of inquiry for candidates to receive certain benefits from the Consistorial Congregation.

At present, the collection *Dataria Apostolica* is organized into twenty-nine series; the index numbers for these are 195 A, 1041–42, and 1046. The series *Processus Datariae* (index no. 1046) contains material on the informative processes conducted by the papal curia in examining candidates' suitability for appointments to particular dioceses. Note that examinations conducted by the dataria followed the same norms and rules that governed those conducted by the Consistorial Congregation. For no apparent reason, several of the processes of inquiry are present in both the *Processus Concistoriales* and the *Processus Datariae*, with the contents and text found in one collection corresponding almost exactly to those in the other.

13. *Delegazione Apostolica negli Stati Uniti*

The Delegazione Apostolica negli Stati Uniti (Apostolic Delegation to the United States) was established in 1893 with four key aims: to strengthen the links between the Holy See and the United States, promote concord among American bishops, restore ecclesiastical discipline, and settle debates over how the children of Catholic immigrants to the United States should be educated (ideally, in the minds of many Church leaders, in parish schools and in the native language of their parents). The archives of the Delegazione Apostolica negli Stati Uniti were transferred to the Vatican Secret Archives in 1979 and consist of 15,000 dossiers in 931 boxes. The collection has two appendices, *Appendice Jugoslavia* and *Appendice Messico*, index nos. 1155A and 1168, respectively.

The collection is divided into twenty-two series numbered as follows: (I) *Delegazione Apostolica*, (II) *Stati Uniti*, (III) *Nazioni Unite*, (IV) *Liste episcopali*, (V) *Affari Esteri*, (VI) *Canada*, (VII) *Filippine*, (VIII) *Messico*, (IX) *Diocesi*, (X) *Diverse*, (XI) *Varie*, (XII) *Società segrete*, (XIII) *Società*, (XIV) *Società cattoliche*, (XV) *Greci orientali*, (XVI) *Stravaganti*, (XVII) *Università Cattoliche*, (XVIII) *Ruteni*, (XIX) *Istituti Religiosi*, (XX) *Finanze*, (XXI) *Collegio Giuseppino*, and (XXII) *Documenti aggiunti*. Researchers can consult index no. 1168, compiled by Claudio De Dominicis, for an inventory of series I–IX. De Dominicis has also published a detailed inventory of material concerning Italian immigration to the United States.

Each series is subdivided into progressively numbered folders. The only exception is (IX) *Diocesi*, which is classified by name of diocese. Given the number and diversity of documents in this series, researchers are encouraged to consult the aforementioned inventories, as well as the two that De Dominicis compiled with Matteo Sanfilippo, which are published in the 1995 and 1996 monographic issues of *Studi Emigrazione (Migration Studies)*.

Researchers should note that the series *Appendice Jugoslavia* (index no. 1155) has documentation about Joseph Patrick Hurley (1894–1967), the bishop of Saint Augustine from 1940 to 1967, who served also as papal nuncio in Yugoslavia from 1946 to 1952.

The series *Appendice Messico* (index no. 1155) consists of thirty-seven folders on Leopoldo Ruiz y Flores (1865–1941), apostolic delegate in Mexico from 1929 to 1937. Following the political turmoil of 1932, he fled to San Antonio, Texas. Because the series *Appendice Jugoslavia* and *Appendice Messico* are currently being reclassified, they are presently unavailable for consultation.

14. *Epistolae ad Principes*

This collection mainly contains papal correspondence written by the secretary of the *Epistolae ad Principes* in cooperation with the cardinal secretary of state on behalf of the pope. The great majority of this correspondence was addressed to bishops, cardinals, princes, or the faithful. The content of the correspondence includes letters of congratulations and gratitude, as well as messages about political and religious matters.

This collection is divided into two series: (1) *Positiones et Minutae* (index no. 1146), which contains 213 volumes covering the years 1823–1969, and (2) *Registra* (index no. 1069 and Sala Indici, Stampati no. 56 [1–3], Schedario Garampi), which contains 316 volumes and three appendices covering the years 1560–1969. Material of American interest is found mainly in the series *Positiones et Minutae*. One example of this (vol. 49, epistola no. 352) is an 1863 letter from Jefferson Davis (1808–89), president of the Confederate States of America during the Civil War (1861–65), to Pope Pius IX (1792–1878). This series also contains three letters that Abraham Lincoln (1809–65), president of the United States from 1861 to mid-April 1865, wrote in 1862 (vol. 47, epistolae nos. 51 and 145) and in 1863 (vol. 50, epistola no. 124).

15. *Epistolae Latinae*

This collection consists of 240 volumes and boxes that cover the period 1823–1914. It is divided into two series: (1) *Positiones et Minutae* (index no. 1148), which contains the original letters written to the pope in Latin, as well as the drafts of the replies, as well as Latin drafts of allocutions and encyclicals, and (2) *Registra* (index no. 1148), which chronologically lists the dates of outgoing letters. It is worth noting that *epistolae latinae* written prior to 1823 are found in certain volumes of the series *Epistolae ad Principes*. An example of the American material contained in this series is the collection of speeches that Pope Leo XIII delivered in 1893 to all the English-speaking pilgrims to the Vatican.[20]

16. *Fondo Benigni*

This collection (index Sala Indici, Stampati no. 62), transferred to the Vatican Secret Archives in 1938, contains the private correspondence of Umberto Benigni (1862–1934), who was a member of Propaganda and of the Affari Ecclesiastici Straordinari (Congregation for Extraordinary Ecclesiastical Affairs) attached to the news bureau of the Secretariat of State and, subsequently a journalist, controversialist, and founder of anti-modernist societies.

Benigni's correspondence is contained in sixty-one boxes that cover the period 1879–1925. The diverse material encompasses correspondence, dispatches from news agencies of many countries, newspaper clippings, and numerous speeches collected by Benigni. Documents are contained in numbered folders and are in neither chronological nor geographical order.

Given the copious material Benigni collected, *Fondo Benigni* is likely to detail thoroughly the status of Catholicism in the United States, particularly with regard to communities of Catholic immigrants. Material of American interest in this collection includes that in dossier no. 2610, perhaps from 1906 with further additions in 1911 and 1913, with information about William Henry O'Connell (1859–1944), bishop of Portland, 1901–6, and archbishop of Boston, 1907–44.[21]

17. *Fondo Missioni*

This collection (index no. 1087, Sala Indici, Stampati no. 101) contains 163 volumes and boxes that cover approximately the period from the late sixteenth century until the first half of the nineteenth century. *Fondo Missioni* belonged originally to the archives of Propaganda

Fide but was removed during the Napoleonic occupation of Rome. Upon its return, the collection was given to the Vatican Secret Archives. Material on North America pertains mainly to the colonial period; especially interesting is the correspondence between Propaganda Fide and Pierre de La Rue (1688–1779), abbot of L'Île-Dieu from 1722 to 1779 and vicar general of the bishop of Quebec from 1734 to 1777, about the French missions in Louisiana during the years 1764–69.

18. *Ospizio Apostolico dei Convertendi*

This collection (index Sala Indici, Stampati no. 69) consists of 759 volumes that cover the years 1673–1904. Since material is arranged in different series, researchers should consult the detailed inventory compiled by Msgr. Sergio Pagano in 1998.[22]

The Ospizio Apostolico dei Convertendi was officially founded in 1673 by the Italian Oratorian priest Mariano Sozzini (1613–80) to care for non-Catholics who went to Rome desiring to become Catholic. Vols. 5 and 7 of this collection contain two registers with details—name, age, nationality, arrival and departure dates, and so on—about those admitted into the Ospizio during the years 1673–1884. For instance, vol. 7 records that on July 3, 1850, William King, an American Lutheran from Arkansas, was admitted into the Ospizio. After abjuring his Lutheranism on July 10, 1850, he was confirmed three days later.[23]

Although only six American names have been found in these registers so far, the abundance of material contained in the other volumes suggests that further material of American interest remains to be found in these.

19. *Piante e Carte Geografiche*

This collection (index no. 1059) was artificially created when the archivists of the Vatican Secret Archives cataloged material originally contained in other archives so that members of the papal curia could enhance their knowledge of the world. As such, the collection holds drawings, original maps, and reproductions of maps, all made between the second half of the eighteenth century and the first half of the nineteenth.

Available here are hemisphere maps of North America made in 1788 by Giovanni M. Cassini, an Italian cartographer (1745–1824); a mid-nineteenth-century map of the American continent; and a reprint of North America that Cassini made in 1825.

20. *Protonotari Apostolici*

This collection (index no. 1064), comprising sixty-six volumes and twenty-four boxes, covers the years 1600–1903. The material included is mostly made up of registers, lists of protonotaries apostolic, and, in some cases, lists of letters of resignation.

21. *Congregazione per i Religiosi*

This collection is divided into five series: (1) *Istituti femminili*, index no. 1288; (2) *Istituti maschili*, index no. 1288; (3) *Ordini*, index no. 1288; (4) *Relicta Congr. Vescovi e Regolari*, index no. 1288; and (5) *Risposte alla circolare sugli studi (1910)*, index no. 1204, Sala Indici, Stampati no. 132. The latter series consists of seventy-eight archival units that cover the years 1908–10. These units contain material from the Congregazioni dei Religiosi, which, following the reform promoted by *Sapienti consilio*, took charge of the tasks belonging to the former Congregazione dei Vescovi e Regolari. Indeed, the new congregation had jurisdiction over all matters—including discipline, granting of privileges, and studies—pertaining to regular orders and religious congregations, both female and male.

The sort of material of American interest found in this series is exemplified by a letter written January 21, 1909, by Father Jean-Baptiste, a member of the Brothers of Sacred Heart active in the United States, in which he requested a dispensation from his vows due to his inability to observe them.[24]

22. *Sacra Romana Rota*

The origins of the Sacra Rota (Roman Rota) remain largely unknown; it seems to have been established at the end of the thirteenth century but was not called the "Rota" until the first half of the fifteenth century. In the early stage, the Sacra Rota was an ecclesiastical court. Although its powers appear to have been unlimited until the mid-sixteenth century, its jurisdiction was gradually circumscribed by the progressive establishment of the Roman congregations. Pope Paul V (1552–1621) entrusted to the Rota matrimonial causes and benefices, including those concerning canonizations, and Pope Benedict XIV (1675–1758) further built up the Rota's power of intervention. At the beginning of the nineteenth century, its activity became limited to the Pontifical States alone, and after 1870 the Rota could intervene only in spiritual matters. Pope Pius X (1835–1914) restored the Rota's jurisdiction over judiciary causes.

At present, the collection *Sacra Romana Rota* is divided into fifteen series: (1) *Appendix*, index no. 1269, Sala Indici, Stampati no. 54; (2) *Causae*, index no. 1299; (3) *Commissiones*, index Sala Indici, Stampati no. 54; (4) *Decisiones*, Sala Indici, Stampati no. 54; (5) *Diaria*, index no. 1303, Sala Indici, Stampati no. 54; (6) *Informationes*, index no. 1286, Sala Indici, Stampati no. 54; (7) *Iura Diversa*, index Sala Indici, Stampati no. 54; (8) *Manualia Actorum*, index no. 1057, Sala Indici, Stampati no. 54; (9) *Miscellanea*, index nos. 1108 and 1269, Sala Indici, Stampati no. 54; (10) *Peritiae*, index no. 1284, Sala Indici, Stampati no. 54; (11) *Positiones*, index nos. 701 and 1072, Sala Indici, Stampati no. 54; (12) *Processus Actorum*, index no. 1247, Sala Indici, Stampati no. 54; (13) *Processus in Admissione Auditororum*, index no. 1300, Sala Indici, Stampati no. 54; (14) *Sententiae*, index Sala Indici, Stampati no. 54; and (15) *Vota*, index Sala Indici, Stampati no. 54.

Given its complex history, the *Sacra Romana Rota* collection contains many volumes and boxes dealing with various matters, and material of American interest is scattered across all the series. For example, the series *Causae* contains documents about numerous matrimonial causes of American Catholics from 1910 to 1922 but also has material on Joseph Meyer, a priest of the Cincinnati diocese, who in 1912 opposed the decision of Bishop Henry Moeller (1849–1925) to remove him from his parish church.[25]

23. *Segreteria dei Brevi*

The Segreteria dei Brevi (the Secretariat of Briefs) originated in the twelfth century as three distinct offices working independently: (1) the Segreteria Apostolica, which drafted common briefs; (2) the Segreteria dei Brevi, which drafted secret briefs; and (3) the Segreteria dei Brevi ai Principi, which was attached to the Secretariat of State and drafted the *Epistolae ad Principes*. In 1678 Pope Innocent XI (1611–89) abolished the Segreteria Apostolica and transferred its tasks to the Segreteria dei Brevi, which, from 1745, also oversaw the granting of requested indulgences. From the seventeenth century onward, the Segreteria dei Brevi supervised and intervened in such matters as the granting of dispensations, indulgences, indults, and titles. In 1908, following the reform carried out by Pope Pius X, the Segreteria dei Brevi became the third section of the Secretariat of State; the first section dealt with extraordinary ecclesiastical matters, the second with ordinary affairs.

The Segreteria dei Brevi collection is divided into six series: (1) *Altare Privilegiatium ad Tempus*, index nos. 1098 and 1099; (2) *Altare Privilegiatium Perpetuum*, index nos. 1098 and 1099; (3) *Indulgentiae ad Tempus*, index nos. 1098 and 1099; (4) *Indulgentiae Perpetuae*, index nos. 1098 and 1099; (5) *Indulta Personalia*, index nos. 1098 and 1099; and (6) *Registra Brevium*, index nos. 289, 315, 740–885, and 1098–1100, Schedario Garampi. The *Registra Brevium*, the main series, classifies various subjects.

Since after the reform of 1908 the Segreteria dei Brevi was no longer an autonomous office, material from 1908 onward is found in the collection *Segreteria di Stato, Brevi Apostolici*. Also, although volumes are not numbered for the period after 1908, each volume contains documents pertaining to a specific month.

Material of American interest is present, particularly dating from the second half of the nineteenth century. At that time the number of briefs increased, partly due to the establishment of new dioceses, partly in response to the growing number of requests from the clergy and the laity, who received new titles such as domestic prelate or protonotary apostolic. Exemplary of such material in the *Registra Brevium* series is the July 1905 brief by which Augusto Maria Colaneri, the Roman-born vicar general of Omaha, was appointed apostolic protonotary *ad instar* at the suggestion of Richard Scannell (1845–1916), bishop of Omaha, 1891–1916.[26]

24. *Segreteria di Stato*

This vast collection is divided into eighty-five series that cover a period dating from the sixteenth century to the early 2000s. It is recommended that researchers consult the Vatican Secret Archives' printed booklet for a complete overview of all the series and related indexes in the *Segreteria di Stato* collection.

The origins of the Segreteria di Stato (the Secretariat of State) remain unclear, so it is difficult to assess its specific powers from its founding in the late Middle Ages until the early modern period. In 1487 Pope Innocent VIII (1432–92) established the position of the *secretarius domesticus* (domestic secretary), who was entrusted with diplomatic correspondence. It was under Pope Leo X (1475–1521), however, that this new officer began to supervise diplomatic correspondence in a more regular manner. In 1537 the Secretariat of State was founded officially.

Given the chronological and thematic breadth of this collection, these archives are divided into two sweeping chronological sections: (1) an old section, the *parte antica*, which covers the period from the sixteenth century to 1810; and (2) a modern section, the *parte moderna*, which covers the period from 1814 onward.

A. *Parte Antica.* The series contained in the *parte antica* are organized according to geographical criteria that improved over the course of the centuries as the Holy See increased its knowledge of the world. During the eighteenth century a good part of the series was reclassified. This reorganization, however, remained incomplete, because the secretaries and cardinals in charge of the Secretariat of State during the sixteenth and seventeenth centuries were also in charge of certain series, such as the *Fondo Albani* or the *Miscellanea Armadi*, which now belong to other collections of the Vatican Secret Archives.

Within the *parte antica* there are five particularly important series that contain material of American interest, especially from the colonial period. The five series are as follows:

(1) *Fiandra* (index nos. 134 and 1026) consists of 250 volumes and covers the years 1553–1795. The nunciature of Brussels was established officially in 1596, though representatives with the rank of nuncio had often resided there, albeit temporarily, before that date. During the seventeenth century, Spanish Flanders, particularly the city of Antwerp, became the great Western news center for the Catholic world. The nuncio to Brussels therefore grew in importance because he was in a position to funnel to Rome accounts and information on England and its colonies, including those in North America. One instance of material of American interest in this series is provided by vol. 135 Ee, which contains information from the Belgian nuncio on the peace between the English and the Creeks in South Carolina in 1762.

(2) *Francia* (index nos. 134 and 1025) consists of 727 volumes that cover the years 1527–1809. Because the nuncio to France resided at one of the most important European Catholic courts, he could collect and send to Rome a great deal of political and religious information about different countries. The series is particularly rich in Canadian material, with 1,050 documents pertaining to New France. There is also material on the American Revolution because the nuncio to France at that time was instrumental in establishing diplomatic relations between the United States and the Holy See. An example of this material is found in vols. 563–70, which contain many details and information about the martial and political activities of the United States and England. Vol. 565 contains a copy of the Declaration of Independence (July 4, 1776).

(3) *Inghilterra* (index nos. 134 and 1071) consists of twelve volumes that cover the years 1575–1704. This series contains many dispatches and letters written by nuncios or other official papal representatives during the reigns of King Charles I (1600–49) and King James II (1633–1701) of England. Material of American interest in this series pertains primarily to

Maryland. For example, vol. 4 contains a report about the religious status of Maryland (fols. 60–63) and an extract of a letter (fols. 64–66) dated May 3, 1641, written by the superior of the Jesuit mission there.

(4) *Spagna* (index nos. 134 and 1025) consists of 490 volumes that cover the years 1524–1808. This series contains the correspondence of the various nuncios in Spain; most material concerns the Spanish colonies in South America and the Caribbean. There are also documents of American interest, such as those in vol. 310, which pertain to the 1804 negotiations that paved the way for the transfer of Florida from Spain to France.

(5) *Nunziatura delle Paci* (index nos. 134 and 1026) consists of fifty-nine volumes and contains the correspondence of special nuncios or ministers at the general peace conferences held between 1628 and 1716. Vol. 49 contains comments on American slave contracts.

B. *Parte Moderna.* Material of the *Segreteria di Stato* collection from the year 1814 onward is ordered by year and is further organized in three hundred rubriche marked by serial numbers, each of which contains one or more dossiers. Each rubrica concerns a specific subject, such as the Saint Peter's alms fee.

Material of American interest is scattered amid the different rubriche, but no. 251 is especially important because it contains material regarding the apostolic delegation to the United States. This rubrica holds the correspondence of Gaetano Bedini (1806–64), the first apostolic delegate sent to the United States, and of Cesare Roncetti, another apostolic delegate, who in 1875 was sent to New York to bring the cardinal's hat to the recently appointed John McCloskey (1810–85), archbishop of the city (1864–85) and the first American cardinal.[27]

A further example of the American material contained by the *parte moderna* of the *Segreteria di Stato* collection is provided by rubrica 280, fascicolo 10. This rubrica contains a valuable report on the status of the American Catholic Church that was compiled by Germano Straniero, papal delegate at the service of James Gibbons (1834–1921), archbishop of Baltimore (1877–1921) and, as of 1886, the second American to be named cardinal.[28]

There is additional material of American interest in other rubriche, particularly material concerning the conditions of Catholic immigrant communities. Researchers may consult the 1995 and 1996 monographic issues of *Studi Emigrazione* (*Migration Studies*) for the two inventories compiled by Matteo Sanfilippo; these provide a general overview of the material available about Catholic immigrants in the United States from the mid-1850s until the early 1920s.

There are three other particularly important series in the modern part of the Secretariat of State:

(1) *Spogli di Cardinali e Officiali di Curia* (index no. 1143 A–B) comprises 533 boxes of documents that belonged to 206 cardinals and members of the papal curia. This series has the official documents as well as the private correspondence of prominent officials of the Holy See who operated in North America. Amid the material of this series are Gaetano Be-

dini's papers, including his reports from the United States in 1854 and his correspondence with American bishops.

(2) *Spoglio Leone XIII* (index no. 1302) consists of official and private documents pertaining to Pope Leo XIII (1810–1903). This series is organized in boxes containing dossiers about various matters. One good example of the sort of material available here is the March 25, 1892, letter that John Ireland (1838–1918), bishop of Saint Paul (1888–1918), sent to Leo XIII about the schools question. Ireland reported that in the United States everyone, except for African Americans and immigrants, was educated. Ireland also stated that compulsory schooling was opposed by Germans who did not want to Americanize, by the Jesuits, and by some conservative bishops like Michael Augustine Corrigan (1839–1902), archbishop of New York (1885–1902.)[29]

(3) *Morte di Pontefici e Conclavi* (index no. 1186, vols. I–IV) consists of seventy-three boxes that cover the period 1846–1922 and contain private letters, condolences, reports by bishops and nuncios, and greetings from politicians on the occasion of one pope's death and the election of his successor. This series is divided into five further subseries: (a) *Pio* IX 1/A-2, (b) *Leone* XIII 3/A-9, (c) *Pio* X 10/A-22/B, (d) *Benedetto* XV 23/A-38/B, and (e) *Appendice* 39. Material of American interest found in this series includes a letter that Theodore Roosevelt (1858–1919), president of the United States from mid-September 1901 to early March 1909, sent to Pius X on August 27, 1903, congratulating him on his election.[30]

25. *Schedario Garampi*

Not a collection at all, the *Schedario Garampi* is an extremely important research tool. This detailed index was compiled by Giuseppe Garampi (1725–92), prefect of the Vatican Secret Archives and of the Archives of Castel Sant'Angelo (1751–72). The *Schedario Garampi* consists of 125 volumes containing more than 800,000 index cards and covering a period from the Middle Ages until the end of the eighteenth century. In some cases, the index cards of the *Schedario Garampi* provide summaries of documents now lost.

The *Schedario Garampi* is divided into ten sections:

(1) *Benefici* (index nos. 445–74) comprises thirty volumes of references for material pertaining to ecclesiastical benefices. These index cards are in alphabetical order by name of diocese.

(2) *Vescovi* (index nos. 475–511) consists of thirty-seven volumes. The index cards are classified both chronologically and alphabetically by Latin name of diocese.

(3) *Miscellanea I* (index nos. 512–534A) consists of twenty-four volumes. The index cards are in alphabetical order by Latin name of diocese. The material listed in this section should be combined with that in the sections *Vescovi* and *Abati*.

(4) *Abati* (index nos. 535–37) consists of three volumes that list 1,500 monasteries in alphabetical order.

(5) *Cronologico* (index nos. 538–49) consists of twelve volumes that provide details about where index cards are located.

(6) *Papi* (index no. 550) consists of one volume with descriptions of briefs, bulls, papal letters, and material from the Archives of Castel Sant'Angelo. The index cards are in alphabetical order by name of pope.

(7) *Cardinali* (index no. 551) consists of one volume of index cards about the cardinals. This volume is arranged in alphabetical order by name of cardinal.

(8) *Offici* (index nos. 552–54) comprises three volumes. The index cards are in alphabetical order by the titles of the different Roman ministries and the tasks of the personnel of the papal curia.

(9) *Chiese di Roma* (index nos. 555–56) consists of two volumes. The first contains index cards organized into three further subseries: (a) cardinals' titles, (b) diaconates, and (c) churches and chapels of Rome. The second volume contains information on other Roman churches.

(10) *Miscellanea II* (index nos. 670–81) consists of twelve volumes that contain the same material as *Miscellanea I*.

BIBLIOGRAPHY

Blouin, Francis Xavier, ed. *Vatican Archives: An Inventory and Guide to Historical Documents of the Holy See.* New York: Oxford University Press, 1998.

Carboni, Luigi. "Gli archivi delle Rappresentanze Pontificie nell'Archivio Segreto Vaticano: Versamenti e nuovi ordinamenti." In *Religiosa Archivorum Custodia: IV Centenario della Fondazione dell'Archivio Segreto Vaticano (1612–2012)*; *Atti del Convegno di Studi, Città del Vaticano, 17–18 aprile 2012*, 273–304. Vatican City: Vatican Secret Archives, 2015.

Castagna, Luca. *A Bridge across the Ocean: The United States and the Holy See between the Two World Wars.* Washington DC: Catholic University of America Press, 2014.

Chiappin, Marcel. "L'archivio della Segreteria di Stato: Il periodo napoleonico." In *Religiosa Archivorum Custodia: IV Centenario della Fondazione dell'Archivio Segreto Vaticano (1612–2012)*; *Atti del Convegno di Studi, Città del Vaticano, 17–18 aprile 2012*, 169–94. Vatican City: Vatican Secret Archives, 2015.

Coco, Giovanni. "Il governo, le carte e la memoria: Aspetti della storia degli archivi della Segreteria di Stato in Epoca contemporanea (1814–1939)." In *Religiosa Archivorum Custodia: IV Centenario della Fondazione dell'Archivio Segreto Vaticano (1612–2012)*; *Atti del Convegno di Studi, Città del Vaticano, 17–18 aprile 2012*, 215–72. Vatican City: Vatican Secret Archives, 2015.

Cummings, Kathleen Sprows. *New Women of the Old Faith: Gender and American Catholicism in the Progressive Era.* Chapel Hill: University of North Carolina Press, 2010.

Cummings, Kathleen Sprows, and R. Scott Appleby, eds. *Catholics in the American Century: Recasting Narratives of US History.* Ithaca, NY: Cornell University Press, 2012.

D'Agostino, Peter. *Rome in America. Transnational Catholic Ideology from the Risorgimento to Fascism.* Chapel Hill: University of North Carolina Press, 2004.

———. "The Triad of Roman Authority: Fascism, the Vatican, and Italian Religious Clergy in the Italian Emigrant Church." *Journal of American Ethnic History* 17 (Spring 1998): 3–37.

De Dominicis, Claudio. *Archives of Apostolic Delegation of United States.* New York: Center for Migration Studies, 1992.

Dieguez, Alejandro M. "Gli archivi delle Congregazioni romane: Nuove acquisizioni e ordinamenti." In *Religiosa Archivorum Custodia: IV Centenario della Fondazione dell'Archivio Segreto Vaticano (1612–2012)*; *Atti del Convegno di Studi, Città del Vaticano, 17–18 aprile 2012*, 305–34. Vatican City: Vatican Secret Archives, 2015.

Doria, Piero. "L'archivio del Concilio Vaticano II all'Archivio Vaticano: Istituzione, inventario e nuove prospettive di ricerca." In *Religiosa Archivorum Custodia: IV Centenario della Fondazione dell'Archivio Segreto Vaticano (1612–2012)*; *Atti del Convegno di Studi, Città del Vaticano, 17–18 aprile 2012*, 497–530. Vatican City: Vatican Secret Archives, 2015.

Ellis, John Tracy. *The Life of James Cardinal Gibbons: Archbishop of Baltimore, 1834–1921*. Milwaukee: Bruce, 1952.

Faggioli, Massimo. *A Council for the Global Church: Receiving Vatican II in History*. Minneapolis: Fortress Press, 2015.

———. *Vatican II: The Battle for Meaning*. New York: Paulist Press, 2012.

Faggioli, Massimo, and Andrea Vicini, SJ, eds. *The Legacy of Vatican II*. New York: Paulist Press, 2015.

Fish, Carl Russell. *Guide to the Materials for American History in Roman and Other Italian Archives*. Washington, DC: Carnegie Institution, 1911.

Florian, Michel. *La Pensée catholique en Amérique du Nord: Réseaux intellectuels et échanges culturels entre l'Europe, le Canada et les Etats-Unis (années 1920–1960)*. Paris: Desclée de Brouwer, 2010.

Fogarty, Gerald P. "Archbishop Francis J. Spellman's Visit to Wartime Rome." *Catholic Historical Review* 100, no. 1 (Winter 2014): 72–96.

———. *The Vatican and the Americanist Crisis: Denis J. O'Connell, American Agent in Rome, 1885–1903*. Rome: Università Gregoriana Editrice, 1974.

———. *The Vatican and the American Hierarchy from 1870 to 1965*. Stuttgart: Anton Hiersemann, 1982.

Gallagher, Charles R. *Vatican Secret Diplomacy: Joseph P. Hurley and Pope Pius XII*. New Haven, CT: Yale University Press, 2008.

Gualdo, Germano, ed. *Sussidi per la consultazione dell'Archivio Vaticano*. Vatican City: Vatican Secret Archives, 1989.

Haskins, Charles H. "The Vatican Secret Archives." *American Historical Review* 2, no. 1 (October 1896): 40–58.

Hoberg, Hermann. "Aggiunte recenti al fondo 'Missioni' dell'Archivio Vaticano." In *Ecclesiae Memoria: Miscellanea in onore del R.P. Josef Metzler O.M.I.*, ed. Willi Henkel, 87–92. Freiburg: Herder, 1991.

———. "Der Fonds Missioni der Vatikanischen Archivs." *Euntes Docete: Commentaria Urbaniana* 21 (1968): 97–107.

———. *Inventario dell'archivio della Sacra Romana Rota (sec. XIV-XIX)*. Vatican City: Vatican Secret Archives, 1994.

Londei, Luigi. "La Segreteria di Stato e la documentazione ad essa afferente conservata presso l'Archivio di Stato di Roma." In *Religiosa Archivorum Custodia: IV Centenario della Fondazione dell'Archivio Segreto Vaticano (1612–2012)*; *Atti del Convegno di Studi, Città del Vaticano, 17–18 aprile 2012*, 195–214. Vatican City: Vatican Secret Archives, 2015.

McGreevy, John T. *Catholicism and American Freedom: A History.* New York: W.W. Norton, 2003.

Melloni, Alberto, ed. *Atlante Storico del Concilio Vaticano II.* Milan: Jaca, 2015.

Pagano, Sergio, ed. *Bibliografia dell'Archivio Segreto Vaticano, nuova versione, X (2000–2002).* Vatican City: Vatican Secret Archives, 2008.

———. "Il fondo di Mons: Umberto Benigni dell'Archivio Segreto Vaticano." *Ricerche per la storia religiosa di Roma* 8 (1990): 347–402.

———. "Ospizio dei Convertendi di Roma fra carisma missionario e regolamentazione ecclesiastica (1671–1700)." *Ricerche per la storia religiosa di Roma* 10 (1998): 313–90.

———. "Paolo V e la fondazione del moderno Archivio Segreto Vaticano (1611–1612)." In *Religiosa Archivorum Custodia: IV Centenario della Fondazione dell'Archivio Segreto Vaticano (1612–2012); Atti del Convegno di Studi, Città del Vaticano, 17–18 aprile 2012,* 305–34. Vatican City: Vatican Secret Archives, 2015.

Pizzorusso, Giovanni. "Un diplomate du Vatican en Amérique: Donato Sbarretti à Washington, La Havane et Ottawa (1893–1910)." *Annali Accademici Canadesi* 9 (1993): 5–33.

———. "Fondo Benigni, Archivio della Congregazione De Propaganda Fide." *Studi Emigrazione/Migration Studies* 32 (1995): 688–721.

———. "Le fonds Benigni aux Archives Secrètes du Vatican." *Annali Accademici Canadesi* 8 (1992): 107–11.

Sanfilippo, Matteo. *L'affermazione del cattolicesimo nel Nord America.* Viterbo: Edizioni Sette Città, 2003.

———. "L'Archivio Segreto Vaticano come fonte per la storia del Nord America anglo-francese." In *Gli Archivi della Santa Sede come fonte per la storia moderna e contemporanea,* ed. Matteo Sanfilippo and Giovanni Pizzorusso, 237–64. Viterbo: Edizioni Sette Città, 2001.

———. *Inventaire des documents d'intérêt canadien dans l'Archivio Segreto Vaticano sous le pontificat de Léon XIII (1878–1903): Délégation Apostolique du Canada, Délégation Apostolique des États-Unis, Epistolae ad Principes et Epistolae Latinae, et autres séries mineures.* Ottawa-Rome: Archives Nationales du Canada-Centre Académique Canadien en Italie, 1987.

———. "Migrants, Bishops and the Vatican: Belgian Immigration in the United States before World War I." *Studi Emigrazione/Migration Studies* (1991): 393–405.

———. *La Santa Sede e l'emigrazione dall'Europa centro-orientale negli Stati Uniti fra Otto e Novecento.* Viterbo: Edizioni Sette Città, 2010.

———. "S. Congregazione Concistoriale." In *Fonti ecclesiastiche per la storia dell'emigrazione e dei gruppi etnici nel Nord America: Gli Stati Uniti (1893–1922),* ed. Matteo Sanfilippo. Monographic issue of *Studi Emigrazione/Migration Studies* 32, no. 120 (December 1995): 663–87.

———. "S. Congregazione Concistoriale." In *Fonti ecclesiastiche romane per lo studio dell'emigrazione italiana in Nord America (1642–1922),* ed. Giovanni Pizzorusso and Matteo Sanfilippo. Monographic issue of *Studi Emigrazione/Migration Studies* 33, no. 124 (December 1996): 603–7.

———. "Segreteria di Stato." In *Fonti ecclesiastiche per la storia dell'emigrazione e dei gruppi etnici nel Nord America: gli Stati Uniti (1893–1922),* ed. Matteo Sanfilippo. Monographic issue of *Studi Emigrazione/Migration Studies* 32, no. 120 (December 1995): 654–61.

———. "Segreteria di Stato." In *Fonti ecclesiastiche romane per lo studio dell'emigrazione italiana in Nord America (1642–1922)*, ed. Giovanni Pizzorusso and Matteo Sanfilippo. Monographic issue of *Studi Emigrazione/Migration Studies* 33, no. 124 (December 1996): 580–88.

———. "Il Vaticano e l'emigrazione nelle Americhe." In *Per le strade del mondo: Laiche e religiose fra Otto e Novecento*, ed. Stefania Bartoloni, 339–63. Bologna: Il Mulino, 2007.

Sanfilippo, Matteo, and Claudio De Dominicis. "Delegazione apostolica degli Stati Uniti." In *Fonti ecclesiastiche per la storia dell'emigrazione e dei gruppi etnici nel Nord America: Gli Stati Uniti (1893–1922)*, ed. Matteo Sanfilippo. Monographic issue of *Studi Emigrazione/Migration Studies* 32, no. 120 (December 1995): 627–49.

Sanfilippo, Matteo, and Daniele Fiorentino, eds. *Gli Stati Uniti e l'Italia nel nuovo scenario internazionale, 1898–1918.* Rome: Gangemi, 2012.

Sanfilippo, Matteo, and Giovanni Pizzorusso. *Dagli indiani agli emigranti: L'attenzione della chiesa Romana al Nuovo Mondo, 1492–1908.* Viterbo: Edizioni Sette Città, 2005.

Venditti, Gianni. "Le Carte Morelli in Archivio Segreto Vaticano." In *Collectanea Archivi Vaticani* 96 (2014): 345–82.

Verhoeven, Timothy. "Transatlantic Connections: American Anti-Catholicism and the First Vatican Council (1869–70)." *Catholic Historical Review* 100, no. 4 (Autumn 2014): 695–720.

NOTES

1. Pietro Fumasoni Biondi to Cardinal Rafael Merry del Val, August 19, 1923, 8, *Materiae diversae, Rerum Variarum* (MDRV) 1923, ACDF: "si sono avute pubbliche ed unanimi manifestazioni di cordoglio da parte dei cittadini di ogni partito ed ogni credo."

2. Marcolino Cicognani to Holy Office, October 1876, MDRV 1884n40, ACDF: "indicevano feste da ballo, e, non senza pericolo di peccato, si abbandonavano ad altri pubblici divertimenti specialmente nei dì festivi, tralasciando di ascoltare la S. Messa e di assistere alle S. Funzioni."

3. Carlo Maria Pedicini to Fabrizio Turriozzi, August 3, 1816, 15, *Dubia varia* (DV) 1814–21, ACDF.

4. The first general congregation of the cardinals was held on January 6, 1622. See fols. 1–4, vol. 22, *Miscellanee diverse*, APF.

5. Nikolaus Kowalsky, OMI, and Josef Metzler, OMI, *Inventory of the Historical Archives of the Congregation for the Evangelization of Peoples or "de Propaganda Fide,"* 3rd ed. (Rome: Pontificia Universitas Urbaniana, 1988), 91–94.

6. Fols. 163–94, vol. 838, rubr. 48, *sottorubr.* 2: *Carolina, Nuova Serie*, APF.

7. Pietro Fumasoni Biondi to Gugliemo Van Rossum, August 15, 1928, fols. 791–808, rubr. 48, *sottorubr.* 1, *America settentrionale, Nuova Serie*, APF.

8. Léon Bouland to Raffaele Cardinal Monaco La Valletta, April 27, 1881, no. 260, vol. 2, Sante Reliquie, Archives of the Vicariate of Rome (Archivio Storico del Vicariato di Roma): "ma paroisse française, la seule qui existe dans la grand ville de Boston, est situé au coeur même du protestantisme."

9. Gianpaolo Rigotti, "L'archivio della Congregazione per le Chiese Orientali: Dalla Costituzione apostolica Romani Pontifices (1862) alla morte del card. Gabriele Acacio Coussa

(1962)," in *Fede e martirio: Le chiese orientali cattoliche nell'Europa del Novecento; Atti del Convegno di storia ecclesiastica contemporanea, Città del Vaticano, 22–24 ottobre 1998*, ed. Aleksander Rebernik, Gianpaolo Rigotti, and Michel Van Parys, OSB (Vatican City: Libreria Editrice Vaticana, 2003), 247–95.

10. Petition from a group of Slovak Catholics to Pope Benedict XV, 1916, 1–3, fasc. 734/32, VIII: *Ruteni Stati Uniti*, Archivio Storico della Congregazione per le Chiese Orientali (Historical Archives of the Congregation for the Oriental Churches).

11. John Rossi to Msgr. Ludwig Kaas, May 25, 1938, unfoliated and unpaginated, D (4) no. 45, *Armadio* 84, Archivio Storico Generale della Fabbrica di San Pietro.

12. Anonymous and undated list of American and Canadian bishops, unfoliated and unpaginated, D (4) no. 51: *Armadio* 84, Archives of the Fabbrica of San Pietro (Archivio Storico Generale della Fabbrica di San Pietro).

13. April 13, 1904, fols. 10–11: *Carteggi Villari*, Vatican Library (Biblioteca Apostolica Vaticana, or BAV).

14. Luigi Villari to Pasquale Villari, November 3, 1909, fols. 20rv–21rv, dossier no. 1, vol. 58, *Carteggi Villari*, BAV: "fu assai bello, e bene accolto, ma il guaio è che la gente a cui dava il consiglio di assistere gli emigrati ignoranti e di farsi intermediari benevoli fra di essi e gli Americani, sono appunto quei 'prominenti' che vivono dell'ignoranza dei cafoni. Il giorno in cui ci sarà un sistema buono e completo di istruzione in tutta l'Italia quella gente lì si troverà senza occupazione!"

15. Protocollo 279/11, fasc. 37, vol. 1911, *Congregazione per i Vescovi, Ponenze*, ASV.

16. Protocollo 821, vol. *Stati Uniti IV, 1919, Congregazione per i Vescovi, Positiones*, ASV.

17. Fasc. 219, *Relationes Dioecesium*, Congregazioni per i Vescovi, ASV.

18. *Visita Apostolica*, 78, *Stati Uniti d'America*, 1928, *Congregazioni per i Vescovi*, ASV: "Il più grande elemento forastiero in New York ed al medesimo tempo il più facile ad americanizzarsi è l'elemento italiano."

19. Honorius Schneider, OFM, to Pope Pius X, December 30, 1904, unfoliated and unpaginated, vol. 591, *Congregazione Disciplina Regolare*, ASV.

20. Nos. 1–23, *registro* 50, vol. 144, *Epistolae Latinae, Positiones et Minutae*, ASV.

21. Dossier no. 2610, scatola 18, *Fondo Benigni*, ASV.

22. Sergio Pagano, "Ospizio dei Convertendi di Roma fra carisma missionario e regolamentazione ecclesiastica (1671–1700)," in *Ricerche per la storia religiosa di Roma* 10 (1998), 313–90.

23. Fols. 231v–232r, vol. 7, *Ospizio dei Convertendi*, ASV.

24. January 21, 1909, protocollo 6604/1909, busta no. 5, *Istituti di Vita Consacrata e Società di Vita Apostolica, Istituti maschili*, ASV.

25. Cincinnati 1912, fasc. 30, busta 47, *Sacra Rota Romana, Causae*, ASV.

26. Fols. 334–37, vol. 6159, *Registra Brevium, Segreteria Brevium*, ASV.

27. Fasc. 1, 1853, rubr. 251, *Segreteria di Stato, parte moderna*, ASV; fasc. 1–2, 1854, rubr. 251, *Segreteria di Stato, parte moderna*, ASV; fasc. 13, 1875, rubr. 251, *Segreteria di Stato, parte moderna*, ASV.

28. Fasc. 10, 1902, rubr. 280, *Segreteria di Stato, parte moderna*, ASV.

29. John Ireland to Leo XIII, March 25, 1892, scatola 11, *Segreteria di Stato, Spoglio di Leone XIII*, ASV.

30. Theodore Roosevelt to Pius X, August 27, 1903, fol. 365r, scatola 10/A, protocollo 658, *Morte di Pontefici e Conclavi, Pio X, Segreteria di Stato*, ASV.

CHAPTER 2

Archives of Religious Orders

This chapter includes profiles of the archives of regular (religious) orders and communities in Rome. Given that, from the early decades of the twentieth century, the majority of the female and male regular orders opened general houses in the city, this section does not provide a comprehensive overview. My research focused on the orders that were active in certain areas of North America since the colonial period. Because of the Jesuits' importance and early presence in North America, the order's general archives, *Archivum Romanum Societatis Iesu*, is the most relevant repository originated by a regular order.

Archivio della Provincia Romana di S. Caterina da Siena (Santa Maria sopra Minerva) /
Archives of the Dominican Roman Province of Saint Catherine of Siena (Santa Maria sopra Minerva)
Address
  Piazza della Minerva 43, 00186 Rome
Contact Details
  Phone: 39-066792255
  Email: archivumsmsm@gmail.com
  Website: www.archivumsmsm.it/contatti-e-servizi

STATUS
Open to researchers Wednesday–Friday, 10:00 a.m.–4:00 p.m. The archives close for Italian national holidays, on April 29–30 for the celebration of Saint Catherine of Siena (1347–80), and for the entire month of August. A broad description of the holdings is posted at www .anagrafebbcc.chiesacattolica.it/anagraficaCEIBib/public/VisualizzaScheda.do?codice_cei= CEI300A00019. Researchers are advised to make an advance appointment with the archivist to be granted access to the material. The majority of the material is in English and Italian. Material post-1939 can be consulted with the archivist's permission.

HISTORY

The Dominican Order was founded by the Spanish priest Domingo Félix de Guzmán (1170–1221) in 1215 and officially recognized by Pope Honorius III (1150–1227) in 1216. From the thirteenth century to the fifteenth, the order spread over continental Europe and the British Isles, also establishing missions in Africa and Asia.

DESCRIPTION OF HOLDINGS

It is difficult to assess when the nucleus of the Archives of the Dominican Roman Province of Saint Catherine of Siena was established. According to a memoir written by Giacomo Reginaldo Quadri, an Italian Dominican, a large group of documents had already been preserved by the mid-eighteenth century. At present, the archives consist of eight thousand volumes covering a period from the first half of the thirteenth century to the last decade of the twentieth.

The holdings are divided as follows: (1) *Fondi Personali*, from the second half of the nineteenth century to the second half of the twentieth; (2) *Provincia Curia Generale*, from the first half of the eighteenth century to the second half of the twentieth; (3) Filippo Crispolti's collection, nineteenth and twentieth centuries; (4) Minerva's collection, mid-sixteenth century through the last decade of the twentieth; (5) *Provincia*, sixteenth century to the twentieth; (6) *Varia*, sixteenth century through twentieth; (7) *Istituto Beato Angelico*, eighteenth century to the twentieth; (8) *Necrologi*, seventeenth century to the twentieth; (9) *Storica*, sixteenth century to the twentieth; and (10) *Pergamene*, parchments from the thirteenth century to the nineteenth.

Material of American interest can be found in the sections *Provincia* (PR CII1) 2, (PR CII1) 4, (PR CII13) 3, and (PR CII13) 7; *Necrologi*, (CM G19) 2; and *Fondi Personali*, CM III19 (6). In addition to this material, the "*archivio di deposito*" contains a volume that includes sermons preached by a destitute American person (*povero*) at the Pontifical North American College. *Provincia* (PR CII1) 2, 4 consists of two catalogs of the Dominican convents and houses of the American Provinces of Saint Joseph and the Most Holy Name of Jesus, established in 1805 and 1850, respectively, for the years 1937–84.[1]

Of particular interest is the section (PR CII13) 3, which contains correspondence between the Italian Dominican Antonino Salvati and his superiors in Rome from 1914 to 1921. His letters vividly depict the religious conditions among Italian immigrants. Salvati emphasized that many of his fellow countrymen wished to become priests. In early February 1921 he wrote, "I think we could have some vocations amid the Italians residents in North America, and make them be educated by our fathers in Canada, where there is a truly religious spirit and good studies." Of a different tone was the letter that Salvati wrote at the end of March 1921, in which he lamented the Church of Saint Catherine of Siena in New York: "Our [Dominican] Fathers would be disposed to grant us the church. By all means, let them grant it! They already lost it! For the archbishop of New York has removed from the jurisdiction of our fathers all the Italians and entrusted them to a secular priest. The bishops, especially of America, don't like to give their parishes to the regulars."[2]

Other material of American interest may be found in the section *Fondi Personali*, CM III19 (6). For more information on relevant sources in this archive, see my section near the beginning of this volume headed "Roman Sources for the History of American Catholicism: A Different Perspective."

BIBLIOGRAPHY
Hinnebusch, W. A., P. Philbert, and R. B. Williams, "Dominicans." In *New Catholic Encyclopedia* 4:854. Farmington Hills, MI: Gale, 2003.

Archivio delle Maestre Pie Filippini
Archives of the Maestre Pie Filippini
Address
   Via della Stazione di Ottavia 72, 00135 Rome
Contact Details
   Phone: 39-0630810786
   Fax: 39-0630818328/0630815544
   Email: segreteriagen@pontificioistitutompf.it
   Website: www.pontificioistitutompf.it

STATUS
Closed.

HISTORY
The Maestre Pie Filippini is a female congregation stemming from the Maestre Pie Venerini. It was officially established in 1692 by Cardinal Marcantonio Barbarigo (1640–1706), bishop of Montefiascone from 1687 to 1706, and by Rosa Venerini (1656–1728). In 1707 Saint Lucia Filippini (1672–1732), a member of Maestre Pie, opened a house in Rome, even though Barbarigo opposed the congregation's expansion beyond his diocese. The Rome opening paved the way for the foundation of the Maestre Pie Filippini, which, from 1707, became an independent congregation. The Maestre Pie Filippini established themselves in the United States in 1910, in compliance with a request made by Luigi Pozzo, pastor of the Saint Joachim Church in Trenton. There, the first five members of the congregation in the United States devoted themselves to assisting the sons of Italian migrants. Despite the initial hostility of the American hierarchy, the Maestre Pie expanded their activity beyond New Jersey. In 1928, the Maestre Pie's mission in Trenton became the Province of Santa Lucia.

DESCRIPTION OF HOLDINGS
Because the archives are closed, this description is based on a short inventory written by Elisabetta Vezzosi for the journal *Studi Emigrazione* in 1996. Material of American interest has not been inventoried and mainly consists of correspondence exchanged between the first Maestre Pie in the United States and their motherhouse in Rome during the period from 1913 to 1921.

BIBLIOGRAPHY

Garroni, Maria Susanna, ed. *Sorelle d'oltreoceano. Religiose italiane ed emigrazione negli Stati Uniti: una storia da scoprire.* Rome: Carocci, 2008.

Marchione, Margherita, MPF. *The Religious Teachers Filippini in America: Centennial, 1910–2010.* Mahwah, NJ: Paulist Press, 2010.

Rocca, Mafaldina, M. P. F. *Grandezza e semplicità di un carisma. Profilo biografico di Suor Rosa Leoni.* Rome: Istituto Maestre Pie Filippini, 1993.

———. "Archivio delle Maestre Pie Filippini." In *Fonti ecclesiastiche romane per lo studio dell'emigrazione italiana in Nord America (1642–1922),* special issue of *Studi Emigrazione* 33, no. 124 (December 1996): 706–8.

Vezzosi, Elisabetta. "Cittadine e mediatrici etniche: le Maestre Pie Filippini negli Stati Uniti." In *Santi, culti, simboli nell'età della secolarizzazione, 1815–1915,* edited by Emma Fattorini, 495–514. Turin: Rosenberg & Sellier, 1997.

Archivio della Congregazione dell'Oratorio di Roma /
Archives of the Congregation of the Oratory in Rome

Address

Via del Governo Vecchio 134, 00186 Rome

Contact Details

Phone: 39-0668801474

Fax: 39-066874797

Email 1: mail.acor@gmail.com

Email 2: info@aco-roma.org

Email 3: consultazione.acor@gmail.com

Website: www.aco-roma.org/home.html

STATUS

Open to researchers. The archives are open from Monday to Friday, 9:00 a.m.–12:30 p.m. The archives close for Italian national holidays and from mid-July until mid-September. A reference letter and an advance appointment with the archivist are necessary to access the material. The material is in English and Italian. Material post-1939 can be consulted with the archivist's permission.

HISTORY

The Congregation of the Oratory was founded by Saint Philip Neri (1515–95) in 1556. In 1575 the first Oratory of Rome was officially recognized by Pope Gregory XIII (1502–85). From the seventeenth century until the early 1800s the Congregation of the Oratory established new foundations in Europe, South America, India, and elsewhere.

DESCRIPTION OF HOLDINGS

The nucleus of the archives was formed in 1580, and two years later it was officially established. At present the archives are subdivided into the following seven broader sections: *Armadio* A, which contains the subsections AI, with forty-six volumes; AII, with forty-five volumes;

AIII, with fifty-six volumes; AIV, with twenty-six volumes; AV, with twenty volumes; AVI, with twenty-seven volumes; AVII, with thirty-five volumes; and AVIII, with sixteen volumes; *Armadio* B, which contains the subsections BI, with nineteen volumes; BII, with sixteen volumes; BIII, with eighteenth volumes; BIV, with thirty-eight volumes; BV, with nine volumes; BVI, with thirty-one volumes; BVII, with fifteen volumes; and BVIII, with four volumes; *Armadio* C, which contains the subsections CI, with forty-one volumes; CII, with thirty-three volumes; CIII, with thirty-six volumes; CIV, with forty-eight volumes; and *Armadio* I, which contains an imprecise number of documents; *Armadio* N, which contains the subsections NI, with thirteen volumes; NII, with twelve volumes; and NIII, with five volumes; *Armadio* O, which contains the subsections OI, with nine volumes; OII, with twelve volumes; and OIII, with eight volumes; *Armadio* P, which contains the subsections PI, with ten volumes; PII, with ten volumes; and PIII, with nine volumes; and *Armadio* Q, which contains the subsections QI, with twelve volumes; QII, with eleven volumes; and QIII, with ten volumes.

Material of American interest is found in *Armadio* QII, vol. 10: *Elenco Congregazione Italiane ed estere*, which contains correspondence exchanged by a group of American secular priests who unsuccessfully sought to open an oratory in the Diocese of New York, with the superior of the Congregation of the Oratory in Rome from 1928 to 1929. An example of this correspondence is provided by a letter that, on January 22, 1929, Peter O'Callaghan, priest in the New York diocese, wrote to Cesare Nanni (1890–1977), superior of the congregation. In it O'Callaghan stressed that the opening of an oratory in the United States would inspire "others of similar mind on this side of the Atlantic who will welcome the opportunity of priestly comradeship and spiritual help."[3]

According to the inventory compiled by Giovanni Morello and Francesco Dante,[4] in Armadio QII, vol. 11, there are some documents on the oratory of Rock Hill, North Carolina, which was the first foundation to be opened in the United States, in 1934. However, this material is missing, and possibly it has been transferred to another section.

BIBLIOGRAPHY
Gallonio, Antonio. *The Life of St. Philip Neri*. San Francisco: Ignatius Press/Family Publications, 2005.
Morello, Giovanni, and Francesco Dante. "L'Archivio della Congregazione dell'Oratorio di Roma alla Chiesa Nuova." *Ricerche per la Storia Religiosa di Roma* 2 (1978): 275–362.

Archivum Romanum Societatis Iesu /
Roman Archives of the Society of Jesus
Address
    Borgo Santo Spirito 4, 00193 Rome
Contact Details
    Phone: 39-0669868636
    Email: arsi-dir@sjcuria.org/arsi-seg@sjcuria.org; arsi-bib@sjcuria.org (for the library)
    Website: www.sjweb.info/arsi

STATUS

The Archivum Romanum Societatis Iesu (ARSI) is open to researchers Monday–Friday, 9:00 a.m.–12:45 p.m. and 2:00 p.m.–4:45 p.m. The archives close for Italian national holidays and from late July until mid-September. A reference letter and an appointment with the archivist are required. Most material is in Latin. Material post-1939 cannot be consulted.

HISTORY

After Saint Ignatius of Loyola (1491–1556) founded the Society of Jesus (the Jesuits) in 1539 and Pope Paul III (1468–1549) officially recognized the order only a year later, the Jesuits became the leading missionary movement of the Catholic Reformation. Between the latter half of the sixteenth century and the early decades of the seventeenth, the Jesuits established missions across continental Europe, Asia, and the Americas, where they arrived in 1611. They established their first North American mission at Port-Royal (now Annapolis Royal), Nova Scotia, where they remained from 1611 to 1613. In 1634 they reached Maryland, where they remained until the order's suppression in 1773. After the order's suppression, they remained there as secular priests. In 1805 five Jesuits affiliated with the Russian province (where the papal order suppressing the Society of Jesus was not implemented) established themselves in Maryland. After the official restoration of the order in 1814, the Jesuits expanded across the United States.

DESCRIPTION OF HOLDINGS

Although ARSI has collected and preserved material since the order's foundation, it was under the supervision of the Spanish Jesuit Juan Alfonso Polanco (1517–76) that documents were first registered and classified. Given that ARSI contains a vast collection spanning the latter half of the sixteenth century to the late decades of the twentieth century, the material is divided into four broad sections: (1) documents of the "old" Society, which cover the period from 1540 to 1773; (2) documents of the "new" Society, which cover the period after 1814; (3) Archives of the Jesuit General Procurator (commonly known as the *Fondo Gesuitico*); and (4) a miscellaneous section containing material that, though not directly related to the Society's central government, is relevant to the order's history.

The material contained in both the "old" and "new" Society sections can be further divided into two sections, the first of which contains material related to assistances and provinces and the second of which contains a range of other documents. The following sorts of material may be found in both the "old" and "new" Society sections of the archives: (1) formulas of final vows; (2) catalogs; (3) *indipetae*, that is, letters of missionaries asking to be sent to the "Indies"; (4) annual and other types of letters; and (5) obituaries.

The *Fondo Gesuitico*, which had been confiscated at the time of the Italian unification, contains the following types of material: (1) documentation related to colleges, (2) letters, (3) censures of Jesuit-authored works, (4) archives of the Roman Jesuit houses and churches, (5) archives of the general procurator, (6) manuscripts, (7) obituaries, (8) printed books, and (9) miscellaneous documents.

The miscellaneous section contains the following types of material: (1) archives of the Jesuit Historical Institute (IHSI); (2) photographs; (3) archives of the Chiesa del Gesù in Rome; (4) archives of the Chiesa di Sant'Ignazio in Rome; (5) archives of the Oratorio del Caravita in Rome; (6) plans of Jesuit buildings from the nineteenth and twentieth centuries; (7) Chinese and Japanese books; (8) seals and medals; and (9) other materials, such as printed books and microfilms. A fuller description of the Roman archives of the Jesuits is posted at www.sjweb.info/arsi/archives.cfm.

Researchers should also consult the inventory of the collection of Jan Philip Roothaan, SJ, (1785–1853), twenty-first superior general of the Society of Jesus from 1829 to 1853. His collection includes 1,829 items contained in sixty-nine folders. A three-volume PDF inventory in Italian is posted for download at the following addresses: (1) www.sjweb.info/arsi /documents/Inventario_Roothaan_Vol1.pdf, (2) www.sjweb.info/arsi/documents/Inventario _Roothaan_Vol2.pdf, (3) www.sjweb.info/arsi/documents/Inventario_Roothaan_Vol3.pdf.

ARSI abounds in material of American interest. Since the Maryland Mission depended on the English Province, researchers interested in the "old" Society period should consult documents of the English (*Angliae*) province, which came from the German Assistancy. Also, several research instruments are available in PDF for those interested in the "old" Society period, namely five catalogs of Jesuits who died between 1640 and 1740 (www.sjweb .info/arsi/documents/Defuncti_1640-1740_vol_I_A_C.pdf) and one catalog of Jesuits who died between 1740 and 1773 (www.sjweb.info/arsi/documents/Defunti_1740-1773.pdf).

American material from the "new" society period is scattered across several sections, and a complete printed inventory of the American Assistancy is available in *Inventario dei documenti inviati alla Curia generalizia parte IIa Nuova Compagnia (1814–)*, finding aid no. 242, pp. 139–40. This inventory also describes the material relating to the eleven American provinces of the Society (Buffalo, California, Chicago, Detroit, Maryland, Missouri, New England, New Orleans, New York, Oregon, and Wisconsin), pp. 141–60.

ARSI also provides access to catalogs of American material from 1774 to 1914, posted in PDF at www.sjweb.info/arsi/Catalog.cfm. These catalogs are divided into three periods: 1811–1830, 1829–53 (catalogs available for the Provinces of Maryland and Missouri), and 1892–1914 (catalogs available for the Provinces of California, Maryland, Missouri, and New Orleans). Roman material about Jesuit activity in Maryland ought to be combined with documents preserved by the Maryland Province Archives.

Generally, the material kept in ARSI should be supplemented by the holdings of its library, the Biblioteca Storica, which boasts a collection of 100,000 books on the society's history. One valuable resource in this library is the *Woodstock Letters* periodical, which describes Jesuit activity in the United States from 1872 to 1969. This collection is available digitally at cdm.slu.edu/cdm/landingpage/collection/woodstock.

Because of numerous transfers and exchanges that occurred between the French occupation of Rome in 1798 and the annexation of the city to the Kingdom of Italy in 1870, an abundance of material on the Jesuits may be found in other archives. For instance, the *Fondo Gesuitico* at the Biblioteca Centrale Nazionale of Italy hosts numerous manuscripts relating to Jesuit missions in North America (www.sjweb.info/arsi/Catalog.cfm), and the *Fondo Gesuiti* section of the Vatican Secret Archives contains material on the Jesuits. (A description of this material is available in the Vatican Secret Archives index room, inventory no. 1077.)

BIBLIOGRAPHY

Burke, James L. *Jesuit Province of New England: The Formative Years*. Boston: Society of Jesus, Province of New England, 1976.

Burke, James L., and Vincent Lapomarda. *Jesuit Province of New England: The Expanding Years*. Boston: Society of Jesus of New England, 1986.

Burns, Robert Ignatius, SJ. *The Jesuits and the Indian Wars of the Northwest*. New Haven, CT: Yale University Press, 1966.

Campeau, Lucien, SJ. *Monumenta Novae Franciae*. 9 vols. Rome: Apud Monumenta Hist. Soc. Iesu, 1967–2003.

Codignola, Luca. "Roman Catholic Ecclesiastics in English North America, 1610–58: A Comparative Assessment." Canadian Catholic Historical Association, *Historical Studies* 65 (1999): 107–24.

Curran, Francis X., SJ. *The Return of the Jesuits: Chapters in the History of the Society of Jesus in Nineteenth-Century America*. Chicago: Loyola University Press, 1966.

Danieluk, Robert, SJ. "Michal Boym, Andrzej Rudomina and Jan Smogulecki—Three Seventeenth-Century Missionaries in China: A Selection of Documents from the Roman Jesuit Archives." In *Monumenta Serica* 59 (2011): 417–24.

Faherty, William B., John J. Hennesey, Gerald L. McKevitt, Charles Edwards O'Neill, and Felix Zubillaga. "Estados Unidos de América." In *Diccionario histórico de la Compañia de Jesús: Biográfico-temático*, 2:1322–36. Madrid-Rome: Institutum Historicum S. I.–Universidad Pontificia Comillas, 2001.

Fortman, Edmund J. *Lineage: A Biographical History of the Chicago Province*. Chicago: Loyola University Press, 1987.

Garraghan, Gilbert, SJ. *The Jesuits of the Middle United States*. 3 vols. Chicago: Loyola University Press, 1938.

Hughes, Thomas, SJ. *History of the Society of Jesus in North America: Colonial and Federal*. 4 vols. New York: Longmans, Green, 1907–17.

Lamalle, Edmond. "L'Archivio di un grande Ordine religioso: L'Archivio generale della Compagnia di Gesù." *Archiva Ecclesiae* 24–25, no. 1 (1981–82): 89–120.

Lapomarda, Vincent A., SJ. *The Jesuit Heritage in New England*. Worcester, MA: College of the Holy Cross, 1977.

———. *The Jesuits in the United States: The Italian Heritage*. Worcester, MA: Jesuits of Holy Cross College, 2004.

McDonough, Peter. *Men Astutely Trained: A History of the Jesuits in the American Century*. New York: Free Press, 1992.

McGloin, John Bernard, SJ. *Jesuits by the Golden Gate: The Society of Jesus in San Francisco, 1849–1969*. San Francisco: University of San Francisco Press, 1972.

McGreevy, John T. *American Jesuits and the World: How an Embattled Religious Order Made Modern Catholicism Global*. Princeton, NJ: Princeton University Press, 2016.

McKevitt, Gerald. *Brokers of Culture: Italian Jesuits in the American West, 1848–1919*. Stanford, CA: Stanford University Press, 2007.

Neyrey, Jerome H. *Southern Jesuit Biographies: Pastors and Preachers, Builders and Teachers of the New Orleans Province*. New Orleans: Acadian House, 2015.

O'Donnell, Catherine. "John Carroll, the Catholic Church, and the Society of Jesus in Early Republican America." In *Jesuit Survival and Restoration: A Global History, 1773–1900*, ed. Robert Aleksander Maryks and Jonathan Wright, 368–85. Leiden: Brill, 2014.

Pasquier, Michael. *Fathers on the Frontier: French Missionaries and the Roman Catholic Priesthood in the United States, 1789–1870*. New York: Oxford University Press, 2010.

Pizzorusso, Giovanni. "Grassi, Giovanni Antonio." In *Dizionario biografico degli Italiani* 57, 625–28. Rome: Istituto della Enciclopedia Italiana, 2002.

Schlafly, Daniel. "The 'Russian' Society and the American Jesuits: Giovanni Grassi's Crucial Role." In *Jesuit Survival and Restoration: A Global History, 1773–1900*, ed. Robert Aleksander Maryks and Jonathan Wright, 353–67. Leiden: Brill, 2014.

Schoenberg, Wilfred P. *Paths to the Northwest: A Jesuit History of the Oregon Province*. Chicago: Loyola University Press, 1982.

Schroth, Raymond A., SJ. *The American Jesuits: A History*. New York: New York University Press, 2007.

Woodstock Letters: A Record of Current Events and Historical Notes Connected with the Colleges and Missions of the Society of Jesus in North and South America. Woodstock, MD: Woodstock College, 1872–1969.

Archivio della Curia Generalizia Agostiniana /
General Archives of the Augustinians
Address
    Via Paolo VI, 00193 Rome
Contact Details
    Phone: 39-06680061
    Fax: 39-0668006299
    Email: archiviogen@osacuria.org
    Website: archivioaugustinians.net

STATUS

The archives are open Monday–Friday, 9:00 a.m.–12:15 p.m. and 3:30 p.m.–6:00 p.m. The archives close for Italian national holidays and from the end of June until early September. Contact the archivists in advance to be granted access to the material; a reference letter is required. The majority of the documents are written in Latin. Material post-1939 cannot be consulted.

HISTORY

The foundations of the order of the Augustinians were laid in 1243, when Pope Innocent IV (1195–1254) invited all the mendicant communities in Tuscany to gather into an order that was to observe the monastic rules of Saint Augustine of Hippo (354–430). The order of the Augustinians was officially established in 1244.

DESCRIPTION OF HOLDINGS

At present the archives consist of five main sections: (1) the archives of the general government of the order, (2) the archives of the convent of Saint Augustine in Rome, (3) the archives of the Congregation of Lombardia, (4) the archives of the convent of Santa Maria del Popolo in Rome, and (5) personal files pertaining to the respective lives of various members of the orders.

The section of the general government is further divided into fourteen subseries: (1) Aa, material on the provinces, congregations, and convents; (2) Bb, registers of the general procurators; (3) Cc, miscellanea; (4) Dd, registers of the generals; (5) Ee, witnesses concerning the beatification of the members of the order; (6) Ff, acts of the meeting of the general chapters of all the provinces; (7) Gg, inventory of the Masses; (8) Hh, original bulls; (9) Li, reports on the economic status of the convents, especially those in Italy; (10) Kk, news on students; (11) revenues of the general fathers; (12) Mm, material on the Biblioteca Angelica; (13) Nn, financial status of the order; and (14) Oo, archives of the Roman province.

Material of American interest is mainly found in the subseries Ff and, more specifically, in Ff59—*Acta Capitolorum Prov Assistentiae Germaniae et Americae 1831–1901*—which contains documents on the Province of Saint Thomas of Villanova in Philadelphia, where the first members of the order arrived in 1796. Material on the twentieth century cannot be consulted at present because it is currently being cataloged. An example of the American material contained in this material is a letter that, at the end of July 1878, Fr. Pacifico, an Italian Augustinian, wrote from Philadelphia to the general in Rome. In it he complained about his American confreres by stating: "I know too well the mood of religious about the imposition of new Italians; the general feeling is that they do not want them."[5]

BIBLIOGRAPHY

Contosta, David R. *Villanova University: American-Catholic-Augustinian.* University Park: Pennsylvania State University Press, 1995.

Di Gregorio, Michael, OSA. "The Mission of the Italian Augustinians in U.S.A." *Analecta Augustiniana* 78 (2015): 117–50.

Ennis, Arthur J. *The Augustinians: A Brief Sketch of Their American History from 1796 to the Present.* Villanova, PA: Augustinian Press, 1985.

———. "The Founding of the Augustinians in the United States (1796)." *Analecta Augustiana* 41 (1978): 285–312.

———. *No Easy Road: The Early Years of the Augustinians in the United States, 1796–1874.* New York: Peter Lang, 1993.

Middleton, Thomas C. *Historical Sketch of the Augustinian Monastery, College and Mission of Saint Thomas of Villanova: Delaware County, Pa. during the First Half Century of Their Existence, 1842–1892.* Villanova, PA: Villanova College, 1893.

Roland, Thomas Francis, OSA. *The Order of Saint Augustine in the United States of America, 1796–1946.* Villanova, PA: Villanova College, 1947.

Sanders, John R. *Before All Else: The History of the Augustinians in the Western United States, 1922–1985.* Villanova, PA: Augustinian Press, 1987.

Tourscher, Francis Edward, OSA. *Old Saint Augustine's in Philadelphia, with Some Records of the Work of the Austin Friars in the United States.* Philadelphia: Peter Reilly, 1937.

Archivio Generale dei Fratelli delle Scuole Cristiane /
General Archives of the Brothers of the Christian Schools
Address
   Via Aurelia 476, 00165 Rome
Contact Details
   Phone: 39-06665231
   Fax: 39-066638821
   Website: www.lasalle.org/en/where-we-are/generalate-2/archives/

STATUS
Open to researchers Monday–Friday, 8:15 a.m.–3:00 p.m., but closed for Italian national holidays and during the summer. Researchers are advised to make an appointment with the archivist in advance to gain access to the material. Most documents are in French. Material post-1939 cannot be consulted.

HISTORY
The Brothers of the Christian Schools, also known as Christian Brothers or Lasallian Brothers, are a French Catholic teaching congregation founded by Saint Jean-Baptiste de La Salle (1651–1719) in 1680. The key aim of the Christian Brothers was to provide assistance and education to poor children. In 1725 Pope Benedict XIII (1649–1730) officially approved the congregation, which was then dissolved during the French Revolution. Napoleon I (1769–1821) reestablished it 1804, and in 1808 the French government recognized the congregation. The Christian Brothers then expanded to continental Europe and beyond. After some unsuccessful attempts to establish themselves in New France during the second half of the eighteenth century, the Christian Brothers arrived at New Orleans in 1817. In 1837 Benoît-Joseph Flaget (1763–1850), bishop of Bardstown, Kentucky, and later of Louisville after the see was transferred there, called on them to found new schools in his diocese.

DESCRIPTION OF HOLDINGS
The archives of the Christian Brothers are divided into thirteen sections. Material of American interest is found in section N: *Documents régionaux et locaux.* This section has 486 boxes, from NS 500 to NS 986; these contain material on the history and activity of the congregation in the United States since its arrival in the 1830s. Amid the material of this section is a February 1837 letter from Bishop Flaget inviting the Christian Brothers to join his diocese. Regarding which missionaries to choose, the bishop suggested, "It would be good that two or three of them should be young enough in order to learn properly the English accent which is difficult for all the strangers."[6]

BIBLIOGRAPHY

Angelus Gabriel, Brother. *The Christian Brothers in the United States, 1848–1948: A Century of Catholic Education.* New York: Declan X. McMullen, 1948.

Battersby, William John. *The Christian Brothers in the United States, 1900–1925.* Winona, MN, Saint Mary's College Press, 1967.

———. *History of the Institute of the Brothers of the Christian Schools in the Nineteenth Century.* London: Waldegrave, 1961–63.

"The Brothers of the Christian Schools in the United States: Half a Century of Work." In *Catholic World* (September 1901): 721–33.

Isetti, Ronald Eugene. *Called to the Pacific: A History of the Christian Brothers of the San Francisco District, 1868–1944.* Moraga, CA: Saint Mary's College of California, 1979.

O'Donoghue, Tom. *Catholic Teaching Brothers: Their Life in the English-Speaking World, 1891–1965.* New York: Palgrave MacMillan, 2012.

Towey, J. *Irish De La Salle Brothers in Christian Education.* Dublin: De La Salle Brothers, 1980.

Archivio Generale dei Cappuccini /
General Archives of the Capuchins
Address
>   Collegio Internazionale San Lorenzo da Brindisi, G. R. A. Km 62,050, 00163 Rome

Contact Details
>   Phone: 39-0666052537
>   Fax: 39-0666052592
>   Email: archivio.generale.ofmcap@gmail.com
>   Website: www.ibisweb.it/bcc/agc/index.html

STATUS

Open to researchers Monday–Friday, 8:30 a.m.–1 p.m. and 2:30 p.m.–5 p.m., and Saturday, 8:30 a.m.–1 p.m. The archives close for Italian national holidays and the entire month of August. Researchers should make an appointment with the archivist in advance to gain access to the material. Most material of American interest is in English, German, or Latin. Material post-1939 can be consulted with the archivist's permission.

HISTORY

The Capuchin Order was founded in 1520 by Matteo da Bascio, an Italian Observant friar (1495–1552) who was persuaded that the Franciscan way of life needed radical reform. In 1528 Pope Clement VII (1474–1534) approved the order, which, from the late sixteenth century onward, began to expand across continental Europe, eventually establishing missions in Africa, the Americas, and Asia.

DESCRIPTION OF HOLDINGS

It is not known when the archives of the Capuchin Order were officially established, although some mid-sixteenth-century documents reference an "Archivio Generale." At present, the archives are organized into twenty-three sections that hold varied material dating from the thirteenth century through to the late decades of the twentieth century. A fuller description of the collections is available at www.ibisweb.it/bcc/agc/conspectus_2009.html.

Material of American interest can be found in two sections: (1) *Calvariensis* contains twenty-four dossiers related to the Capuchin Province of Wisconsin, which was the first to be erected in the United States, in 1852, and formally established in 1882; (2) *Pennysilvanica* comprises four sections, G 97 I, G 97 II, G 97 XIII, G 97 XIV, which contain material related to the Pennsylvania province, erected in 1873 and formally established in 1882. Additional material is available in the sections G 147, *Neoeboracensis-Novae Angliae*; G 151, *Neojerseyensis*; and G 195, *Texiana*. In the section H, *Missioni*, there is a box, no. 10, titled *America Septentrionalis*, which contains material relating to the activity of Ignazio Persico (1823–95), an Italian Capuchin who was active in the diocese of Charleston starting in 1867 and bishop of Savannah from 1870 to 1873.

Section G 97 II is of particular importance because it provides details on the Capuchins' activity and impact among the American people between the second half of the nineteenth century and the first three decades of the twentieth. For instance, this section contains an anonymous request addressed in 1917 to Venanzio de Lisle-en-Rigault, the Capuchin minister general from 1914 to 1920. The document addressed the problem of the Capuchin beard: "As a matter of fact, Catholics as well as non-Catholics are so accustomed to see priests clean-shaven, with neither moustache nor whiskers, that it often requires some effort to convince them that we are priests." The letter explains that "in the United States we have charge of parishes. Hence we must mingle with the laity far more than do our brethren in religion elsewhere; and here likewise this regulation more than once proves a hindrance to efficiency … if it must be a question of sacrificing time-honoured custom, we believe the Catholic Church herself sets the best and safest example. As a kind mother she wisely moderates her laws even in serious matters of discipline and adapts them to varying conditions."[7]

Of similar tenor is a letter that James Malone, state senator in Kansas, sent to Venanzio de Lisle-en-Rigault in 1917 about the problem of the Capuchins' whiskers: "In the majority of cases in the United States, the social and public functions of communities are presided over and controlled by non-Catholics. The Capuchins are seldom recognized or invited to participate in the exercises on these occasions. Why? They are kind, gentle and lovable, devoting their lives to the spiritual welfare of their fellowmen. There is, in my judgement, only one reason for the objections set forth: 'WHISKERS.' Because the appendages on their face, which the people refer to as hairy entanglements, are repulsive to the American idea of appearance."[8]

BIBLIOGRAPHY

Baer, Campion R., and Celestine N. Bittle. *A Romance of Lady Poverty Revisited: A History of the Province of Saint Joseph of the Capuchin Order*. Milwaukee: Bruce, 1933.

Barbato, Robert. *In the Land of the Pioneer: A History of the Capuchin Franciscans in the Western United States*. Berkeley, CA: Province of Our Lady of the Angels, 1985.

Celestino, Pietro, OFM Cap. "Il cardinale missionario cappuccino Ignazio Persico." In *Studi e ricerche francescane* 10 (1981): 115–32.

Cuthbert of Brighton, OFM Cap. *The Capuchins: A Contribution to the History of the Counter Reformation*, 2nd ed. 2 vols. Port Washington, NY: Kennikat, 1971.

D'Alatri, Mariano, OFM Cap, and Ignatius McCormick, OFM Cap, eds. *The Capuchin Way: Lives of Capuchins*. Pittsburgh, PA: North American Capuchin Conference, 1985.

Lenhart, John Mary. "The Capuchin Prefecture of New England (1630–1656)." *Franciscan Studies* 24 (1943): 21–46.

Lexicon capuccinum: promptuarium historico-bibliographicum ordinis fratrum minorum capuccinorum (1525–1950). Rome: Bibliotheca Collegii Internationalis S. Laurentii Brundusini, 1951.

Messmer, Sebastian Gebhard, OFM Cap. *The Establishment of the Capuchin Order in the United States*. New York: The Catholic Historical Society, 1906.

Miller, Norbert H. "Capuchins in New York, Pennsylvania, Kentucky, Saint Louis, and Part of Baltimore: Pioneer Capuchin Missions in the US." *Franciscan Studies* 10 (1932): 170–234.

———. *Pioneer Capuchin Missionaries in the United States (1784–1816)*. Washington, DC: Catholic University of America Press, 1930.

Roemer, Theodore. "Pioneer Capuchin Letters." *Franciscan Studies* 16 (1938): 4–156.

Vogel, Claude L., OFM Cap. "Capuchins in French Louisiana (1722–1766)." *Franciscan Studies* 8 (1928): 1–95.

———. *The Capuchins in French Louisiana, 1722–1766*. Ville Platte, LA: Provincial Press, 1998.

———, ed. *Franciscan History of North America: Report on the Eighteenth Annual Meeting, Santa Barbara, California, August 2–4, 1936*. Washington, DC: Capuchin College, 1937.

Wolf, James C. "The Midwest Capuchin Province of St. Joseph, Detroit, Michigan: Its History and Its Archives." *Michigan Historical Review* 27, no. 1, special issue, *Detroit 300* (Spring 2001): 137–51.

Archivio Generale della Congregazione della Missione /
General Archives of the Congregation of the Mission
Address
   Via dei Capasso 30, 00164 Rome
Contact Details
   Phone: 39-066613061
   Email: archives@cmglobal.org

STATUS

The archives are open Monday–Friday, 9:00 a.m.–12:30 p.m. and 3:00 p.m.–5:00 p.m., and by appointment on Saturday. Generally, researchers should contact the archivist in advance to gain access to the material, most of which is in Italian. Material post-1939 can be consulted with the archivist's permission.

HISTORY

The Congregation of the Mission, also known as Lazarists or Vincentians, is a Catholic society of apostolic life of priests and brothers founded by Saint Vincent de Paul (1581–1660) in 1624. In 1626 it obtained archiepiscopal recognition, and the society was constituted as a congregation in 1633.

DESCRIPTION OF HOLDINGS

There is no detailed inventory at present because all material is currently being reorganized. Material of American interest is mainly found in the diary of Giuseppe Rosati (1789–1843), bishop of Saint Louis, 1826–43, which covers the period from August 1, 1831, to December 1836. Further material of American interest is available in the twenty-volume section titled *Felice De Andreis Collection*. Felice De Andreis (1778–1820) was an Italian Vincentian active as missionary and vicar general of the New Orleans diocese from 1816 to 1820.

Amid his collection there are two volumes titled *America: Lettere Parte I* and *America: Lettere Parte II*. *Parte I* contains a series of letters written by De Andreis, but also letters by Monsignor Louis-Guillaume-Valentin Dubourg (1766–1833), bishop of Louisiana and the Floridas from 1815 to 1826 and apostolic administrator of Mississippi from mid-August of 1825 to mid-January 1826. This volume also contains a series of letters written by eleven Vincentian missionaries active in the United States from 1818 to 1839.

America: Lettere Part II contains seventy-nine letters written by Bishop Rosati and series of letters written by Benoît-Joseph Flaget (1763–1850), bishop of Bardstown and then bishop of Louisville after the see was transferred there. This volume also contains statistics on the Catholic clergy in US dioceses in 1840.

One example of the American material in the volume *America: Lettere Parte I* is a particular letter that De Andreis wrote in late November 1816. In it the missionary observed:

The seeds of unbelief and irreligion have not penetrated here. Each one loves his own faith, whether true or false. It is true that the Catholics are very few and that magnificent temples are built by Quakers, Presbyterians, Episcopalians, Methodists and the Protestants of a thousand different sects that keep multiplying daily. This happens because of a dearth of missionaries. The Protestants themselves respect and welcome Catholic priests beautifully, even more than they do their own ministers. We ourselves have experienced this. In more and more places there has been a kind of violence to collect the harvest that is already white. An entire heretic family, after hearing only two words of exhortation, knelt down and tearfully begged us to remain at least a while with them to instruct them and others were moved to renounce [their heresy]. It makes one very compassionate to see the great extent of the region where there are cities and villages with many Catholic families who never see a priest. The same is true when we see a Catholic area without a pastor, since no priest can be had, which then forces them to seek out a minister and they all become Protestants. O God, what desolation! And with so many priests living in idleness in Italy and in Rome itself, who here would do an immense good by simply saying mass, teaching catechism with a book in hand, and baptizing. Unfortunately, among the other things introduced among the heretics, there is such a great negligence in baptizing that many adults remain unbaptized, and a huge number of infants die without baptism. Any miserable priest with a little zeal and good will, anywhere he stayed, would surely be able in a short time to found a parish of good Catholics.[9]

Researchers should note that copies of De Andreis's letters and, more broadly, those of the other Vincentian missionaries active in the United States, can also be found in the archives of the Congregation for the Propagation of the Faith and in the *Annales de la Con-grégation de la Mission*, which can be downloaded from the following website: via.library .depaul.edu/annales/.

The archives also contain a considerable amount of material on the cause of beatification for Elizabeth Ann Bayley Seton. This material consists of the following documents:

(1) Two volumes containing the transcribed copies of the acts pertaining to her cause and process of beatification.

(2) Two small books, dated 1940 and 1941, that include additional transcribed copies of documents about her beatification process.

(3) A book containing a small collection of printed letters of postulation written by the following cardinals: William O'Connell, archbishop of Boston; Francis Joseph Beckman, archbishop of Dubuque; Francis Moeller, archbishop of Cincinnati; Rudolph Aloysius Gerken, archbishop of Santa Fe; Richard O'Gerow, bishop of Natchez; Urban J. Vehr, bishop of Denver; Carol O'Reilly, bishop of Scranton; Thomas K. Gorman, bishop of Reno; and Joseph Edward McCarthy, bishop of Portland. The concluding part of the book contains the letters of Charles L. Souvay, superior general of the Congregation of the Mission, Mother Vincentia M. Renna of the Sister of Charity of Saint Vincent de Paul, and Sister M. Chaplain, superior general of the Sisters of Charity of Saint Vincent de Paul. The book also lists thirty-five American bishops who wrote similar letters to support Seton's beatification.

(4) A volume of transcribed copies of documents, dated 1961, on the beatification process initiated by the Diocese of New Orleans.

(5) A volume, no. 364, of documents and testimonies written by a series of doctors collected on behalf of the Diocese of Baltimore.

(6) A volume, no. 366, of further transcribed copies, dated 1961, on the process of beatification initiated at Baltimore.

(7) Two volumes, nos. 1069 and 1070, both dated 1968, containing transcribed copies of the documents on Seton's process of beatification initiated by the Diocese of New York.

(8) A volume, no. 365, dated 1961, which contains another set of the transcribed copies of documents and testimonies compiled by doctors on the miracles done through Seton's intercession.

(9) A volume, no. 363, dated 1961, which contains further transcribed copies of the documents on the process begun by the Diocese of Baltimore.

(10) A printed book, dated 1962, titled *Baltimoren: Beatificationis et canonizationis ven. Servae Dei Elisabeth Annae Bayley Viduae Seton Fundatricis Congr.nis Sororum a Charitate Sancti Joseph in America Septentrionali; Positio Super Miraculis*, which contains a series of documents written by the Congregation of the Rites.

(11) A printed book, dated 1974, titled *Baltimoren: Beatificationis et canonizationis ven. Servae Dei Elisabeth Annae Bayley Viduae Seton Fundatricis Congr.nis Sororum a Charitate*

Sancti Joseph in America; Positio Super Miraculo, containing transcribed copies from the Congregation of the Rites.

(12) Two volumes, both dated 1959, titled *Baltimoren: Beatificationis et canonizationis servae Dei Elisabeth Annae Bayley Viduae Seton; Fundatricis Congr.nis Sororum a Charitate Sancti Joseph in America Septentrionali; Nova Positio Super Virtutibus.*

(13) a small volume, dated 1941, titled *Baltimoren: Beatificationis et canonizationis servae Dei Elisabeth Annae Bayley Viduae Seton; Fundatricis Congr.nis Sororum a Charitate Sancti Joseph in America; Positio super non cultu.*

(14) A small volume, dated 1959, titled *Baltimoren: Beatificationis et canonizationis servae Dei Elisabeth Annae Bayley Viduae Seton; Fundatricis Congr.nis Sororum a Charitate Sancti Joseph in America Septentrionali; Novissima positio super virtutibus.*

(15) A book, dated 1963, titled *Baltimoren: Beatificationis et canonizationis ven. Servae Dei Elisabeth Annae Bayley Viduae Seton; Fundatricis Congr.nis Sororum a Charitate Sancti Joseph in America Septentrionali; Novissima positio super miraculis.*

(16) A volume, dated 1963, titled *Baltimoren: Beatificationis et canonizationis ven. Servae Dei Elisabeth Annae Bayley Viduae Seton; Fundatricis Congr.nis Sororum a Charitate Sancti Joseph in America Septentrionali; Positio super tuto.*

(17) A small volume, dated 1965, entitled *Baltimoren: Canonizationis ven. Servae Dei Elisabeth Annae Bayley Viduae Seton; Congr.nis Sororum a Charitate Sancti Joseph in America Septentrionali fundatricis; Positio super causae reassumptione.*

(18) A small booklet, published in 1975, providing details on the Mass that Pope Paul VI celebrated on September 14, 1975, for the solemn canonization of Elizabeth Ann Bayley Seton.

(19) A printed report, dated 1958, titled *Baltimoren: Beatificationis et canonizationis ven. Servae Dei Elisabeth Annae Bayley Viduae Seton; Fundatricis Congr.nis Sororum a Charitate Sancti Joseph in America († 1821); Relazione presentata all'E.mo Sig. Card. Gaetano Cicognani prefetto della S. Congregazione dei Riti dal Rev.mo P. Relatore Generale sulla seduta della sezione storica del 13 Novembre 1967.*

(20) A small book, dated 1974, titled *Compendium vitae virtutum ac miraculorum necnon actorum in causa canonizationis beatae Elisabeth Annae Bayley Viduae Seton: Fundatricis Sororum a Caritate S. Iosephi in America; E tabulario Sacrae Congregationis pro Causis Sanctorum.*

(21) A small volume, dated 1974, titled *Baltimoren: Canonizationis Beatae Elisabeth Annae Bayley Viduae Seton; Fundatricis Congr.nis Sororum a Charitate Sancti Joseph in America; Relatio et vota congressus peculiaribus super miro die 8 Octobris an. 1974 habiti.*

(22) An unpublished, undated paper written by Don Gino Franchi titled "Riflessioni su S. Elisabetta Anna Seton: L'amore di Cristo ci spinge."

(23) A folder containing the following documents: (a) a letter, dated June 25, 1979, written by Sr. Delort, archivist of the Congregation of the Mission in Paris and addressed to William W. Sheldon, general procurator of the Congregation in Rome; (b) a series of receipts pertaining to the expenses paid to collect material on Seton's cause by the Congregation of the Rites; and (c) a small volume, dated 1963, titled *Sanctissimi Domini Nostri Ioannis Divina*

Providentia Papae XXIII litterae apostolicae quibus venerabilis dei famula Elisabeth Anna Bayley vid. Seton: Instituti Sororum a Caritate S. Ioseph in America Septentrionali fundatrix beata renuntiatur.

(24) A printed report, dated 1939, titled *Baltimoren: Beatificationis et canonizationis servae Dei Elisabeth Annae Seton; Fundatricis Congr.nis Sororum a Charitate Sancti Joseph in America; Relazione sommaria presentata all'E.mo Signor Card. Carlo Salotti prefetto della S. Congregazione dei Riti dal R.mo P. Relatore Generale sulla documentazione relativa alla causa.*

(25) Two printed documents, both dated 1939, written by Salvator Natucci, general promotor of the faith.

(26) Two printed summaries, dated 1933 and 1935, on the decisions made by the theologians who examined Seton's written works.

(27) A printed volume, dated 1961, titled *Baltimoren: Beatificationis et Canonizationis ven. Servae Dei Elisabeth Annae Bayley Viduae Seton; Fundatricis Congr.nis Sororum a Charitate Sancti Joseph in America; Positio super validitate processuum.*

(28) A volume, printed in 1939, titled *Baltimoren: Beatificationis et Canonizationis Servae Dei Elisabeth Annae Bayley Viduae Seton; Fundatricis Congr.nis Sororum a Charitate Sancti Joseph in America; Positio super causae introductione.*

(29) A volume containing letters written by the American cardinals and addressed to the pope during the years 1924–39.

(30) A volume, published in 1957, titled *Baltimoren: Beatificationis et Canonizationis Servae Dei Elisabeth Annae Bayley Viduae Seton; Fundatricis Congr.nis Sororum a Charitate Sancti Joseph in America; Positio super virtutibus ex officio disposita.*

(31) A folder containing a mixed group of documents. These include (a) letters and extracts from newspapers; (b) five small booklets on the celebration of the bicentenary of Seton's birth; (c) one small book published in 1971 in commemoration of the 150th anniversary of her death; (d) a short summary of her life, published in 1974; (e) a report, published in 1974, titled *Baltimoren: Canonizationis Beatae Elisabeth Annae Bayley Viduae Seton; Fundatricis Congr.nis Sororum a Charitate Sancti Joseph in America; Relatio et Vota Congressus peculiaris super miro die 8 Octobris an. 1974 habiti*; and (f) a report, published in 1974, titled *Baltimoren: Canonizationis Beatae Elisabeth Annae Bayley Viduae Seton; Fundatricis Congr.nis Sororum a Charitate Sancti Joseph in America; Animadversiones promotoris generalis fidei super dubio; An et de quo miraculo constet in casu et ad effectum de quoagitur.*

BIBLIOGRAPHY

Codignola, Luca. "The Holy See and the Conversion of Aboriginal People in North America, 1760–1830." In *Ethnographies and Exchanges: Native Americans, Moravians and Catholics in Early North America*, ed. Anthony Gregg Roeber, 77–96. University Park: Penn State University Press, 2008.

McNeil, Betty Ann, DC. *The Vincentian Family Tree.* Chicago: Vincentian Studies Institute, 1996.

Pasquier, Michael. "When Catholic Worlds Collide: French Missionaries and Ecclesiastical Politics in Louisiana." In *God's Empire: French Missionaries and the Modern World*, ed. J. P. Daughton and Owen White, 29–46. New York: Oxford University Press, 2012.

Poole, Stafford, CM, and Douglas Slawson. *Church and Slave in Perry County, Missouri, 1818–1865*. Lewiston, NY: Edward Mellen, 1986.

Ricciardelli, Raffaele. *Vita del Servo di Dio, Felice de Andreis, fondatore e primo superiore della Congregazione della Missione negli Stati Uniti d'America*. Rome: Industria Tip. Romana, 1923.

Rybolt, John E., CM. *The American Vincentians: A Popular History of the Congregation of the Mission in the United States, 1815–1987*. Brooklyn, NY: Vincentian Studies Institute, 1988.

———. *Frontier Missionary, Felix De Andreis, 1778–1820, Correspondence and Historical Writings*. Chicago: Vincentian Studies Institute, 2005.

———. *The Vincentians: A General History of the Congregation of the Mission*. Vols. 3–4. New York: New City Press, 2014.

Slawson, Douglas J. "Catholic Revivalism: The Vincentian Preaching Apostolate in the United States." In *Embodying the Spirit: New Perspectives on North American Revivalism*, ed. Michael J. McClymond, 211–52. Baltimore: John Hopkins University Press, 2004.

Udovic, Edward, CM. *Jean-Baptiste Étienne and the Vincentian Revival*. Chicago: Vincentian Studies Institute, 2001.

Archivio Curia Generale Figlie di Santa Maria della Provvidenza /
General Archives of the Daughters of Saint Mary of Providence

Address

   Piazza di San Pancrazio 9, 00152 Rome

Contact Details

   Phone: 39-065809918

   Fax: 39-065809918

   Email: centroricercaroma@gmail.com

   Website: www.cgfsmp.org/cr.html

STATUS

Open to researchers. Since the archives do not keep regular hours, contact the archivist in advance to arrange a meeting and be granted access to the material. The archives close for Italian national holidays and the summer period. Material is in Italian. Material post-1939 cannot be consulted.

HISTORY

The foundations of the Congregazione delle Figlie di S. Maria della Provvidenza (CGFMDP), the Daughters of Saint Mary of Providence, also known as Guanellians, were laid in 1872 when Carlo Coppini, the parish priest of Pianello del Lario, in the Lombardy region, founded a hospice, known as Sacred Heart, to assist orphans and elderly people. In 1878, Marcellina Bosatta (1847–1934), the hospice's director, and her sister, Chiara Bosatta (1858–87), together with other volunteers, decided to form a religious community to be known as the Ursulines. Saint Luigi Guanella (1842–1915) replaced Coppini as parish priest in 1881 and took charge of the hospice's direction. Guanella expanded the activity of the hospice and of the congregation, which then took the name of the Daughters of Saint Mary of Providence. The constitutions and rules of the congregation were approved officially in 1917.

The arrival of the Daughters of Saint Mary of Providence in the United States followed from a request made by James Edward Quigley (1854–1915), archbishop of Chicago from 1903 to 1915. In 1910 Quigley contacted Aristide Leonori (1856–1928), an Italian engineer and friend of Guanella's, seeking nuns to serve the Italian community's orphans and elderly people. Between December 1912 and February 1913, Guanella visited the most important cities of the northeastern United States, paving the way for the first mission to begin in May 1913, when the first group of six Guanellian sisters arrived in Chicago.

DESCRIPTION OF HOLDINGS

Material of American interest is found in two broad sections: (1) *Case d'America*, which contains five folders on the history of the religious houses opened between 1918 and 1956, and (2) *Raccolta di lettere delle prime suore d'America, anni 1913–1935*, which contains twenty-seven folders of correspondence sent by sisters in the United States to their superiors in Italy.

Amid this correspondence is a letter that Rosa Bertolini wrote to Marcellina Bosatta in 1919 about the difficulty of recruiting new novices. According to Sr. Bertolini, "In America it is almost a miracle to have any. Nuns almost steal the girls, they are so scarce."[10] Researchers should note that additional material on the Daughters of Saint Mary of Providence may be found in the archives of the Chicago province and in the archives of the Archdiocese of Chicago. More information is available at www.dsmpic.org and at archives.archchicago.org.

BIBLIOGRAPHY

Carrozzino, Michela, CGFSMP. "Le Guanelliane a Chicago (1913–1940)." In *Per le strade del mondo: Laiche e religiose fra Otto e Novecento*, ed. Stefania Bartoloni, 415–35. Bologna: Il Mulino, 2007.

Cerri, Maria Giuseppina. "L'espansione missionaria Guanelliana negli Stati Uniti d'America." In *Figlie di S. Maria della Provvidenza e Servi della Carità nei vent'anni successivi alla morte del Fondatore*, ed. Alejandro Dieguez, 321–59. Rome: Nuove Frontiere Editrice, 2003.

Guanella, Luigi. *Le vie della Provvidenza: Autobiografia di un santo*. Cinisello Balsamo: Edizioni San Paolo, 2011.

Hillman, Jim, and John Murphy. *Images of America: Indiana's Catholic Religious Communities*. Charleston, SC: Arcadia, 2009.

Archivio Generale dei Carmelitani Scalzi (OCD) /

General Archives of the Discalced Carmelites (OCD)

Address

　　Corso d'Italia 38, 00198 Rome

Contact Details

　　Phone: 39-0685443241

　　Fax: 39-068559342

　　Email: archgen@ocdcuria.org

　　Website: agocd.com

STATUS

Open Monday–Friday, 9:00 a.m.–1:00 p.m. The archives close for Italian national holidays and from mid-July until mid-September. Contact the archivists in advance to arrange a meeting and be granted access to the material. Before visiting, researchers must fill out an online form at agocd.com/come-accedere-all-agocd. Researchers also must send to archgen @ocdcuria.org a reference letter from their supervisors and a scanned copy of their identification document. Material of American interest is mainly in English, French, Italian, or Latin. Material post-1939 can be consulted with the archivist's permission.

HISTORY

The origins of the Discalced Carmelites can be traced back to the thirteenth century, when a small group of European men began to gather around Mount Carmel in the Holy Land. Between 1206 and 1214, this group became a community with written rules. During the fourteenth and fifteenth centuries, however, the Carmelite community progressively lost its initial religious fervor, necessitating spiritual reform. The first to promote this reform was Saint Teresa of Ávila (1515–82), who in 1562 founded in Ávila a small monastery of nuns who took the name Discalced Carmelites. In 1568 Saint John of the Cross (1542–91), with the help of Teresa of Ávila, founded the monastery of Duruelo, thus establishing the male branch of the Discalced Carmelites. With the brief *Pia Consideratione* of June 22, 1580, Pope Gregory XIII (1502–85) recognized the Discalced Carmelites as a separate province of the Carmelite Order.

DESCRIPTION OF HOLDINGS

The nucleus of these archives was possibly created between the late 1560s and the early 1570s, when Saint Teresa of Ávila herself encouraged the keeping of the documents pertaining to the order's activity. At present the general archives are organized into twenty sections; researchers, however, must take into account that this subdivision is to be revised.

Material of American interest is mainly found in the section *A. Archivio Antico—vols. 1–560*, which contains a subsection titled *Missiones*. This subsection consists of twenty-three series. Series no. 11 is divided into four parts:

(1) *430/f America: Missio Mexicana-Californiae*, 1586–88, which contains copies from the *Archivo General de Indias* in Spain.

(2) *270/l Louisiana*, which contains eleven documents on the establishment and development of the mission in Louisiana during the eighteenth and nineteenth centuries. The Discalced Carmelites had opened this first mission in Louisiana in 1720.

(3) *270/½ Virginia seu Nova Anglia: Missio; Circa missionem proiectatam in Virginia*, which contains a copy of a document from Propaganda that was written by the English Discalced Carmelite Simon Stock (born Thomas Doughty, 1576–1652), about the possibility of establishing a mission in Virginia.

(4) *272/f/2 Virginia seu Nova Anglia: Documenta quoad missionem in Virginia et Avellonia*, which contains another copied Propaganda document written by Stock; the general

archives of the Discalced Carmelites contain twenty of Stock's original letters. The majority of his correspondence, however—seventy-three letters—are found in the archives of Propaganda. Most of Stock's letters have been transcribed and published by Luca Codignola.[11]

Series no. 14 contains further American material, namely documents on the first three permanent convents that the Discalced Carmelites founded in the United States: The convent in Baltimore was established in 1790, that in Saint Louis in 1863, and that in New Orleans in 1887.

Additional material of American interest is found in series no. 19, *Acta Definitori generali*, which contains the decisions made by the order's general chapters regarding its missions.[12] This series contains ten documents subdivided as follows: document no. 1 concerns the general chapter's decision to decline the bishop of Toronto's 1872 invitation to the members of the Irish Discalced Province to found a convent there; document nos. 2–9 contain material on the short-lived convent that the Discalced Province of Bavaria established at Paterson, New Jersey, from 1875 to 1877; and document no. 10 deals with the general chapter's 1887 decision to deny the prior of the Dublin convent's request for permission to found a church and convent in New York.

One example of the American material contained here is an anonymous and undated report addressed to the superior in Rome about the first convent that the female Discalced Carmelites opened in Baltimore in 1790. The document shows that the Carmelites desired greater knowledge of the original rules set by Saint Teresa of Ávila. The report states that "there are, of course, more particulars of the little usages and customs of the Order than are contained in either Constitutions, Ceremonial or Manual. Now the seal of St. Teresa's daughter in Baltimore to imitate their holy mother in all things, makes them earnestly desire to know every minutiae of what has been handed down as her practice, or of what, by proper authority, has been deduced from her writings, and thus established. Where shall we obtain this information?"[13]

A further example is a letter from Sr. Mary Magdalene of Jesus Crucified, prioress of the Carmelite Monastery of Baltimore, to Father Silverio da Santa Teresa (1878–1954), superior general of Discalced Carmelites, written in early October 1946. In this letter Sr. Mary Magdalene informed the superior that the prioress of the Iloilo convent in the Philippines needed American nuns: "The American nuns seem to be wanted for the offices of Prioress, Mistress of Novices, etc; A number of the Nuns with a real missionary spirit are most anxious to go, although they are fully aware of the difficulties they may have to face. We are not thinking much about the difficulties, but trying to do God's will each day and leave the future in his kind hands."[14]

BIBLIOGRAPHY

Ahedo, Óscar I. Aparicio, OCD. *Archivio della casa generalizia dell'ordine dei Padri Carmelitani Scalzi*. Rome: Casa Generalizia Carmelitani Scalzi, 2011.

Codignola, Luca. *The Coldest Harbour of the Land: Simon Stock and Lord Baltimore's Colony in Newfoundland, 1621–1649*. Montreal: McGill-Queen's University Press, 1988.

Fortes, Antonio, OCD, ed. *Acta Definitori gen. OCD Congregationis s. Eliae (1863–1875) et totius Ordinis (1875–1920)*. Rome: Teresianum, 1984.

———. *Las Misiones del Carmelo Teresiano, 1584–1799: Documentos del Archivo General de Roma*. Rome: Teresianum, 1997.

———. *Las Misiones del Carmelo Teresiano, 1800–1899: Documentos del Archivo General de Roma*. Rome: Teresianum, 2008.

July, Myron, OCD. *Carmel Came: A History of the American Carmelite Province of the Most Pure Heart of Mary, 1864–1900*. Downers Grove, IL: Aylesford Priory, 1964.

Rohrbach, Peter-Thomas, OCD. *Journey to Carith. The Story of the Carmelite Order*. Washington, DC: ICS Publications, 1966.

Archivio Generale dell'Ordine dei Frati Predicatori (Domenicani) /

General Archives of the Order of Friars Preachers (Dominicans)

Address

Piazza Pietro d'Illiria 1, 00153 Rome

Contact Details

Phone: 39-0657940555/39-06579401

Fax: 39-065750675

Email: archivum@curia.op.org

Website: www.op.org/en/content/archivum

STATUS

Open to researchers Tuesday–Thursday, 9:00 a.m.–6:30 p.m., and closed for Italian national holidays and from the end of July until mid-September. Researchers should make an appointment with the archivist in advance and should send the archivist desired documents' series numbers to verify their availability and accessibility; only reserved documents will be provided on the research day. Researchers can consult the archives' database at archivum.op.org/htm/iniziale.php. Documents are in English, French, Italian, or Latin. Material post-1939 cannot be consulted.

HISTORY

The Dominican Order was founded by the Spanish priest Domingo Félix de Guzmán (1170–1221) in 1215. It was officially recognized by Pope Honorius III (1150–1227) in 1216. From the thirteenth century to the fifteenth, the order spread over continental Europe and the British Isles and established missions in Africa and Asia.

DESCRIPTION OF HOLDINGS

The Archivum Generale Ordinis Praedicatorum (AGOP or General Archives of the Dominican Order) were established when the order was founded. At present they are divided into twenty-one sections that contain a diverse mix of bulls, decrees, acts of the general chapters, registers of letters of the master generals, material on female congregations, correspondence with the missions, and other items.

Material of American interest can be found in the sections AGOP IX.128a, AGOP IX.128b, and AGOP IX.128c, which contain a series of catalogs about the status of the Dominican Order in North America for the period from 1873 to 1900.

AGOP IV.278, register no. 2, vol. 1, contains the 1859–62 correspondence of Vincent Jandel, master general from 1850 to 1872, with Joseph Kelly, American provincial; AGOP IV.281, register no. 5, vol. 1, contains another set of correspondence of Jandel with the members of the American province for the years 1860–69. AGOP X.2240 contains documentation on the life and beatification process of the Dominican Sr. Mary Reparata Rose (née Marie Gautier, 1892–1927); AGOP XI.27000 and AGOP XI.28000 have material on the convents of Ponchatoula and Springfield; and AGOP XII.4.1700 provides information on the activity of the Dominican Sisters of the Sick Poor and of the convent of the Immaculate Conception at Ossining, New York, for the years 1890–1911. Series AGOP XII.4.1700 also has other sections devoted to Dominican female convents in America. AGOP XIII.03156 contains material on the Province of Saint Joseph, the first to be established in the United States, for the years 1891–1907.

Additional material is found in other series, though this material mainly covers the post–World War II period and is therefore not available for consultation.

BIBLIOGRAPHY

Fortini, Reginaldo, OP, Ramón Hernández, OP, and Anny Palliampikunnel, OP. *Catalogus Analyticus Archivi Generalis Ordinis Praedicatorum*. 6 vols. Rome: Sancta Sabina, 2002.

McGreal, Mary Nona. *The Order of Preachers in the United States: Dominicans at Home in a Young Nation, 1786–1865*. Strasbourg: Éditions du Signe, 2001.

O'Daniel, Victor F. *The Dominican Province of Saint Joseph: Historical-Biographical Studies*. New York: National Headquarters of the Holy Name Society, 1942.

———. *The First Two Dominican Priories in the United States: Saint Rose's Priory, near Springfield, KY; Saint Joseph's Priory, Somerset, OH*. New York: Holy Name Society, 1947.

———. *The Right Rev. Edward Dominic Fenwick, O.P.: Founder of the Dominicans in the United States, Pioneer Missionary in Kentucky, Apostle of Ohio, First Bishop of Cincinnati*. Washington, DC: Dominicana, 1920.

Parmisano, Fabian Stan. *Mission West: The Western Dominican Province, 1850–1966*. Oakland, CA: Western Dominican Province, 1995.

Petit, Loretta. *Friar in the Wilderness: Edward Dominic Fenwick, O.P.* Chicago: OPUS, 1994.

Pizzorusso, Giovanni. "Archives générales de l'Ordre des frères prêcheurs (Dominicains)." In *L'Amérique du Nord française dans les archives religieuses de Rome, 1600–1922*, ed. Pierre Hurtubise, Luca Codignola, and Fernand Harvey, 115–17. Quebec: Les Éditions de l'IQRC, 1999.

Sanfilippo, Matteo. "Archivio Generale dell'Ordine dei Predicatori." In *Ecclesiastical Sources for the History of Immigration and Ethnic Groups in North America: United States (1893–1922)*. Monographic issue of *Studi Emigrazione/Etudes Migrations* 32, no. 120 (December 1995): 725.

Vidmar, John. *Fr. Fenwick's "Little American Province": 200 Years of the Dominican Friars in the United States*. New York: Dominican Province of Saint Joseph, 2005.

Walz, Maximilian, CPPS. *Life of Sister Mary Reparata Rose of the Sacred Heart, OP: The Child of My Sacrament Love*. New York: José L. Morales, 1972.

Archivio Storico Generale dell'Ordine dei Frati Minori (Curia Generalizia) /
General Archives of the Order of Friars Minor (Curia Generalizia)
Address
   Via di Santa Maria Mediatrice 25, 00165 Rome
Contact Details
   Phone: 39-0668491425
   Fax: 39-066380292
   Email: archivum@ofm.org
   Website: www.ofm.org

STATUS

Open to researchers Monday, Wednesday, and Friday, 2:00 p.m.–6:30 p.m. The archives are closed on Italian federal holidays and June 30–September 20. A broad description of the holdings was posted at www.anagrafebbcc.chiesacattolica.it/anagraficaCEIBib/public/VisualizzaScheda.do?codice_cei=CEI300A00021. Researchers should make an appointment with the archivists in advance to be granted access to the material. Documents are written in English or Italian. Material post-1939 cannot be consulted.

HISTORY

The origin of the Franciscans goes back to 1209, the year when Saint Francis of Assisi (1181/1182–1226) founded the order (the Order of Friars Minor), which was officially recognized by Pope Innocent III (1160/1161–1216) in 1210. After the later creation of splinter groups such as the Capuchins, the Conventual Franciscans, and the Poor Clares, the members of this order were commonly known as Franciscans or Observants. Between the fifteenth century and the sixteenth, other branches were established within the Observants' family. These branches were known as the Recollects in France, the Reformed in the Italian Peninsula, and the Discalced in Spain. Pope Leo XIII (1810–1903) dissolved these branches in 1897.

DESCRIPTION OF HOLDINGS

The nucleus of the Franciscan archives, hosted in the Franciscan convent of Aracoeli, was destroyed during the first Napoleonic occupation of Rome (1798–99). At present the archives are divided into five sections: (1) *Segreteria Generale*, containing 3,780 volumes for the period from the sixteenth century to the first half of the twentieth; (2) *Procura Generale*, consisting of 350 volumes for the period from the mid-sixteenth century until the first half of the twentieth; (3) *Missioni*, with 310 volumes for the period from the first half of the sixteenth century until the middle of the twentieth; (4) *Fondi Ausiliari*, consisting of 5,675 volumes for the period from the first half of the seventeenth century to the first decade of the twenty-first; and (5) *Fondi Speciali*, with 1,000 volumes from the first half of the thirteenth century to the first decade of the twenty-first.

Material of American interest can be found in the sections *Segreteria Generale* and *Missioni*. In the section *Segreteria Generale* there is a volume titled *America Settentrionale*,

California, devoted to the Franciscan College of Santa Barbara in the years 1870–85. This volume contains relevant information about the college, particularly about the personnel who trained and worked there. The volume also provides crucial details about the problems that the Franciscans faced while seeking to establish the Province of Santa Barbara, officially founded in 1915. A significant example of these difficulties is provided by the 1878 letter that Giuseppe Romo, an Italian Franciscan active in California, addressed to Bernardino dal Vago da Portogruaro, minister general from 1869 to 1889. The former stated, "I am sure that California can easily support in due form not only this college, but a province, if we were allowed to beg freely; but some priests are so malicious that they wrote a report to Msgr. Amat [Thaddeus Amat y Brusi (1810–78), bishop of Los Angeles] saying that we, under the pretext of helping the orphans, do the begging for our own advantage."[15]

Other material of American interest is available in the section *Missioni*, which includes a volume devoted to the Province of the Immaculate Conception in the years 1848–69. The papers collected in this volume contain crucial references to the earlier activity of the Franciscans in the United States. For more information on relevant sources in this archive, see this volume's preface.

BIBLIOGRAPHY

Bacigalupo, Leonard, OFM. *A Francisca Saga: The History of the Province of the Immaculate Conception U.S.A.* New York: Provincialate, 1986.

Bluma, Dacian, OFM, and Theophilus Chowaniec, OFM. *A History of the Province of the Assumption of the Blessed Virgin Mary.* Pulaski, WI: Franciscan Publishers, 1967.

Carmody, Maurice John, OFM. *The Leonine Union of the Order of Friars Minor 1897.* Saint Bonaventure, NY: Franciscan Institute, 1994.

Conlan, Patrick, OFM. "John Benedict Daly, OFM." *Journal of the Old Athlone Society* 2, no. 5 (1978): 55.

Faulkner, Anselm, OFM. "Letters of Charles Bonaventure Maguire, O. F. M. (1768–1833)." *Clogher Record* 10 (1979–81): 284–303, and 11 (1982–83): 77–101, 187–213.

Geiger, Maynard, OFM. *The Roots of the Franciscan Province of Saint Barbara.* Santa Barbara, CA: Santa Barbara Mission, Archive-Library, 1990.

Habig, Marion A. *Heralds of the King; the Franciscans of the St. Louis-Chicago Province, 1858–1958.* Chicago: Franciscan Herald Press, 1958.

Historia Missionum Ordinis Fratrum Minorum. Vol. 3: *America Septentrionalis.* Rome: Secretariatus Missionum OFM, 1968.

McCloskey, Patrick, OFM. *God Gives His Grace: A Short History of St. John the Baptist Province.* Cincinnati: The Province, 2001.

Monti, Dominic. *Francis and His Brothers: A Popular History of the Franciscan Friars.* Cincinnati: Saint Anthony Messenger Press, 2009.

Pandzic, Basilio, OFM. "L'archivio generale dell'ordine dei frati minori." In *Il Libro e le biblioteche: Atti del primo congresso bibliologico francescano internazionale, 20–27 febbraio 1949,* 223–37. Rome: Pontificium Athenaeum Antonianum, 1950.

Robinson, Jack Clark. "The Franciscan Friars of New Mexico: Three Borderlands Trails to Vatican II, 1957–1985." PhD diss., University of California, Santa Barbara, 2009.

White, Joseph M. *Peace and Good in America: A History of Holy Name Province, Order of Friars Minor, 1850s to the Present.* New York: Holy Name Province and Academy of American Franciscan History, 2004.

Archivio Generale degli Oblati di Maria Immacolata /
General Archives of the Missionary Oblates of Mary Immaculate
Address
   Via Aurelia 290, 00165 Rome
Contact Details
   Phone: 39-06398771
   Fax: 39-0639375322
   Email: archives@omigen.org
   Website: www.omiworld.org

STATUS
The archives are open Monday–Friday, 9:00 a.m.–1:00 p.m. They are closed on Italian national holidays and during the summer. Researchers must contact the archivist in advance to have access granted to the material; a reference letter is required. Most documents are in English or French. Material post-1939 cannot be consulted.

HISTORY
The Missionary Oblates of Mary Immaculate was a male congregation officially founded in France in 1816 by Saint Charles-Joseph-Eugène de Mazenod (1782–1861). In 1826 the congregation was officially approved by Pope Leo XII (1760–1829). In the early days of the congregation, the Oblates devoted themselves to preaching and ministry in the poorest, most rural areas of Provence. From 1841 onward they expanded beyond Europe and established missions in North America. In that year they arrived in the Province of Québec and proceeded toward western Canada. Missions were established on the Pacific coast (1845), in Texas and northern Mexico (1847), and in Oregon (between 1849 and 1852). Starting in 1851, they were also active in the eastern part of the United States, where they established residences in Buffalo and Plattsburgh, New York.

   In the early 1860s, 105 Oblates were active in Canada and the United States. The American province, established in 1833, was divided in 1904 into an Eastern province and a Southern province. The Oblates founded three more provinces between 1921 and 1963: the Saint John the Baptist province, the Central province, and the Western province.

DESCRIPTION OF HOLDINGS
Researchers must take into account that, since the archives are currently being reorganized, the current location of documents is provisional. At present the archives are divided into nine sections: (1) *congress and meetings*; (2) *various items*; (3) *education*; (4) *founder*; (5) *general administration*; (6) *general chapters*; (7) *international scholasticate*; (8) *provinces, delegations, and missions*; and (9) *regions*.

Material of American interest is mainly to be found in section 8, which contains documents on the five provinces. This documentation is arranged in five different boxes, subdivided as follows: (1) USA central province B-250 A-D; (2) USA eastern province B-247; (3) USA northern province B-249 A-B; (4) USA southern province B-4, 248 A–G; and (5) USA western province B-251.

One example of the American material available in this section is a report written in 1867 by the Oblate Missionaries active at that time in the area between Texas and Mexico. Its opening words depict a gloomy situation: "The Church had descended the last step of the destruction's scale. The abomination sat in the sanctuary. Religion was only a scandalous pantomime. The pestiferous influence had exercised its ravages in all classes on a wide range. The two banks of the Rio Grande were drowned by a flood of iniquity. Dilapidated churches, scandals emanating from high places, ignorance and corruption of the people, abandoned sacraments, such was the picture presented by the border to the arrival of the Oblates."[16]

It must be noted that the material pertaining to the American provinces consists of some original documents but, most of the time, of copies that come from the archives in the United States. Additional material of American interest is to be found in the collection of yearly letters that the Oblate superiors addressed to their missionaries. Correspondence for the years from 1862 to 1878 was posted at www.omiworld.org/en/missions.

Further relevant material is available in the two-volume *Lettres aux correspondants d'Amérique*, which contains the correspondence de Mazenod exchanged with the North American missionaries from 1841 to 1860. This material was also posted at www.omiworld .org/en/ecrits-oblats.

Researchers should note that in the archives of Propaganda, series *Congressi, America Centrale*, it is possible to find the correspondence between the Oblate missionaries active in the United States and the Roman ministry. Moreover, the letters and reports compiled by the Oblate missionaries are printed in the issues of the *Annales de la Propagation de la Foi* (this journal is available online via the National Library of France, gallica.bnf.fr/ark:/12148 /cb34348166d/date, collection *Gallica*).

BIBLIOGRAPHY

Atlas O.M.I. Rome: Curia Generalizia, 1990.

Barton, Barbara. *Pistol Packin' Preachers: Circuit Riders of Texas.* Lanham, MD: Taylor Trade Publications, 2005.

Historical Dictionary of the Oblates of Mary Immaculate. Rome: Association of Oblate Studies and Research, 2008.

Martínez, Anne M. *Catholic Borderlands: Mapping Catholicism onto American Empire, 1905–1935.* Lincoln: University of Nebraska Press, 2014.

Mazenod, Charles-Joseph-Eugène de. *Lettres aux correspondants d'Amérique.* Vols. 1–2. Rome: Postulation générale O. M. I., 1977.

Oblates of Mary Immaculate, Central United States Province. *Oblates of Mary Immaculate: 50 Years in the Central United States, 1924–1974.* Belleville, IL: National Shrine Our Lady of the Snows, 1974.

Waggett, George M. *The Oblates of Mary Immaculate in the Pacific Northwest, 1847–1878.* Philadelphia: American Catholic Historical Society, 1953.

Wild, Joseph C., OMI. *Men of Hope: The Background and History of the Oblate Province of Our Lady of Hope (Eastern American Province).* Boston: Missionary Oblates of Mary Immaculate, 1967.

Woestman, William H. *The Missionary Oblates of Mary Immaculate: A Clerical Religious Congregation with Brothers.* Ottawa: Faculty of Canon Law, Saint Paul University, 1995.

Archivio Generale delle Missionarie del Sacro Cuore di Gesù /

General Archives of the Missionary Sisters of the Sacred Heart of Jesus

Address

   Via Cortina d'Ampezzo 269, 00135 Rome

Contact Details

   Phone: 39-0635505721/39-0635505949

   Email: segreteria@msccuria.191.it

   Website: www.msccabrini.org/index.php/it/la-congregazione

STATUS

Closed. The majority of the documents are in Italian.

HISTORY

The congregation of the Missionary Sisters of the Sacred Heart of Jesus was founded by Saint Francesca Saverio Cabrini (1850–1917), commonly known as Mother Cabrini, in 1880. In 1889 Mother Cabrini and her fellow sisters moved to the United States, where they assisted communities of Italian migrants. More precisely, the Missionary Sisters organized catechism and education classes for Italian immigrants and provided for the needs of the many orphans, establishing schools and orphanages. In 1909 Mother Cabrini became an American citizen. In 1938 she was beatified, and in 1946 she was canonized by Pope Pius XII (1876–1958), thus being the first American citizen to be canonized as a saint of the Catholic Church.

DESCRIPTION OF HOLDINGS

Material of American interest is found in seven boxes that are arranged in the following order: (1) Memorie: Burbank, Los Angeles; (2) Memorie: Cresco, Newark, Radnor, Scranton, San Donato Philadelphia; (3) Memorie: Chicago, Columbus, Des Plaines, School of the Assunta; (4) Memorie: Denver, Seattle orphanage; (5) Memorie: New Orleans house; (6) Memorie: St Philips orphanage; and (7) New York.

For more information on relevant sources in this archive, see my section near the beginning of this volume headed "Roman Sources for the History of American Catholicism: A Different Perspective."

BIBLIOGRAPHY
Bartoloni, Stefania, ed. *Per le strade del mondo: Laiche e religiose fra Otto e Novecento*. Bologna: Il Mulino, 2007.
De Maria, Saverio, MSC. *Vita e opere di Santa Francesca Saverio Cabrini*. Rome: Suore Missionarie del Sacro Cuore di Gesù, 2001.
Garroni, Maria Susanna, ed. *Sorelle d'oltreoceano: Religiose italiane ed emigrazione negli Stati Uniti: Una storia da scoprire*. Rome: Carocci, 2008.
Maynard, Theodore. *Too Small a World: The Life of Mother Cabrini*. Milwaukee: Bruce Publishing, 1945.
Sullivan, Mary Louise, MSC. *Mother Cabrini: Italian Immigrant of the Century*. New York: Center for Migration Studies, 1992.

Archivio Generale dei Redentoristi /
General Archives of the Redemptorists
Address
   Via Merulana 31, 00185 Rome
Contact Details
   Phone: 39-06494901
   Fax: 39-064466012
   Email: archivio.gen@cssr.com
   Website: www.cssr.com

STATUS
Open to researchers Monday–Friday, 9:00 a.m.–12:00 p.m. and 3:00–6:00 p.m. The archives close for Italian national holidays and from July until the end of August. Researchers should make an appointment with the archivist in advance to access the material. Most material is in English or German. Material post-1939 cannot be consulted.

HISTORY
The Congregazione del Santissimo Redentore (CSsR or Congregation of the Most Holy Redeemer ["the Redemptorists"]) was founded in 1732 by Saint Alfonso Maria de' Liguori (1696–1787), bishop of Sant'Agata dei Goti from 1762 to 1775. The congregation sought to provide material and spiritual assistance to the poor in rural areas. The congregation was officially recognized in 1749 by Pope Benedict XIV (1675–1758). From the late eighteenth century onward, the congregation expanded into continental Europe. In 1832 the first group of Redemptorists arrived in New York, and the American province was founded in 1850.

DESCRIPTION OF HOLDINGS

The nucleus of the Redemptorists' archives was established in Pagani, in the Naples region. Its first archivist was Fr. Giovanni Giuseppe Sabelli, who compiled the first inventory of material for the years 1747–1848. In 1856 the archives were transferred to Villa Caserta in Rome.

Initially the holdings of the archives were divided into two broad sections: *Generalia* and *Provincialia*. These sections were further subdivided into thirty-nine sections. Material of American interest is plentiful, particularly in the section *Provincialia*, which has documents on the American province. In this section is material related to the Baltimore province (the oldest one), the Denver province, and the Vice-Province of Richmond. Given the abundance of material, researchers are advised to consult the five detailed inventories on the Baltimore and Saint Louis provinces compiled by Dr. Patrick J. Hayes, archivist of the Redemptorist Province of Baltimore; these were posted at www.redemptorists.net/province -archives.cfm.

Amid the material relating to the United States are copies of the papers of Augustine Francis Hewit (1820–97), a former member of the congregation and one of the founders of the Paulist Fathers.[17] Of particular interest is a letter that Patrick Lynch (1817–82), bishop of Charleston from 1857 to 1882, wrote to Hewit in early April 1858. In it Lynch agreed to provide support to Hewit and his newly formed missionary society: "I have just had the pleasure of receiving your letter of the 6th . . . with the copy of your victorious decree. I trust you will be able now to devote yourself to the missions with fervor and unembarrassed in any way; [o]ne thing, too, I think of importance. Have your first home in a diocese, where the Redemptorist Fathers can have no issue with you whatever. Your first years of existence should be freed from all contact with them."[18]

BIBLIOGRAPHY

Arboleda, Hernan, CSSR. "Archivio Storico Generale CSSR." In *Spicilegium Historicum Congregationis Ssmi Redemptoris* 30, no. 1 (1987): 205–8.

Byrne, John F. *The Redemptorist Centenaries, 1732–1932.* Philadelphia: Dolphin, 1932.

Curley, Michael J., CSSR. *Cheerful Ascetic: The Life of Francis Xavier Seelos, C. Ss. R.* New Orleans: Redemptorists, Seelos Center, 2002.

———. *The Provincial Story: A History of the Baltimore Province of the Congregation of the Most Holy Redeemer.* New York: Redemptorist Fathers, Baltimore Province, 1963.

———. *Venerable John Neumann, C. SS. R., Fourth Bishop of Philadelphia.* Washington, DC: Catholic University of America Press, 1952.

Donlan, Francis. *Southeastern Redemptorist Heritage, 1926–1986.* New Smyrna Beach, FL: The Redemptorists, 1986.

Hanley, Boniface. *Paulist Father, Isaac Hecker: An American Saint.* Mahwah, NJ: Paulist Press, 2008.

Hayes, Patrick J., ed. *The Civil War Diary of Father James Sheeran: Confederate Chaplain and Redemptorist.* Washington, DC: Catholic University of America Press, 2016.

Hoegerl, Carl W. *Sincerely, Seelos: The Collected Letters of Blessed Francis Xavier Seelos.* New Orleans: The Redemptorists, Seelos Center, 2008.

Laverdure, Paul. "Early American Redemptorists in British North America, 1834–1863." In *Catholic Historical Review* 80, no. 3 (1994): 476–96.

Licking, William. *Reminiscences of the Redemptorist Fathers: Rev. John Beil, Rev. Patrick Mc-Givern, Rev. John O'Brien, Rev. Leopold Petsch.* Ilchester, MD: Redemptorist College, 1891.

Skinner, Thomas L., CSSR. *The Redemptorists in the West.* Saint Louis: Redemptorist Fathers, 1933.

Wuest, Joseph. *Annales Congregationis SS. Redemptoris, Provinciae Americanae.* 5 vols, 1888–1924. Ilchester, MD: Congregationis Sanctissimi Redemptoris, 1914.

Archivio Generale della Società del Sacro Cuore /
General Archives of the Society of the Sacred Heart
Address
    Via San Francesco di Sales 18, 00165 Rome
Contact Details
    Phone: 39-0668808506
    Email 1: arcgenrscj@gmail.com
    Email 2: arcgen@rscjroma.org
    Website: rscjinternational.org/general-archives

STATUS

Open to researchers Monday–Friday, 9:00 a.m.–12.45 p.m. and 2:00 p.m.–4:45 p.m. The archives close for Italian national holidays and from July 27 to September 11. Researchers are advised to make an appointment with the archivists in advance to gain access to the material. The majority of the documents are written in French and English. Material post-1939 cannot be consulted.

HISTORY

The Society of the Sacred Heart of Jesus was officially co-founded in 1800 by Madeleine Sophie Barat (1779–1865) and Joseph-Désiré Varin (1769–1850) in Paris. Initially the Society was known as *Dames de la Foi* (Women of Faith) or *de l'Instruction chrétienne* (Christian instructors). In 1818 the first American mission was established in Saint Charles, Missouri, through the efforts of Saint Rose Philippine Duchesne (1769–1852). In 1819 the Society founded its first novitiate at Florissant, Missouri.

DESCRIPTION OF HOLDINGS

The archives are divided into nine main series and several subseries. The nine series are (A) *Society as canonical institute*, with four subseries; (B) *relations of the Society with the church*, with six subseries; (C) *internal history of the Society*, with twelve subseries; (D) *external history of the Society*, with three subseries; (E) *legal and financial affairs*, with six subseries; (F) *Audio-Visual material*, with four subseries; (G) *Society Memorabilia*, with three subseries; (H) *Special Collections*, with two subseries; and (I) *Library*, with twenty subseries.

Material of American interest can be found in the series *C-I-Central Government*, subseries CIII_1_USA, which contains five boxes (DOC-000.705, DOC-000.710, DOC-000.711, DOC-000.712, and DOC-000.713) on the early history of the Society of the Sacred Heart in Louisiana.

Of particular interest among the documents related to the early activity of the Society are the observations made by Elizabeth Galitzine, assistant general and provincial, during her visit to the houses in North America between 1840 and 1843. She encouraged all the members "carefully to avoid having any air of repulsion and of boredom towards the country, its customs, and its laws that you dislike. It will become impossible to have a warm reception by the Americans if we hurt their national pride. Do not make any detrimental comparisons of America to other countries. Be particularly attached to the citizens of the towns where our houses are located."[19]

BIBLIOGRAPHY

Callan, Louise, RSCJ. *Philippine Duchesne: Frontier Missionary of the Sacred Heart, 1769–1852*. Westminster, MD: Newman, 1957.

———. *The Society of the Sacred Heart in 19th Century France, 1800–1865*. Cork, Ireland: Cork University Press, 2012.

———. *The Society of the Sacred Heart in North America*. London: Longmans, Green, 1937.

Kilroy, Phil. *Madeleine Sophie Barat, 1779–1865: A Life*. Cork, Ireland: Cork University Press, 2000.

Mooney, Catherine M., RSCJ. *Philippine Duchesne: A Woman with the Poor*. New York: Paulist Press, 1990.

Paisant, Chantal, ed. *Philippine Duchesne et ses compagnes: Les années pionnières, 1818–1823; Lettres et journaux des premières missionnaries du Sacré-Coeur aux États-Unis*. Paris: Les Éditions du Cerf, 2001.

Archivio Generale dei Servi di Maria /

General Archives of the Servants of Mary

Address

Viale XXX Aprile 6, 00153 Rome

Contact Details

Phone: 39-0658391637

Email: archiviosm@mar.urbe.it

STATUS

Open to researchers Tuesday, Wednesday, and Thursday of the first and third weeks of each month, 9:00 a.m.–6:00 p.m. The archives close for Italian national holidays and from July until early September. Researchers are advised to make an appointment with the archivist in advance to gain access to the material. The documents are in English, Italian, or Latin. Material post-1939 cannot be consulted.

The archives are located in the same building as the library of the Pontificia Facoltà Teologica Marianum, which contains the most complete collection of works on the Servants of Mary. The library is open Monday–Friday, 8:00 a.m.–6:30 p.m., and Saturday, 8:30 a.m.–12:30 p.m.; it is closed from mid-July until mid-September. A catalog is available at oseegenius1.urbe.it/mar.

HISTORY

The order of the Servants of Mary ("the Servites") was founded between 1230 and 1240 when a group of seven Florentine merchants gathered together and left Florence to retire to Monte Senario for a life of communion and poverty. The order was officially approved by Pope Benedict XI (1240–1304) in 1304. In the thirteenth century the order expanded across continental Europe. Antonino M. Grundner, a Servite of the Tyrolese province, began in 1852 to work amid the communities of German immigrants in New York. He subsequently moved to eastern Pennsylvania and then to Philadelphia, where he became parish priest of Saint Alphonsus Church. Despite his intense activity, Grundner did not establish any permanent foundation.

In 1870 Joseph Melcher (1806–73), first bishop of Green Bay, Wisconsin, invited the Servites to work in his diocese. That year four Servites under the guidance of Fr. Agostino Morini (1826–1909) took charge of Saint Charles Church in Menasha, Wisconsin. In 1874 Thomas Patrick Roger Foley (1822–79), bishop coadjutor of Chicago, invited the order to serve among Chicago's growing number of Italian immigrants. The city in this way became the center of Servite activity in the United States. The American province was established in 1909.

DESCRIPTION OF HOLDINGS

The earliest form of the archives was established in the thirteenth century, but only after the second half of the sixteenth century did the general archives of the order begin regularly to be organized and kept in Rome. Although the archives contain a considerable amount of material pertaining to the order's activity in the United States, there is no detailed inventory of this activity. Amid the material of American interest, three series are of particular relevance: (1) the *Epistula Priorum Generalium*, containing letters sent to the Servites' general; (2) *USA Addolorata*, with material on the eastern province; and (3) *USA San Giuseppe*, with material on the western province.

The series *Epistula Priorum Generalium* contains Morini's correspondence from his time in Chicago; one particular letter he sent to Rome in mid-January 1887 clearly reveals his general disappointment with the Italian immigrants. For more information on Morini's correspondence and relevant sources in this archive, see my section near the beginning of this volume headed "Roman Sources for the History of American Catholicism: A Different Perspective."

Given that the material is scattered and still to be cataloged, researchers should combine the order's Roman material with the material the order has preserved in the United States. Contact details of the American province are available at www.servite.org/contact.aspx.

BIBLIOGRAPHY

Benassi, Vincenzo, Odir Jacques Dias, and Faustino M. Faustini. *I Servi di Maria: Breve storia dell'ordine.* Rome: Le Missioni dei Servi di Maria, 1984.

Borntrager, Conrad, OSM. "The Arrival of the Servites in Denver, March 18, 1904, and Saint Frances Xavier Cabrini." In *Studi Storici dell'Ordine dei Servi di Maria* 61–62, no. 2 (2011–12): 675–716.

———. "The First Servite Foundation in Eastern United States (Oakland, New Jersey, 1918)." In *Studi Storici dell'Ordine dei Servi di Maria* 35, nos. 1–2 (1985): 177–90.

———. "The First Servite Foundation in the Pacific Northwest of the United States: Diocese of Baker City, Oregon." In *Studi Storici dell'Ordine dei Servi di Maria* 39, nos. 1–2 (1989): 199–212.

D'Agostino, Peter R. "Italian Ethnicity and Religious Priests in the American Church: The Servites, 1870–1940." In *Catholic Historical Review* 80, no. 4 (October 1994): 714–40.

———. "When Friars Become Missionaries: An Interpretive Review of Scholarship on Italian Servites in Chicago." In *Studi Storici dell'Ordine dei Servi di Maria* 43, nos. 1–2 (1993): 93–109.

Dias, Odir Jacques, and Andrea Dal Pino, OSM. *Storia e inventari dell'archivio generale o.sm.,* 2nd ed. Rome: Archivum Generale Ordinis Servorum, 1972.

Morini, Austin, OSM. *The Foundation of the Order of Servants of Mary in the United States of America (1870–1889),* ed. Conrad Borntrager, OSM. Rome: Edizioni Marianum, 1993.

Archivio Generale della Società dell'Apostolato Cattolico (Pallottini) /
General Archives of the Society of the Catholic Apostolate (Pallottines)

Address

Piazza di San Vincenzo Pallotti 204, 00186 Rome

Contact Details

Phone: 39-066819469

Fax: 39-066876827

Email: isvp@sac.info

Website: www.sac.info

STATUS

Closed for reorganization at the time of this writing. Researchers may use the library, which is open on Monday, Tuesday, and Thursday, 10 a.m.–5 p.m. Researchers must contact the director, Fr. Jan Kupka, in advance to make an appointment to access the library.

HISTORY

The Società dell'Apostolato Cattolico (SAC, Society of the Catholic Apostolate, better known as the Pallottines), was founded in 1835 by the Roman priest Vincenzo Pallotti (1795–1850). In 1844 the Society established a community of priests in London devoted to assisting Italian migrants. In 1884 the Pallottines arrived in New York, where they established the Church of Our Lady of Mount Carmel. This soon became a key institution for the assistance of the Italian community.

DESCRIPTION OF HOLDINGS

Because the archives are closed, this description is based on a short inventory written by Maria Susanna Garroni for the journal *Studi Emigrazione* in 1996. Material of American interest may be found the section called *Catalogus Piae Societatis Missionum*, which contains catalogs of the Society's missions and provinces. The 1923 catalog provides a description and history of the American-Italian province. Six parish churches were attached to it: in New York, Our Lady of Mount Carmel and Saint Anne; in New Jersey, Saint Joseph in Hammonton, Saint Philip Neri in Newark, and one in Union Hill; and, in Massachusetts, one in Fall River.

The archives contain some material on Italian immigration to America in the section named *Societas ante 1909, Armadio* 18. In it there are two subsections, cassetto 1 and cassetto 2. Cassetto 1 has five different boxes that contain documents on the Church in London and on the Church of the Sacred Hearts of Jesus and Mary in New York. Cassetto 2 contains two boxes labeled New York and Newark. The New York box consists of four dossiers. Dossier no. 1 contains five letters that Michael Augustine Corrigan (1839–1902), archbishop of New York from 1885 to 1902, wrote to Carlo Mario Orlandi, vicar general of the Society of the Catholic Apostolate, during the years 1891–1908; dossier no. 2 has material on the Sacred Congregation for the Regulars for the years 1884–1906; dossier no. 3 holds letters related to the coronation of the image of the Virgin of Mount Carmel and a brief account of the Pallottine mission in New York since 1884; and dossier no. 4 contains financial accounts of the Church of Our Lady of Mount Carmel.

Additional material on the Pallottines' activity in America and on the Church in London can be found in the archives of Propaganda Fide and in the Archivio Storico del Vicariato di Roma, the Archives of the Vicariate of Rome.[20]

BIBLIOGRAPHY

Avella, Steven M. *Like an Evangelical Trumpet: A History of the Mother of God Province of the Society of the Catholic Apostolate*. Milwaukee: Pallottine Fathers and Brothers, Mother of God Province, 1998.

Garroni, Maria Susanna. "Archivio Generale della Società per l'Apostolato Cattolico (Pallottini)." *Fonti ecclesiastiche romane per lo studio dell'emigrazione italiana in Nord America (1642–1922)*. Special issue of *Studi Emigrazione* 33, no. 124 (December 1996): 703–4.

———, ed. *Sorelle d'oltreoceano: Religiose italiane ed emigrazione negli Stati Uniti; Una storia da scoprire*. Rome: Carocci, 2008.

McCarthy, Donald F., SAC. *A Patchwork Quilt: Pallottines in the USA*. 2 vols. Dublin: Eprint.ie, 2013.

Molle, Pietro. *La chiesa italiana di Londra: La storia dei primi Pallottini in Inghilterra*. Todi, Italy: Tau Editrice, 2014.

Orsi, Robert A. *The Madonna of 115th Street: Faith and Community in Italian Harlem, 1880–1940*. New Haven, CT: Yale University Press, 1985.

Our Lady of Mount Carmel Shrine-95th Celebration: Solemn Pontifical Coronation-Diamond Jubilee, 1904–1979. New York: Pallottine Fathers, 1979.

NOTES

1. The catalog of the Saint Joseph Province covers the years 1937, 1947, and 1983–84. The catalog of the Most Holy Name of Jesus Province covers the years 1937, 1946, and 1950–52. See *Provincia*, (PR CII1) 2, (PR CII1) 4, Archives of the Dominican Roman Province of Saint Catherine of Siena (Santa Maria sopra Minerva).

2. Antonino Salvati to minister general, March 21, 1921, (PR CII13) 3, Archives of the Dominican Roman Province of Saint Catherine of Siena, *Provincia*: "Forse i nostri padri sarebbero disposti a cederci S. Caterina di New York. Altro che cederla, l'hanno già perduta! Perché l'arcivescovo di New York ha sottratto alla giurisdizione dei nostri padri tutti gli italiani e gli ha affidati ad un prete secolare! I vescovi, specialmente d'America, non amano di dare le loro parrocchie ai religiosi."

3. Peter J. O'Callaghan to Cesare Nanni, New York, January 22, 1929, 38–39, *Armadio* QII 10-*Elenco Congregazioni Italiane ed estere*, Archives of the Congregation of the Oratory in Rome.

4. Giovanni Morello and Francesco Dante, "L'Archivio della Congregazione dell'Oratorio di Roma alla Chiesa Nuova," in *Ricerche per la Storia Religiosa di Roma* 2 (1978): 275–362.

5. Father Pacifico, Order of Saint Augustine (OSA), to the Augustinians' general, July 26, 1878, fols. 94rv–95rv, Ff59 *Acta Capitolorum Prov Assistentiae Germaniae et Americae, 1831–1901*, General Archives of the Augustinians: "Conosco troppo bene l'animo di religiosi circa l'imposizione di nuovi Italiani; il sentimento generale è che non si vogliano."

6. Benoît-Joseph Flaget, bishop of Bardstown, to the superior of the Christian Brothers, February 18, 1837, D.1, NS 500 Historique, General Archives of the Brothers of the Christian Schools: "Il faisait à propos que deux ou trois d'entre eux fussent assez jeunes pour bien faiser la prononciation Anglaise qui est assez difficile pour tous les étrangers."

7. Anonymous request to Venanzio de Lisle-en-Rigault, Capuchin minister general, 1917, ii–iv, G 97 II, *Pennysilvanica*, General Archives of the Capuchins (Archivio Generale dei Cappuccini or AGC).

8. John Malone, state senator in Kansas, to Venanzio de Lisle-en-Rigault, August 16, 1917, unfoliated and unpaginated, G 97 II, *Pennysilvanica*, AGC.

9. Felice De Andreis, CM, to Peter Dahmen, November 29, 1816, pp. 21–24, section D, Part I, vol. 1, De Andreis Collection, General Archives of the Congregation of the Mission: "I semi di incredulità, ed irreligione qui non sono penetrati. Ciascuno ama la sua credenza, o buona, o falsa ch'ella sia. E' vero che i cattolici sono assai pochi, ed ovunque torreggiano anche magnifici templi di Quaccheri, di Presbiteriani, di Episcopaliani, di Metodisti, e di Protestanti di mille diverse sette, che van pullulando di nuovo di giorno in giorno, ma ciò proviene per mancanza di missionari. I Protestanti stessi rispettano, e fanno le più belle accoglienze di preti Cattolici più che ai loro ministri. Lo abbiamo noi stessi sperimentato in più e più luoghi ci è stata fatta una specie di violanza per fermarci a raccogliere una messe già biondeggiante. Una famiglia intiera di eretici al solo intendere due parole di esortazione si buttò a terra in ginocchio colle lagrime agli occhi per pregarci a restar almeno qualcuno fra di loro per istruirli. Più altri sono indotti ad abiurare. Fa compassione estrema trovare un estensione immensa di paese, ove sono città, e villaggi con moltissime famiglie cattoliche, che non vedono mai un prete, e qualche paese cattolico per non restar senza pastore, non potendo aver un prete chiamarono un ministro, e si

fecero protestanti. Oh Dio! Che desolazione! Tanti preti che vivono oziosamente in Italia, e in Roma stessa qui con solo dir la Messa, far il catachismo col libro in mano, e battezzare farebbero un bene immenso, giacché infelicemente fra le altre cose s'è introdotta fra gli eretici una gran negligenza sull'articolo di battezzare, che se ne trova moltissimi non battezzati ed una infinità di bambini muoiono senza battesimo. Qualunque miserabile prete con un po' di zelo, e di buona volontà in qualunque luogo si fisse è sicuro in poco tempo di fermarsi una Parrocchia di buoni cattolici."

10. Rosa Bertolini to Marcellina Bosatta, April 3, 1919, vol. 8, 1919, *Raccolta di lettere delle prime suore d'America, anni 1913–1935*, General Archives of the Daughters of Saint Mary of Providence (Archivio Curia Generale Figlie di Santa Maria della Provvidenza): "In America è quasi un miracolo ad avere qualcuna. Tutte le suore quasi se le rubano le ragazze, tanto sono scarse."

11. Luca Codignola, *The Coldest Harbour of the Land: Simon Stock and Lord Baltimore's Colony in Newfoundland, 1621–1649* (Montreal: McGill-Queen's University Press, 1988).

12. All the documents contained in the series *Acta Definitori generali* were edited and published by Antonio Fortes. See Antonio Fortes, OCD, ed., *Acta Definitori gen. OCD Congregationis s. Eliae (1863–1875) et totius Ordinis (1875–1920)* (Rome: Teresianum, 1984).

13. Anonymous and undated report submitted to the superior general of the Discalced Carmelites, fols. 1rv.2rv, ser. no. 14-OCD, in *Missiones*, General Archives of the Discalced Carmelites (Archivio Generale OCD [Ordine dei Carmelitani Scalzi] or AOCD).

14. Sister Mary Magdalene of Jesus Crucified to Father Silverio da Santa Teresa, Baltimore, October 9, 1946, unfoliated and unpaginated, ser. no. 14-OCD, in *Missiones*, AOCD.

15. Giuseppe Romo, OFM, to Franciscan minister general, April 26, 1878, fols. 176rv–177r, *America Settentrionale, California, 1870–1885*, I, SK 41, General Archives of the Franciscan Order (Archivio Storico Generale dell'Ordine dei Frati Minori, AGOFM-Storico): "Io son sincero che la California può sostenere benissimo, non solo questo collegio, ma una provincia in forma, se ci si permette la libera questua; ma è tanta la malignità di alcuni preti, ch'hanno fatto rapporto a Monsignor Amat, dicendo, che noi altri, sotto pretesto degli orfani, facciamo la questua per noi medesimi."

16. Report of the missions of Texas and Mexico, May 31, 1867, pp. 2–3, section 8, *provinces, delegations, missions*, southern province USA-Reports (1867–1877), Archivio Generale degli Oblati di Maria Immacolata: "L'Eglise était descendue au dernier échelon de l'échelle de dégradation. L'abomination siégeait dans le sanctuaire. La religion n'était plus qu'une pantomine scandaleuse. L'influence pestifère avait exercé ses ravages dans toutes les classes, sur un rayon d'immense étendue. Les deux rives du Rio Grande étaient noyées par un déluge d'iniquités. Eglises délabrées, scandales émanant des hauts lieux, ignorance et corruption du peuple, sacraments abandonnées, tel est le tableau que présentait la frontière à l'apparition des Oblates."

17. The originals are in the Archives of the Paulist Fathers in New York.

18. Patrick Lynch to Augustine Francis Hewit, April 10, 1858, pp.1–4, doc. IX 028, *Provincia Americana, Personalia*, Hewit Papers, 1849–1858, General Archives of the Redemptorists (Archivio Generale dei Redentoristi).

19. Visit of Mother Elizabeth Galitzine, 1840–1843, C-III *Provinces*, General Archives of the Society of the Sacred Heart: "eviter avec soin de laisser paraitre meme par un air de dégout et d'ennui que le pays, ses coutumes, ses lois, ses moeurs ne plaisent pas; on ne trouverait plus d'accès favorable auprès des Americains si on blessait leur orgueil national. N'établir avec d'autres pays aucune comparaison défavourable à l'Amérique. Se montrer particulierèment affectionnée aux habitants des villes où sont nos maisons."

20. *Lettere*, vols. 334–58 et passim, APF; 1.341, XII, Opera della propagazione della fede, Archivio Storico del Vicariato di Roma (Archives of the Vicariate of Rome).

CHAPTER 3

Archives of Religious Colleges

This chapter contains profiles of the archives of religious colleges. The material contained in these repositories provides a wealth of detail on students as well as staff. At the same time, it sheds light on the networks these institutions established with their respective countries. Unfortunately, it has not been possible to access the archives of the Pontifical North American College because the material there is being reorganized.

Archivio del Collegio San Clemente /
Archives of the Irish Dominican College, San Clemente
Address
    Via Labicana 95, 00184 Rome
Contact Details
    Phone: 39-067740021
    Fax: 39-0677400201
    Email: segreteria@basilicasanclemente.com
    Website: basilicasanclemente.com/eng

STATUS
Open to researchers, who are advised to make an appointment with the rector in advance to access the material. There is no online catalog, and documents are in English, Italian, or Latin. Material post-1939 cannot be consulted.

HISTORY
The origins of the Irish Dominican College of San Clemente can be traced back to 1667, when Giovanni Battisti de Marinis (d. 1669), minister general of the Dominican order, responded to the destructive Cromwellian conquest of Ireland by giving John O'Connor, procurator of the Irish province, permission to found new convents in continental Europe. In 1677 the church

and the convent of San Clemente, together with those of San Sisto Vecchio, were officially handed from the Italian to the Irish Dominican province. This step led to the establishment of the first Irish Dominican College in Rome.

Suppressed in 1798 during the French conquest of Rome, the convent was restored in 1799. From that year onward, a small community of Irish Dominicans lived at the college of San Clemente. Due to the second Napoleonic invasion of Rome, the convent was again suppressed in July 1810. After Napoleon's final defeat, the college was returned to the Irish Dominicans in the summer of 1814. In the second half of the nineteenth century, a portion of the church and convent of San Sisto Vecchio was given to the missionary congregation of the Dominicans nuns founded by Maria Antonia Lalia (1839–1914).

DESCRIPTION OF HOLDINGS

The archives of the Irish Dominican College of San Clemente can be divided into five parts: (1) conventual records, (2) documents of more general Irish ecclesiastical interest, (3) personal records and letters, (4) transcripts of documents from other archives, and (5) some printed pamphlets. Material of American interest can be found in the conventual and the personal records. The former are important because they provide information on the Roman experience of John Thomas Troy (1739–1823), bishop of Dublin from 1786 to 1823; Richard Luke Concanen (1747–1810), first bishop of New York from 1808 to 1810; and John Connolly (1750–1825), second bishop of that city from 1814 to 1825. The *Liber de Ratione Studiorum Generalis*, a bound manuscript volume of 163 pages, is the most relevant source of information about the aforementioned clerics because, in the case of Troy and Connolly, it sheds light on their education, particularly how they progressed in their studies.

The personal records are more strictly related to the beginnings of the Irish Dominicans' activity in America. Of particular interest in this series is the leather-bound manuscript that contains the letter-book and the journal of Fr. Francis O'Finan (1772–1847), former student and prior of San Clemente from 1816 to 1819, who in 1835 was appointed bishop of Killala. Indeed, from 1823 until 1838 O'Finan acted as "Roman" intermediary for various bishops, among whom were Edmund Burke (1753–1820), bishop of Sion and vicar apostolic of Halifax, and Connolly (see above).

The section of the personal records also includes a collection of letters addressed to O'Finan from his confrere Edward Fenwick, first bishop of Cincinnati (1768–1832), as well as a bundle of eight documents, letters, and newspapers pertaining to the missionary activity of the Irish Dominican Charles Dominic Ffrench (1775–1851) in New Brunswick during the years from 1818 to 1829.

Additional material of American interest related to San Clemente's college can be found in the archives of Propaganda in the series *Scritture riferite nei Congressi, Collegi Vari*, vol. 58.

BIBLIOGRAPHY

Boyle, Leonard E., OP. *San Clemente Miscellany I: The Community of SS. Sisto e Clemente in Rome, 1677–1977; With a Chapter by Hugh Fenning, O.P.* Rome: Apud S. Clementem, 1977.

Codignola, Luca. "The Policy of Rome towards the English-Speaking Catholics in British North America, 1750–1830." In *Creed and Culture: The Place of English-Speaking Catholics in Canadian Society, 1750–1930*, ed. Terrence Murphy and Gerald Stortz, 100–25. Montreal: McGill-Queen's University Press, 1993.

Fenning, Hugh. "The Books of Receptions and Professions of SS Sixtus and Clement in Rome, 1676–1792." *Collectanea Hibernica* 14 (1971): 13–35.

Kearns, Conleth. "Archives of the Irish Dominican College, San Clemente, Rome: A Summary Report." *Archivium Hibernicum* 18 (1955): 145–49.

O'Daniel, V. F. "The Right Rev. Richard Luke Concanen, O.P., the First Bishop of New York (1747–1810)." *Catholic Historical Review* 1, no. 4 (January 1916): 400–421.

Power, Thomas P., ed. *The Irish in Atlantic Canada, 1780–1900.* Fredericton: New Ireland Press, 1991.

Tancrell, Luke, OP, ed. *Edward Dominic Fenwick Papers, 1803–1832: Founding American Dominican Friar and Bishop.* New York: Dominican Publications, 2005.

Archivio del Collegio di Sant'Isidoro, Roma /

Archives of the Irish Franciscan College of Saint Isidore, Rome

Address

Via degli Artisti 41, 00187 Rome

Contact Details

Phone: 39-064885359

Fax: 39-064884459

Email: biblioteca.wadding@gmail.com

Website: www.stisidoresrome.com

STATUS

Open. An appointment is required because hours change often; updated schedules should be available on the college webpage. At present there are two catalogs of the library's collection: (1) www.stisidoresrome.com/files/Inventario_Biblioteca_Wadding.pdf and (2) www.ibisweb.it/Wadding.

An inventory of the archival holdings, albeit incomplete, has been posted in PDF format at www.stisidoresrome.com/files/W_Section.pdf. Documents are in English, Italian, or Latin. Material post-1939 can be consulted with the archivist's permission.

HISTORY

Saint Isidore's College was officially founded in 1625 by the Irish Franciscan Luke Wadding (1588–1657). This was the first Irish college established in the city, and it prepared friars for missionary work in Ireland. In 1798, during the first French occupation of Rome, the college was closed. Between 1802 and 1806, Saint Isidore's resumed its activities, which enabled numerous friars to be educated and ordained in Rome. The college was again closed from 1809 to 1814, during the second French occupation of Rome, but thereafter remained open.

DESCRIPTION OF HOLDINGS

The nucleus of the archives of Saint Isidore's College was established soon after the foundation of the college. In 1793 a group of manuscripts extremely important for Irish history was transferred to Rome from Saint Anthony's College of Louvain. During the second French occupation of Rome, the college was sold and a considerable part of the archives was transferred to Paris. Although the material was returned to Rome in 1817, several registers and valuable codices were lost or sent to the wrong owner during the years 1810–14. In 1872 various manuscripts and rare books were transferred to the British Embassy in Rome, and from there dispatched to Ireland. In 2008 the Irish Franciscan province decided to keep the Gaelic manuscripts, which came mainly from Louvain, and half of the archival collections of Saint Isidore's and to donate them to the Archives of the Mícheál Ó Cléirigh Institute of the University College Dublin.

The archives of Saint Isidore's College consist of three main types of documents: (1) Mass registers covering the years 1666–1990; (2) account books for the years 1683–1861; and (3) registers of the *discretorium*, which recorded the meetings of the guardian with the friars appointed to help him, for the years 1741–1977. In addition to this material, there is a large collection of documents and papers, called *Section W*, which covers a period spanning the early sixteenth century up to World War II.

Material of American interest can be found in the second register of the *discretorium*, for the years 1741–1878. This register provides details on the activity of Saint Isidore's staff, particularly Michael Francis Egan (1761–1814) and Michael MacCormick (d. 1820). The former was guardian from 1787 to 1790 and in 1808 was appointed bishop of Philadelphia; the latter was guardian from 1782 to 1783 and corresponded with Archbishop John Carroll (1735–1815) of Baltimore. This register also provides information on the college's professors and students who left Rome for work in North America. This was the case of Charles Bonaventure Maguire (1768–1833), who, during the late 1790s and the early 1810s, taught at Saint Isidore's; in 1817 he went to the United States, where he helped establish Saint Patrick's Cathedral in Pittsburgh. In addition, the register details the activity of James Louis O'Donel (1738–1811) and Patrick Lambert (1755–1816). O'Donel was, from 1784 to 1795, the first prefect apostolic of Newfoundland, and from 1796 to 1806 the first bishop of that diocese. Lambert was the second bishop of Newfoundland from 1807 to 1817. O'Donel studied at Saint Isidore's during the 1750s, while Lambert served as guardian in 1783–84.

Section W, no. 32, includes a bundle of documents from the German commander in Rome during World War II. Most of these documents are propaganda pamphlets written and published by the Nazi army in response to the bombing campaign that Anglo American forces led against Rome during the years 1943–44.

BIBLIOGRAPHY

Byrne, Cyril J., ed. *Gentlemen-Bishops and Faction Fighters: The Letters of Bishops O'Donel, Lambert, Scallan and Other Irish Missionaries.* Saint John's, Newfoundland: Jesperson, 1984.

Codignola, Luca. "Roman Catholic Conservatism in a New Atlantic World, 1760–1829." *William and Mary Quarterly*, 3rd ser., 64, 4 (October 2007): 717–56.

Conlan, Patrick, OFM. "Missions and Missionaries." In *The Irish Franciscans, 1534–1990*, ed. Edel Bhreathnach, Joseph MacMahon, OFM, and John McCafferty, 271–86. Dublin: Four Courts, 2009.

———. *St. Isidore's College, Rome.* Rome: Istituto Pio XI, 1982.

Faulkner Anselm, OFM. "Letters of Charles Bonaventure Maguire, O. F. M. (1768–1833)." *Clogher Record* 10 (1979–81): 284–303, and 11 (1982–83): 77–101, 187–213.

Millett, Benignus, OFM. "The Archives of St. Isidore's College, Rome." *Archivium Hibernicum* 40 (1985): 1–13.

Murphy, Terrence, and Cyril J. Byrne, eds. *Religion and Identity: The Experience of Irish and Scottish Catholics in Atlantic Canada; Selected Papers from a Conference on Roman Catholicism in Anglophone Canada: The Atlantic Region, Held at Saint Mary's University, 19–22 September 1984.* St John's, Newfoundland: Jesperson, 1987.

White, Joseph M. *Peace and Good in America: A History of Holy Name Province Order of Friars Minor, 1850s to the Present.* New York: Holy Name Province and Academy of American Franciscan History, 2004.

Archivio di Santa Maria dell'Anima /

Archives of the Pontifical Institute of Santa Maria dell'Anima

Address

Via della Pace 20, 00186 Rome

Contact Details

Phone: 39-0668281802/39-0668801394

Fax: 39-0668281886

Email: archiv@santa-maria-anima.it

Website: www.pisma.it/wordpress/?page_id=918

STATUS

Open to researchers on Wednesday and Friday, 3:00 p.m.–6:00 p.m., but closed on Italian national holidays and throughout the summer period. Researchers are advised to make an appointment with the archivist in advance to access the material. Most documents are written in German. Material post-1939 can be consulted with the archivist's permission.

HISTORY

The church of Santa Maria dell'Anima was probably founded in 1350 and served as a hospice for the German community in Rome. In 1406 Pope Innocent VII (1339–1406) endowed the hospice with a letter of protection, thus placing it under direct papal control. In 1444 Pope Eugenius IV (1383–1447) granted to Santa Maria dell'Anima the right to care for the spiritual welfare of the German pilgrims and of the poor through the regular cele-bration of the Mass and the administration of other sacraments. In 1859 a college for the training of secular clergy was founded adjacent to the church.

DESCRIPTION OF HOLDINGS
Material of American interest can be found in the section named "Hudal-Papers." This im-portant section consists of ninety-three boxes covering the years from 1922 to 1952. (A full inventory is available in the archives.) It contains the correspondence of Alois Hudal (1885–1963), rector of Santa Maria dell'Anima from 1923 to 1952 and bishop of Aela from 1932 onward, who played a key role in the relationship between the Holy See and promi-nent figures of Nazi Germany from the early 1920s until the late 1950s. In particular, Hudal was influential in the development of a migratory network meant to assist former Nazis, and also many Croatian families, who fled Europe and established themselves in North and South America after World War II.

Of these papers the letter that Hudal sent on March 8, 1951, to Harry Truman (1884–1972), the American president from 1945 until early 1953, is of special significance. In it the bishop petitioned Truman to "exercise your high influence in favour of Baron von Neurath, former German minister of Foreign Affairs, who is 78 years old and since long years impris-oned in Spandau = Berlin; The fact seems to justify, in a certain manner, my appealing to Your Excellency's Christian heart and my asking of a quick and, God grant it, successful intervention. It would earn gratitude, sympathy and admiration among Christian and honest-minded Germans and Your Excellency's name would illuminate, as the name of a humanitarian and Christianly thinking statesman, the darkness of hatred and moral confu-sion of our times and would enter the history of the truly Great Personalities."[1]

BIBLIOGRAPHY
Chenaux, Philippe. "Pacelli, Hudal, et la question du nazisme (1933–1938)." In *Rivista di Storia della Chiesa in Italia* 1 (January–June 2003): 133–54.
Goñi, Uki. *The Real Odessa: How Perón Brought the Nazi War Criminals to Argentina.* London: Granta, 2002.
Ickx, Johan. "The Roman 'Non Possumus' and the Attitude of Bishop Alois Hudal towards the National Socialist Ideological Aberrations." In *Religion under Siege: The Roman Catholic Church in Occupied Europe (1939–1950)*, ed. Lieve Gevers and Jan Bank, 1:315–44. Leuven: Peeters, 2007.
Matheus, Michael. *S. Maria dell'Anima: Zur Geschichte einer deutschen Stiftung in Rom.* Berlin: Walter De Gruyter, 2010.
Phayer, Michael. *The Catholic Church and the Holocaust, 1930–1965.* Bloomington: Indiana University Press, 2000.
Sanfilippo, Matteo. "Los papeles de Hudal como fuente para la historia de la migración de alemanes y nazis después de la segunda guerra mundial." In *Estudios Migratorios Latino-americanos* 43 (1999): 185–209.
Spatzenegger, Hans. "Das Archiv von Santa Maria dell'Anima in Roma." In *Römische historiche Mitteilungen* 25 (1983): 133–54.

Archivio del Pontificio Collegio Irlandese /
Archives of the Pontifical Irish College
Address
   Via dei Santi Quattro 1, 00184 Rome
Contact Details
   Phone: 39-06772631
   Fax: 39-0677263323
   Email 1: rector@irishcollege.org
   Email 2: ufficio@irishcollege.org
   Website: www.irishcollege.org/archive

STATUS

Closed since September 2009; access not permitted. Researchers can consult the online catalogs, which include all the material preserved in the college, at www.irishcollege.org/archive
/holdings. For the early modern period, most documents are written in Italian and in Latin.
From the nineteenth century onward, most material is written in English. Material post-
1939 cannot be consulted.

HISTORY

The Irish College of Rome was co-founded by the Irish Franciscan Luke Wadding (1588–
1657) and Cardinal Ludovico Ludovisi (1595–1632) in early 1628. In early 1635 the college,
initially under the control of the Irish Franciscans of Saint Isidore's College, was handed
over to the Jesuits. They managed it until 1772, when it passed into the hands of Luigi
Cuccagni (1740–98), a Pontifical States layman, who administered the seminary until it
closed in 1798 due to the French occupation of Rome. In 1826 former student Michael
Blake (1775–1860) reopened the college, becoming its first rector since the closure. The college became a pontifical institution in 1948. Today the college is the last Irish college on the
European continent to function as a diocesan seminary.

DESCRIPTION OF HOLDINGS

The archives of the Pontifical Irish College can be subdivided into three broad parts. The
first includes the so-called papers of the early period of the college's administration. This
collection of papers pertains to the college's foundation and Jesuit periods and covers the
years 1628–1798. The second part includes documents related to Michael Blake, rector
from 1826 to 1828; Paul Cullen (1803–78), rector from 1850 to 1891; and Tobias Kirby
(1804–95), rector from 1894 until 1901. The third part covers the years 1904–30 and includes all the papers related to John Hagan (1873–1930), vice rector from 1904 to 1919 and
rector from 1919 to 1930.

   In the collection of Cullen Papers, the series known as *CUL/OCO* is particularly useful:
It contains the correspondence exchanged between Cullen and Michael O'Connor (1810–72),
who served as vice rector of the Irish College in 1833–35. In 1843 O'Connor was appointed

bishop of Pittsburgh, a position he held until May 1860. Although this collection includes only thirty letters (1834–47), it sheds light on the state of religion in Pittsburgh before and after the diocese's establishment, particularly on the political and practical problems its bishop faced. One example of these problems can be gleaned from a letter that O'Connor sent to Cullen on November 27, 1844, about his baggage, clearly stating that he did not wish it opened by a parcel of "ruffianly" customs officers, especially not in his absence.

Additional material on American Catholicism from this period can be found in a series known as *CUL/Ame-The American Letters*, a collection of 138 items relating to the years 1824–49. Most letters in this collection were addressed to Cullen or O'Connor by prominent members of the American hierarchy, such as the bishops of Charleston, Chicago, Detroit, and New York. This extremely important correspondence paints a vivid portrait of the emerging Catholic Church in the United States, with keen observations of the financial and logistic problems facing the bishops. One example is a mid-September 1833 letter from John Power (1792–1849), vicar general of New York, to Cullen, in which Power remarked that the local bishop, Jean Dubois (1764–1842), had bought a farm, intending to build a seminary, but later realized in the midst of its construction that he had no money to complete it. Another example is the letter that John England (1786–1842), the bishop of Charleston, wrote to Cullen on December 16, 1833, in which he reported that his diocese was in excellent order and had considerably improved.

Researchers wishing to consult the *CUL/OCO* and the *CUL/Ame-The American Letters* series should make use of the most recent calendars and catalogs. These are posted at (1) www.irishcollege.org/archive/online-catalogues/ and (2) www.irishcollege.org/wp-content/uploads/2011/02/Cullen-Supplements.pdf.

The above finding aids should replace the selective calendars compiled by Anton Debeveč in vols. 7, 10–11, and 13 of the *United States Documents in the Propaganda Fide Archives*.

In contrast with the Cullen Papers, material on American Catholicism in the Kirby Papers is more difficult to trace because it is scattered within a collection of more than 20,000 items covering the period from 1831 to 1895. At present the material is divided into two main parts: the *Kirby Collection* (KIR/), which represents the core of this collection, with 19,803 catalogued items covering the years 1836–95. The second part is the *New Collection*, which includes the papers that were taken from the archive by Cardinal Francis Patrick Moran of Sydney (1830–1911), who intended to write a biography of his uncle, Paul Cullen.

The Kirby letters concern many diverse matters that, for the most part, are not exclusively related to the American church. Kirby could, in one letter, receive answers to a variety of questions concerning distant places with absolutely no connection to each other. A clear example of this is a letter that a certain Sebastian A. Duarte penned to Kirby in mid-January 1851 describing his journey to Malta and briefly referencing the archbishop of New York, who was likely to be made a cardinal.

The letters that were written by prominent American bishops tend to be mainly simple greetings or, more often still, requests for Kirby to favor the admission of certain applicants to the Urban College of Propaganda Fide or to the Pontifical North American College. There are therefore very few detailed reports that provide a clear view of the status and development of American Catholicism; the only notable exceptions are accounts Kirby received of the state of religion in California and New Mexico (1850) and in Milwaukee (1856).

For a preliminary overview of the Kirby Papers, researchers may consult calendars and catalogs at the following web pages:

> www.irishcollege.org/wp-content/uploads/2011/02/Kirby-Catalogue-Part-1-Intro +undated+incomplete.pdf
>
> www.irishcollege.org/wp-content/uploads/2011/02/Kirby-Catalogue-Part-2-1836 -1860.pdf
>
> www.irishcollege.org/wp-content/uploads/2011/02/Kirby-Catalogue-Part-3-1861 -1866.pdf
>
> www.irishcollege.org/wp-content/uploads/2011/02/Kirby-Catalogue-Part-4-1867 -1873.pdf
>
> www.irishcollege.org/wp-content/uploads/2011/02/Kirby-Catalogue-Part-5-1874 -1879.pdf
>
> www.irishcollege.org/wp-content/uploads/2011/02/Kirby-Catalogue-Part-6-1880 -1886.pdf
>
> www.irishcollege.org/wp-content/uploads/2011/02/Kirby-Catalogue-Part-7-1887 -1890.pdf
>
> www.irishcollege.org/wp-content/uploads/2011/02/Kirby-Catalogue-Part-8-1891 -1895.pdf

The material on American Catholicism in the Hagan Papers is rather more limited than that in the Cullen and the Kirby collections. Indeed this collection, which is divided into seven parts and covers the years from 1904 to 1930, details the status of the Catholic clergy in Australia and New Zealand rather than in North America. Hagan established and developed strong relationships with members of the Irish clergy in these colonies in particular because they provided one-fifth of the students who entered the Irish College during his period as vice rector and rector.[2]

Even though most documents deal with the British Commonwealth, the material of American interest in the Hagan Papers should not be overlooked, for it provides insight into Hagan's political role, particularly his close relationship with fellow countrymen who, during the 1920s, were active in the United States to gain support for the Irish Cause. A tangible example is a March 10, 1921, letter that Stanislaus Dempsey, an Irish priest based in San Francisco, sent Hagan to inform him that the newly founded American Association for the Recognition of the Irish Republic would command many votes once its power was felt in Washington.

As in the cases of the Cullen and the Kirby Papers, researchers can avail themselves of the online catalogs of the Hagan Papers at the following web pages:

www.irishcollege.org/wp-content/uploads/2011/02/Hagan-Catalogue-Part-1-Intro
-+-1904-1919.pdf

www.irishcollege.org/wp-content/uploads/2011/02/Hagan-Catalogue-Part-2-1920
-1922.pdf

www.irishcollege.org/wp-content/uploads/2011/02/Hagan-Catalogue-Part-3-1923
-1926.pdf

www.irishcollege.org/wp-content/uploads/2011/02/Hagan-Catalogue-Part-4-1927
-1930-+-HAG-2-6.pdf

BIBLIOGRAPHY

Barr, Colin. "The Irish College Rome, and the Appointment of Irish Bishops to the United States, 1830–1851." In *The Irish College, Rome, and Its World*, ed. Keogh Dáire and Albert McDonnell, 102–15. Dublin: Four Courts, 2008.

Corish, Patrick. "Irish College, Rome: Kirby Papers; Guide to Materials of Public and Political Interest." *Archivium Hibernicum* 30 (1972): 29–116.

———. "Irish College, Rome: Kirby Papers; Guide to Materials of Public and Political Interest, 1836–1861." *Archivium Hibernicum* 31 (1973): 1–94.

———. "Irish College, Rome: Kirby Papers; Guide to Material of Public and Political Interest, 1884–1894 with Addenda, 1852–1878." *Archivium Hibernicum* 32 (1974): 1–62.

Hanly, John. "Records of the Irish College, Rome, under Jesuit Administration." *Archivium Hibernicum* 28 (1964): 13–75.

———. "Sources of the History of the Irish College, Rome." *Irish Ecclesiastical Record* 102, series 5 (1964): 28–34.

Hanly, John, and Vera Orschel. "Calendar of 17th-and 18th-c. Documents at the Archives of the Irish College, Rome (with Index)." *Archivium Hibernicum* 63 (2010): 7–263.

Olden, Michael. "Tobias Kirby (1804–1895): The Man Who Kept Papers." In *The Irish College, Rome, and Its World*, ed. Keogh Dáire and Albert McDonnell, 131–48. Dublin: Four Courts, 2008.

Orschel, Vera. "Archives of the Pontifical Irish College, Rome: History and Holdings." In *The Irish College, Rome and Its World*, ed. Keogh Dáire and Albert McDonnell, 267–78. Dublin: Four Courts, 2008.

Szarnicki, Henry A. *Michael O'Connor: First Catholic Bishop of Pittsburgh ... 1843–1860 (A Story of the Catholic Pioneers of Pittsburgh and Western Pennsylvania)*. Pittsburgh: Wolfson, 1975.

Archivio del Pontificio Collegio Scozzese /
Archives of the Pontifical Scots College
Address
    Via Cassia 481, 00189 Rome
Contact Details
    Phone: 39-063366801
    Fax: 39-0633668025
    Email: office@scotscollege.it
    Website: scotscollege.org

STATUS

Open. Contact the vice rector, Fr. Gerald Sharkey (at vicerector@scotscollege.it), in advance to make an appointment and be granted access to the material. The majority of the material is in English and in Latin. Material post-1939 can be consulted with the archivist's permission.

HISTORY

The Pontifical Scots College was officially founded by Pope Clement VIII (1536–1605) primarily to train Scottish seminarians who were to return to Scotland as missionary priests after completing their studies. From 1615 until 1773, the college was administered by the Society of Jesus. From 1773 until 1798, the year of the French occupation of Rome, the college was placed under the control of the Italian rectors. From 1800 onward, all the rectors came from the ranks of the Scottish secular clergy.

DESCRIPTION OF HOLDINGS

The archives of the Scots College contain material pertaining to the history of the college from the early seventeenth century through to the early 1980s. At present the material is arranged in 106 boxes and nine binders. Researchers should note that the material in Rome should be combined with that contained in the series *SCA CA/3* of the collection titled *GB 3380 Scottish Catholic Archives*, which is preserved in the Special Collections Centre of the Sir Duncan Rice Library of the University of Aberdeen. More information about material on the Scots College of Rome is posted at www.abdn.ac.uk/library/about/special/scottish-catholic-archives.

Material of American interest is very limited and is found in boxes 39/9, 42/31, 48/264, and 48/320–22. It mainly consists of correspondence that was exchanged between William Clapperton (1886–1969), rector from 1922 to 1960, and the Sisters of Saint Joseph of Peace of Newark, who were entrusted with the housekeeping of the college from 1928 onward. One example of this correspondence is a letter that Clapperton addressed to Mother Monica, one of the sisters, on November 29, 1939, warning her of difficulties the sisters could face due to the increasingly unsafe political situation in Europe. He told her that "the difficulty of getting the Sisters out of the country in case of war, has been met up by a large extent by an assurance from the Italian government, given to the Holy See, that in case of necessity ecclesiastics and religious would be allowed to leave the country in a quiet and orderly manner. I hope it will not be necessary for us to leave this country at all; in any case it would be difficult for the Sisters to go to America under present conditions, and they are safer here than in England as long as Italy remains neutral."[3]

BIBLIOGRAPHY

McCluskey, Raymond, ed. *The Scots College Rome, 1600–2000.* Edinburgh: John Donald, 2000.

Archivio del Venerabile Collegio Inglese /
Archives of the Venerable English College

Address
  Via di Monserrato 45, 00186 Rome
Contact Details
  Phone: 39-066868546/066865808
  Fax: 39-066867607
  Email: schwarzenbachfellow@vecrome.org
  Website: www.vecrome.org/the-archives.html

STATUS

Closed at the time of this writing. As of February 2015, the material is being reorganized to facilitate production of an electronic catalog of the collections; this reorganization should be complete in 2018. The material is mainly in English or Latin.

HISTORY

The Venerable English College was officially established in 1579 in compliance with a bull issued by Pope Gregory XIII (1502–85). The leading figure behind the college's foundation was Cardinal William Allen (1532–94). In 1576 he set the agenda for transforming the moribund Hospice of Saint Thomas, which had been a key structure for housing English pilgrims who went to Rome during the Middle Ages, into a seminary to train missionary priests and send them back to England. From its founding, the college was run by the Jesuits, who managed it until 1773, when it was handed over to the care of Italian seculars. Between 1798 and 1818, because of the disarray caused by the French presence in Rome, the college was closed. It was reopened by Robert Gradwell (1777–1833), rector from 1818 until 1828.

DESCRIPTION OF HOLDINGS

Material of North American interest can be found in three different sections. The first, titled *Scritture 63/1-5, Canadian Agency*, contains 411 folios housed in seven folders that cover the period from the end of April 1817 until late August 1885. This section sheds light on the internal dynamics of Canadian dioceses, particularly Montreal, and on troubles with the Jesuits and the Séminaire de Saint Sulpice. These papers also provide details on the activity of Robert Gradwell and Cardinal Nicholas Wiseman (1802–65),[4] who acted as intermediaries between the Catholic Church in England or the United States, respectively, while they were rectors of the English College.

   The second section containing American material is titled *Scritture 69/1-13, Baltimore Agency*. It comprises 290 folios for the period from February 1821 to October 1834. The material in this section sheds light on the history of the Baltimore diocese, providing information particularly about problems that emerged between the restored Jesuits and the Irish immigrant clergy and about the administration of the Catholic Church's goods. This section is also relevant for reconstructing the intermediary roles Gradwell and Wiseman played between the Roman Curia and the American clergy.

The third section containing American material is titled *Scritture 69/14-16, Philadelphia Agency*. It has twenty-three documents concerning the period from March 1829 to May 1835. This section provides information on the Diocese of Philadelphia, Gallicanism in America, and troubles between the secular and regular clergy and the Jesuits.[5]

Until the new catalog is made available, researchers must rely on the calendar compiled by Anton Debevec (1977), which provides a short summary of the items included in the college's Baltimore Papers and Philadelphia Papers.[6]

BIBLIOGRAPHY

Fothergill, Brian. *Nicholas Wiseman*. London: Faber, 1963.

Gasquet, Francis Aidan. *A History of the Venerable English College, Rome: An Account of Its Origins and Work from the Earliest Times to the Present Day*. London: Longmans, Green, 1929.

Kenneally, Finbar, ed. *United States Documents in the Propaganda Archives: A Calendar*. Vol. 7. Washington, DC: Academy of American Franciscan History, 1977.

Schofield, Nicholas, ed. *A Roman Miscellany: The English in Rome, 1550–2000*. Leominster, England: Gracewing, 2002.

Williams, Michael E. *The Venerable English College Rome: A History, 1579–1979*. London: Associated Catholic Publications, 1979.

NOTES

1. Alois Hudal to US President Harry Truman, March 8, 1951, fol. 377r, Hudal Papers, Archivio di Santa Maria dell'Anima (Archives of the Pontifical Institute of Santa Maria dell'Anima).

2. Seventy-one out of 349 students who entered the Irish College of Rome from 1904 to 1930 were from outside of Ireland. In Australia, of the eleven dioceses involved, Goulburn and Brisbane stand out (with fourteen and thirteen students, respectively). In North America, only Saint John's, Newfoundland, sent students with any regularity (four); such US Irish hubs as Boston and New York are not represented at all, and other dioceses like those of Ontario, Cheyenne, Los Angeles, and San Francisco sent only one student apiece.

3. Rector William Clapperton to Mother Monica, November 29, 1939, unfoliated and unpaginated, box 48/231, Archives of the Pontifical Scots College of Rome.

4. Wiseman was rector of the English College from 1828 to 1840.

5. I owe all these details to the generosity of Professor Maurice Whitehead.

6. The items of Baltimore Papers calendared by Debevec are nos. 2250–2329; the items of Philadelphia Papers are nos. 2330–53. See Kenneally, *United States Documents*, vol. 7, Appendix 3, 343–59.

CHAPTER 4

Other Civil and Religious Archives

This chapter consists of profiles of other civil and religious archives that preserve material of American interest. It also includes non-Catholic archives, such as those of the Keats-Shelley House, the Episcopal Church of St. Paul's Within the Walls, and the Non-Catholic Cemetery in Rome. The choice to include these archives was dictated by the fact that they contain documents on the American presence in Rome since the mid-nineteenth century.

Archivio Doria Pamphilj /
Doria Pamphilj Archives
Address
    Via del Corso 305, 00186 Rome
Contact Details
    Phone: 39-066797323
    Fax: 39-066780939
    Email: archivio@doriapamphilj.it
    Website: www.doriapamphilj.it/roma/en/l-archivio-doria-pamphilj

STATUS
Open to researchers on Tuesday and Wednesday, 10 a.m.–1 p.m. The archives close for Italian national holidays and from June 29 or 30 until September 12 or 13. Researchers are advised to make an appointment with the archivist in advance to be granted access to the material. Also, researchers should send the archivist the specific series numbers of documents for verification, availability, and accessibility. Only documents reserved in this way are available to researchers. Most documents are written in Italian or Latin. Material post-1939 cannot be consulted.

A detailed catalog of the Doria Pamphilj archives may be consulted at the Soprinten-denza archivistica per il Lazio, which is open Monday–Friday, 9 a.m.–3 p.m. To consult this catalog, researchers must make an appointment with Dr. Mariapina Di Simone at sa-laz @beniculturali.it or mariapina.disimone@beniculturali.it.

HISTORY

The Doria-Pamphilj family was established by two noble weddings: the first occurred in 1627, when Giovanni Andrea Doria II (1607–40) married Maria Polissena Landi (1608–79); the second occurred in 1671, when Giovanni Andrea Doria III (1653–1737) married Anna Pamphilj (1652–1728).

DESCRIPTION OF HOLDINGS

The Doria Pamphilj archives are the result of several archives' merging together. Added to the material of the original Doria archives was material from the Landi, the Pamphilj, the Aldobrandini, and the Facchinetti families. The archives presently comprise 7,115 volumes from the ninth century through the twentieth. There are six key sections in the archives: (1) *Doria-Pamphilj*, which contains 5,500 volumes dating from the fifteenth century to the nineteenth; (2) *Libro mastro dei feudi*, with 687 volumes from the sixteenth to the nineteenth century; (3) *Mandati di casa Pamphilj*, with 140 volumes for the years 1661–1763; (4) *Archiviolo*, with 349 volumes for the period 1451–1870; (5) *Feudi*, with 350 volumes for the period from the sixteenth century to the nineteenth; and (6) *Pergamene*, with eighty parchments for the years 1513–1766.

There is material of American interest in the section *Doria-Pamphilj*, particularly on shelf 37, in box 2; shelf 53, in boxes 12–14; and shelf 93, in box 91. These boxes contain cor-respondence addressed to Cardinal Giuseppe Maria Doria Pamphilj (1751–1816), nuncio in France from 1773 until mid-February of 1785, secretary of state from 1797 to 1799, and pro-prefect of Propaganda in 1815. Although initial research in this section has not yielded any material of American interest, it seems likely, given the nuncio's role in the American negotiations, that such material may be found elsewhere. Additional material of American interest related to Cardinal Doria Pamphilj can be found in the archives of Propaganda.

BIBLIOGRAPHY

Codignola, Luca. *Guide of Documents Relating to French and British North America in the Archives of the Sacred Congregation "de Propaganda Fide" in Rome, 1622–1799*. Ottawa: National Archives of Canada, 1991.

Sanfilippo, Matteo. "Doria." In *Die Grossen Familien Italien*, ed. V. Reinhardt, 225–36. Stuttgart: Kroner, 1992.

Vignodelli, Rubrichi Renato. "Il fondo detto 'L'Archiviolo' dell'archivio Doria Landi Pamphilj in Roma." In *Miscellanea della Società Romana di Storia Patria* XXII (1972): 7–18.

Archivio Storico di San Paolo fuori le Mura /
Archives of Saint Paul Outside the Walls

Address

Via Ostiense 186, 00146 Rome

Contact Details

Phone: 39-065410341

Fax: 39-064547784939

Email: archivio@abbaziasanpaolo.org

Website: www.abbaziasanpaolo.org

STATUS

Open to researchers Monday, 9:00 a.m.–12:15 p.m., and Friday, 2:30 p.m.–5:30 p.m. The archives close for Italian national holidays and from early July until the end of September. To consult the material, an appointment with the archivist is required. The majority of the material is in English or Latin. Material post-1939 cannot be consulted.

HISTORY

The abbey of San Paolo fuori le Mura (Saint Paul Outside the Walls) was founded in the sixth century, and the early formation of the archives dates back to the abbey's founding. The current archives are a combination of three different collections: the *Archivio Storico*; the *Archivio of the Procura Generale Cassinese*, whose activity can be traced back to the mid-seventeenth century; and the "current" archives, which hold the material from 1872 onward.

DESCRIPTION OF HOLDINGS

At present the archives are subdivided into the following seven sections: (I) *Bolle*, (II) *Basilica*, (III) *Monastero*, (IV) *Diocesi*, (V) *Congregazione Cassinese*, (VI) *Archivio Vaticano*, and (VII) *Varia*.

The collection of the Archivio Storico that proves most relevant for the history of American Catholicism is in section III: *Monastero*, which features a collection of documents on the most prominent abbots who resided at San Paolo fuori le Mura. This collection includes the correspondence of the Irish Benedictine Dom Bernard Smith (1812–92), who had a prominent role in Rome. From 1850 to 1855 he served as vice rector of the Irish College, and around this time he was also named professor of dogmatic theology at the Urban College and consultor to the Sacred Congregation of the Index. In addition, he was appointed consultor to the Oriental Congregation in 1862, to the Holy Office in 1874, and to Propaganda Fide in 1880. Smith also played a crucial role because he acted as pontifical agent for a number of Australian, English, Irish, and North American bishops and clerics.

Smith's correspondence is located on shelf no. 27 of the Archivio Storico and is divided into twenty-two volumes, five volumes of which have material on North America

(Canada and the United States) for the years from 1840 to 1892. The five volumes on North America are subdivided as follows: Smith I, 1840–1861: America, Canada; Smith II, 1862–1876: America; Smith III, 1877–1884: America; Smith IV, 1885–1892: America; Smith V, America *Varie.*

Because of his role in Rome, Smith was in contact with numerous members of the American Catholic hierarchy who wrote him to ask that he promote or hasten their requests to the pope. The letters addressed to Smith vividly portray the emerging contrasts between different immigrant communities. Smith corresponded with a number of laypeople as well, in particular with some members of the Seton family on a variety of issues. For more information on Smith's correspondence, see my section near the beginning of this volume titled "Roman Sources for the History of American Catholicism: A Different Perspective."

Amid the papers of vol. V, dossier no. 53 provides clear insight into the Roman and Italian experiences of Robert Seton (1839–1927), the first American to receive the Roman Prelatura, who in 1903 was consecrated archbishop of Heliopolis. The dossier includes two documents: a diary that covers the period from 1863 to October 1864, when Seton was a student at the Pontifical North American College, and a small booklet titled *Journal from Leghorn to Baltimore,* which describes his return journey from Italy to the United States. This dossier also contains documents on Eliza MacBride, an American nun, and lists of the students enrolled at the North American College for the years 1864–65.

Additional material on American Catholicism is found on shelf no. 19, in the volume named *Miscellanea.* In this volume is a bundle of letters written by Paolo Marella (1895–1984), an Italian cleric who worked as auditor for the apostolic delegation to Washington from 1922 to 1933, when he was named the apostolic delegate to Japan. Marella's letters are a valuable source because they offer a double perspective: that of the cleric and that of the Italian immigrant adapting to a new society. A letter that Marella sent to Rome in March 1922 exemplifies this dual perspective. In it he reported, "It [Washington, DC] is full of Protestants of any sect. When I see the boys on the street I pity to think that the great majority of them are heretic," and also wrote that "there is no noise as in Rome; cars rarely honk the horn, the traffic is regulated by the police."[1]

BIBLIOGRAPHY
Baiocchi, Stefano, OSB. "L'Archivio dell'Abbazia di S. Paolo." Unpublished inventory, 1966. This is an inventory that can be consulted only within the archives.
Fogarty, Gerald P., SJ. *The Vatican and the Americanist Crisis: Denis J. O'Connell, American Agent in Rome, 1885–1903.* Rome: Università Gregoriana Editrice, 1974.
McNamara, Robert F. *The American College in Rome (1855–1955).* New York: Christopher Press, 1956.

Archivio di San Paolo entro le Mura /
Archives of Saint Paul Within the Walls Episcopal Church
Address
   Via Napoli 58, 00184 Rome

Contact Details
    Phone: 39-064883339
    Fax: 39-064814549
    Email: rector@stpaulsrome.it
    Website: www.stpaulsrome.it/homepage

STATUS

Open to researchers. There is no fixed schedule for the days the archives are open, so an appointment is required to gain access to the material. Documents are in English. Material post-1939 may be consulted with the archivist's permission.

HISTORY

The Protestant Episcopal Church in the United States of America, the American church of the Anglican Communion, was organized after the War of American Independence (1775–83), during which it separated from the Church of England, whose members were required to swear allegiance to the British monarch. The first Mass celebrated in Rome according to the liturgy of the Episcopal Church was held in 1859 in a private house close to the Spanish Steps. In the same year, William Chauncy Langdon (1831–95), an American clergyman, arrived in Rome and founded the first Episcopalian church of the city under the name of Grace Church. In 1860 Langdon was elected as the first rector. In 1871 the name of the church was changed to Saint Paul's Within the Walls, and the following year construction of a new building began on via Nazionale.

DESCRIPTION OF HOLDINGS

The archives of the Episcopal Church of Saint Paul's Within the Walls are divided into two main sections: (1) vestry records from 1859 onward, which provide information on the church's administration, its financial status, and the members of the Episcopalian community in Rome, and (2) baptism registers.

    Researchers should note that there is no inventory and that the material in Rome should be combined with the collection of the Lowrie Papers preserved at the Firestone Library of Princeton University (details on this collection are available at findingaids.princeton.edu/collections). Walter Lowrie (1868–1959) was rector of Saint Paul's Within the Walls from 1907 to 1930.

BIBLIOGRAPHY

Elliot, John. "The Protestants in Rome." *Ecclesiology Today* 33 (May 2004): 3–8.

Holmes, David L. *A Brief History of the Episcopal Church*. Harrisburg, PA: Trinity Press International, 1993.

Lowrie, Walter. *Fifty Years of Saint Paul's American Church, Rome: Some Historical Notes and Descriptions*. Rome, 1926.

Millon, Judith Rice. *St Paul's Within-the-Walls in Rome: A Building History and Guide, 1870–2000*. Rome: Edizioni dell'Elefante, 2001.

Nevin, Jenkins Robert. *St. Paul's within the Walls: An Account of the American Chapel at Rome, Italy; Together with the Sermons Preached in Connection with Its Consecration, Feast of the Annunciation, March 25, 1876.* New York: D. Appleton and Company, 1878.

Archivio della Keats-Shelley House /
Archives of the Keats-Shelley House
Address
> Piazza di Spagna 26, 00187 Rome

Contact Details
> Phone: 39-066784235
> Email: info@keats-shelley-house.org
> Website: www.keats-shelley-house.org/it

STATUS

Open to researchers by appointment only. Researchers should contact the archivist and send a reference letter in advance to be granted access to the material, most of which is in English.

HISTORY

The Keats-Shelley House was officially opened in 1909 by a group of prominent American, English, and Italian scholars to preserve the memory of English poets John Keats (1796–1821) and Percy Shelley (1792–1822) and the house where the latter briefly lived prior to his death. Among the founders were Robert Underwood Johnson (1853–1937), president of the New York Committee of the Italian War Relief Fund of America from 1918 to 1919 and American ambassador to Rome from April 1920 to July 1921, and Harry Nelson Gay (1870–1932), a Harvard University historian and specialist in the Italian Risorgimento.

DESCRIPTION OF HOLDINGS

At present the archives of the Keats-Shelley House consist of nine boxes divided as follows: (1) Box 1, Keats, Severn and Associates; (2) Box 2, Percy Bysshe Shelley, Mary Wollstonecraft Shelley, Thomas Medwin, and William Godwin; (3) Box 3, miscellaneous correspondence; (4) Box 4, Byron Papers; (5) Box 5, Charles Cowden Clarke; (6) Box 6, William Wetmore Story, Brownings, and Lowell; (7) Box 7–8, letters concerning the founding of the archives and the collection; (8) Box 8, concerning the graves; and (9) Box 9, letters and autographs of distinguished people.

Material of American interest is mainly to be found in boxes 1, 5–6, and 7–8. One example of the sort of material available is a letter that Theodore Roosevelt (1858–1919), president of the United States from 1901 to 1909, sent to Johnson on January 5, 1906, promising his support for the opening of the house.[2] Another example is a letter that Harold Woodbury Parson, an American art expert who lived in Rome, sent to Gay in late November 1919. In it Parson stated: "Our subscriptions make a fairly good showing after all, when one considers the really limited number of Americans in Italy at this time."[3]

BIBLIOGRAPHY

Brown, Sally. "An Echo and a Light unto Eternity: The Founding of the Keats-Shelley House." In *Keats and Italy: A History of the Keats-Shelley House in Rome*, 51–67. Rome: Edizioni Il Labirinto, 2005.

Browning, Robert, Elizabeth Barrett Browning, William Wetmore Story, Emelyn Story, James Russell Lowell, and Gertrude Reese Hudson. *Browning to His American Friends: Letters between the Brownings, the Storys, and James Russell Lowell*. London: Bowes and Bowes, 1965.

Fiorentino, Daniele. "Ambasciatori e aristocratici: Stati Uniti e Italia durante la presidenza di Theodore Roosevelt." In *Stati Uniti e Italia nel nuovo scenario internazionale, 1898–1918*, ed. Daniele Fiorentino and Matteo Sanfilippo, 23–46. Rome: Gangemi Editore, 2012.

Archivio del Museo Centrale del Risorgimento /
Archives of the Museo Centrale del Risorgimento

Address

Complesso del Vittoriano, Piazza Venezia, 00186 Rome

Contact Details

Phone: 39-066793598

Fax: 39-066782572

Email: ist.risorgimento@tiscalinet.it

Website: www.risorgimento.it/index.php?section=archivio

STATUS

Open to researchers on Monday, Thursday, and Friday, 9:00 a.m.–1:15 p.m., and Tuesday and Wednesday, 9:00 a.m.–5:15 p.m. The archives close for Italian national holidays and during the month of August. Researchers should make an appointment with the archivist in advance to access the material and should send the archivist the specific series numbers of documents to verify their availability and accessibility. Most documents are written in Italian.

HISTORY

The archives of the Museo Centrale del Risorgimento contain material related to the history of the Italian Risorgimento and to the period, commonly known as "Liberal Italy," when the Kingdom of Italy was unified. At present the material is contained in 1,132 boxes and 1,093 volumes covering a period from 1830 to the early decades of the twentieth century.

DESCRIPTION OF HOLDINGS

The material of American interest contained by the archives of the Museo Centrale del Risorgimento is mainly political in nature. For example, the collection related to Giuseppe Garibaldi (1807–82) is rich in content due to the numerous prominent figures in North America with whom Garibaldi established links. Particularly worth noting among the Garibaldi material is a letter he sent in early October 1861 to Abraham Lincoln (1809–65), president of United States from 1861 to 1865.[4]

The archives of the museum have a large amount of material—fifteen boxes holding 1,847 documents—on the activity in Italy of Gaetano Bedini (1806–64), the first apostolic delegate sent to the United States. The archives also contain thirty-three documents related to Alessandro Gavazzi (1809–89), one of the most prominent Protestant preachers in Italy.

Another significant collection is that created by Henry Nelson Gay (1870–1932), Harvard University historian and one of the leading experts on the Italian Risorgimento. The first part of this collection (buste [folders] 545–55) deals with his investigations into key figures and facts of the Risorgimento. The second section (buste 715–30) contains the archives of the Società Nazionale Italiana, a political movement that supported the unification of the Kingdom of Italy. This part has material concerning the diplomatic relationships established with the American government by Giuseppe La Farina (1815–63), one of the most prominent figures of the Società Nazionale. In the Gay section is a printed copy of the *Life of the Most Reverend John Hughes* (1866), written by John Hassard.[5] Researchers must take into account that Gay also donated a collection of ten thousand books from his private library; this collection is now held by the Centro Studi Americani (centrostudiamericani.org).

BIBLIOGRAPHY

Fiorentino, Daniele. "Ambasciatori e aristocratici: Stati Uniti e Italia durante la presidenza di Theodore Roosevelt." In *Stati Uniti e Italia nel nuovo scenario internazionale, 1898–1918*, ed. Daniele Fiorentino and Matteo Sanfilippo, 23–46. Rome: Gangemi Editore, 2012.

Menghini, Mario. "Enrico Nelson Gay e la storia del Risorgimento Italiano." *Rassegna Italiana* 130 (1933): 430–33.

Musmanno, Michelangelo. "The Library for American Studies in Italy." *Rivista d'America e d'Italia* 13–14 (1925).

Pizzo, Marco, ed. *L'Archivio del Museo Centrale del Risorgimento: Guida ai fondi documentari.* Rome: Gangemi Editore, 2007.

Archivio del Cimitero Acattolico /
Archives of the Non-Catholic Cemetery
Address
   Via Caio Cestio 6, 00153 Rome
Contact Details
   Phone: 39-065741900
   Fax: 39-065741320
   Email 1: mail@cemeteryrome.it
   Email 2: direttore@cemeteryrome.it
   Website: www.cemeteryrome.it

STATUS
Open to researchers by appointment only. Researchers are advised to contact the director in advance to access the material. Due to the nature of the material contained in these

archives, researchers are advised to consult the database of the cemetery's burials (at www .cemeteryrome.it/infopoint/encerca.asp) for the exact names of those buried there. Material is written mainly in English, but there are also documents in German, Italian, Russian, and Swedish. Material post-1939 cannot be consulted.

HISTORY

The Non-Catholic Cemetery in Rome dates back to 1716, when it served as an unofficial burial place for several members of the exiled Stuart court. From that time a growing number of non-Catholic foreigners were buried in that area. In 1821 Pope Pius VII (1742–1823) forbade further burials in front of the Pyramid of Caius Cestius but granted an adjoining piece of land surrounded by a wall, which became the New Cemetery.

DESCRIPTION OF HOLDINGS

The archives of the Non-Catholic Cemetery in Rome contain material relating to the people buried there. The earliest documents date back to the 1820s, and material consists primarily of bureaucratic certificates of death or nationality. At present the database of the cemetery lists the names of 622 American citizens buried there from the 1830s until the present.

It must be noted that from the early 1830s onward, burials of American citizens in the Non-Catholic Cemetery were overseen by the American consul in conjunction with the cardinal secretary of state. The first example of a consul's involvement is in the burial of William Henry Elliot, an American Protestant from New York, who died in Rome in 1833.[6] The consul's involvement may also be seen in material concerning the death and burial of Jacob L. Martin, an American representative appointed to the Holy See, who arrived in Rome in early August 1848 and died at the end of the same month.[7]

BIBLIOGRAPHY

Menniti Ippolito, Antonio. *Il Cimitero Acattolico di Roma: La presenza protestante nella città del papa*. Rome: Viella, 2014.

Menniti Ippolito, Antonio, and Paolo Vian, eds. *The Protestant Cemetery in Rome: The Parte Antica*. Rome: Unione Internazionale degli Istituti di Archeologia, Storia e Storia dell'Arte in Roma, 1989.

Stanley-Price, Nicholas. *The Non-Catholic Cemetery in Rome: Its History, Its People, and Its Survival for 300 Years*. Rome: Non-Catholic Cemetery in Rome, 2014.

Stevens, Revalee, and Robert Kim Stevens. *North American Records in Italy: The Protestant Cemetery of Rome*. Baton Rouge: Oracle Press, 1981.

Archivio Centrale dello Stato /

Central Archives of the State
Address
　　Piazzale degli Archivi 27, 00144 Rome

Contact Details
> Phone: 39-06545481
> Fax: 39-065413620
> Email: acs@beniculturali.it
> Website: acs.beniculturali.it

STATUS

The archives are open Monday–Friday, 9:00 a.m.–6:45 p.m., and Saturday, 9:00 a.m.–1:00 p.m., and close for Italian national holidays and during the whole month of August. Researchers must provide identification to gain access to the documents; applications to access material may be submitted only Monday–Thursday, 9:40 a.m.–12:20 p.m., and Friday, 9:40 a.m.–1:30 p.m. Most material is in Italian. Material post-1939 can be consulted.

HISTORY

The archives were established by the Italian government in 1874 as a repository for original copies of the decrees and laws issued by different ministries. From 1874 until 1952, however, Central Archives was not an independent agency but was jointly administered with the Archivio dello Stato di Roma (State Archives of Rome). In 1953 the duties of the Archivio Centrale dello Stato were officially established, and it gained complete autonomy.

DESCRIPTION OF HOLDINGS

Given the particular focus of the Archivio Centrale, most material contained in it concerns the bureaucratic activity of the various ministries and key politicians of the Italian government. A fuller inventory of the different archival collections is posted in PDF format at search.acs.beniculturali.it/OpacACS/resources/pdf/Guida_ai_fondi_ACS_2012 _Pubblico.pdf. Researchers can also consult the online catalog at search.acs.beniculturali .it/OpacACS.

Ten sections contain material relevant to the study of American Catholicism:

(1) *Archivi di Enti Pubblici e Società* (1856–1994) contains a twenty-five-box collection named *Consorzio di credito per le opere pubbliche* (CREDIOP), on the system of Italian loans and their conversion in the United States, 1923–78.

(2) *Nuclei documentali in copia* (1509–1947) contains 8,519 microfilm reels of documents of the Allied Control Commission (the originals are now at the US National Archives in College Park, Maryland), the Collection of Italian Military Records, the Allied Intelligence Bureau, and the US Department of State.

(3) *Archivi degli Organi Di Governo e Amministrativi dello Stato, Ministero per il commercio con l'estero* contains eighty-seven boxes pertaining to the Italian financial commission, which, from late November 1944 until 1967, was based in Washington, DC.

(4) *Archivi delle Personalità della Politica e della Pubblica Amministrazione* contains material relating to the 1917 Italian Mission to Washington, DC, which was led by Francesco

Saverio Nitti (1868–1953), then the Italian secretary of the treasury and later the prime minister (1919–20).

(5) *Casellario politico centrale* contains 5,615 boxes for the period 1894–1945, with personal information on emigrants compelled to flee Italy for political reasons—including 138 Italians who went to America. An online inventory of the *Casellario* is available at dati.acs.beniculturali.it/CPC.

(6) *Archivi della Personalità della Politica e della Pubblica Amministrazione* contains ten boxes of the 1913–52 correspondence of Carlo Sforza, foreign minister of Italy, 1920–21 and 1947–51. This collection sheds light on the role Sforza played in the establishment and development of the North Atlantic Treaty.

(7) *Ministero dell'Interno, D.G. Pubblica Sicurezza, Div. AA. GG. RR, Massime, I4, Istruzioni di Polizia Militare*, box nos. 74–89, and *Ministero dell'Interno, Direzione Generale Pubblica Sicurezza, Divisione Affari Generali e Riservati, Cat. A 16, Stranieri e Ebrei stranieri, Affari Generali* (1930–1956), box nos. 23–62, contain material on the refugee camps the American government supported in Italy after World War II.

(8) *Archivi di Personalità della Cultura* contains eighty-three boxes for the years 1919–43, concerning Cornelio di Marzio (1896–1944), a prominent member of the Fascist party abroad.

(9) *Ministero della Cultura Popolare* has two collections:
   (a) *Direzione Generale Servizi della Propaganda, poi per gli Scambi Culturali*, with 292 boxes for the period 1930–44.
   (b) *Gabinetto*, 396 folders for the period 1926–45, with material about Fascist propaganda in Italian communities abroad, including those in the United States.

(10) *Archivi degli Organi e delle Istituzioni del Regime Fascista* (1862–1945) holds the collection *Segreteria Particolare del Duce* (1922–45), with 4,227 boxes that cover the period 1922–1945 and contain additional material on Fascist propaganda in North America.

BIBLIOGRAPHY

Caruso, Alfio. *Il piano Marshall e la Sicilia: Politica ed economia*. Turin: G. Giappichelli Editore, 2013.

Cova, Alberto, ed. *Il dilemma dell'integrazione: L'inserimento dell'economia italiana nel sistema occidentale, 1945–1957*. Milan: Franco Angeli, 2008.

Fracchiolla, Domenico. *Un ambasciatore della "nuova Italia" a Washington: Alberto Tarchiani e le relazioni tra l'Italia e gli Stati Uniti, 1945–1947*. Milan: Franco Angeli, 2012.

Luconi, Stefano. *From Paesani to White Ethnics: The Italian Experience in Philadelphia*. Albany: State University of New York, 2001.

Miller, James Edward. *The United States and Italy, 1940–1950*. Chapel Hill: University of North Carolina Press, 1986.

Paparazzo, Amelia, ed. *Calabresi sovversivi nel mondo: L'esodo, l'impegno politico, le lotte degli emigrati in terra straniera (1880–1940)*. Soveria Mannelli: Rubbettino Editore, 2004.

Pretelli, Matteo. *La via fascista alla democrazia americana: Culture e propaganda nelle comunità italo-americane*. Viterbo: Edizioni Sette Città, 2012.

Rossini, Daniela. *Donne e Propaganda internazionale: Percorsi femminili fra Italia e Stati Uniti nell'età della Grande Guerra.* Milan: Franco Angeli, 2015.

Sanfilippo, Matteo. "Per una storia dei profughi stranieri e dei campi di accoglienza e di reclusione nell'Italia del secondo dopoguerra." *Studi Emigrazione/Migration Studies* 43, no. 164 (2006): 835–56.

Archivio di Stato di Roma /
Archives of the State of Rome

Address

Corso Rinascimento 40, 00186 Rome

Branch Office: Via di Galla Placidia 93, 00159 Rome

Contact Details, Archives

Phone: 39-06672356

Fax: 39-0668190871

Email: as-rm@beniculturali.it

Website: www.archiviodistatoroma.beniculturali.it

Contact Details, Branch Office at Galla Placidia

Phone: 39-064370019

Fax: 39-064370019

Email: mariatemide.bergamaschi@beniculturali.it

STATUS

The archives are open to researchers Monday–Friday, 9:00 a.m.–6:00 p.m., and Saturday, 9:00 a.m.–1:00 p.m. On Saturday only reserved material may be consulted. The branch office is open Monday, Tuesday, Wednesday, and Friday, 9:00 a.m.–2:00 p.m., and Thursday, 9:00 a.m.–5:00 p.m. Precise references to material are available in the online catalog: ricerca.archiviodistatoroma.beniculturali.it/OpacASRoma. Researchers should contact the director to gain access to material at the branch office at Galla Placidia. Most material is in Italian.

HISTORY

The Archivio di Stato di Roma was officially established on December 31, 1871, to preserve three key types of documents: (1) the acts of the central departments of the Holy See, (2) the archived materials of Roman notaries before 1871, and (3) the archived materials of public offices located in the district of Rome, from the periods before and after the annexation of the city to the Kingdom of Italy.

DESCRIPTION OF HOLDINGS

Material of American interest is scattered across different sections of the archives, with most of it contained in the section *Organi e Uffici Preunitari, Camerlengato* (1816–54),

Parte II (1824–54), *Titolo V-Affari esteri*. This section has fifteen folders on the diplomatic activity of the American and papal consuls in the United States and the Italian Peninsula, particularly at Civitavecchia and Leghorn, during the first half of the nineteenth century. Especially important in this section is folder no. 328, which contains a detailed description by Giovanni Battista Sartori (1768–1854), consul of the Holy See in the United States, titled *Notizie sulla politica e amministrazioni, nonmmeno che sul commercio di quel Regno*. Additional material on the American consuls is found in the section *Organi e Uffici Preunitari*, more specifically in the subseries *Camerlengato* (1816–54); *Parte II* (1824–54); in *Titolo VI-Poste*; and in *Titolo IX-Marina*. Further material may be found in the section *Organi e Uffici Periferici Postunitari*, subseries *Luogotenenza generale del re per Roma e le provincie romane*; *Amministrazione dell'interno*, nos. 1–30; and *L. Affari politici*, October 16, 1870–February 3, 1871, dossier 48. In the section *Organi e Uffici Preunitari*, subseries *Congregazione degli studi 1816–1870, Personale-Istanze*, there is material on Samuele Tayella and Giacomo Tetta, Italian priests active in the Diocese of Erie, Pennsylvania.

The Archivio di Stato di Roma also has also a library (open Monday–Friday, 9:30 a.m.– 1:00 p.m., and Tuesday and Wednesday, 2:00 p.m.–5:00 p.m.), which contains the diary (*manoscritto* 504) of Alessandro Gavazzi (1809–89), in which he describes his permanent residence in the United States and Canada.

Researchers interested in the American and Canadian zouaves who fought in the papal army during the Italian Risorgimento should take into account that the matriculation records of the soldiers are held in the branch office at Galla Placidia.

BIBLIOGRAPHY

Coulombe, Charles A. *The Pope's Legion: The Multinational Fighting Force That Defended the Vatican*. New York: Palgrave MacMillan, 2008.

Fiorentino, Daniele. *Gli Stati Uniti e il Risorgimento d'Italia, 1848–1901*. Rome: Gangemi Editore, 2013.

Fiorentino, Daniele, and Matteo Sanfilippo, eds. *Le relazioni fra Stati Uniti e Italia nel periodo di Roma capitale*. Rome: Gangemi Editore, 2011.

Marraro, Howard Rosario. *American Opinion on the Unification of Italy: 1846–1861*. New York: Columbia University Press, 1969.

Sanfilippo, Matteo. "Fuggitivi e avventurieri: Volontari nord-americani tra Garibaldi e Pio IX; Una proposta di ricerca." *Ricerche di Storia Politica* 1 (March 2007): 67–78.

Stock, Leo F., ed. *Consular Relations between the United States and the Papal States: Instructions and Despatches*. Washington: American Catholic Historical Association, 1945.

Archivio Storico Capitolino /
Archives of the City of Rome
Address
> Piazza dell'Orologio 4, 00186 Rome

Contact Details
  Phone: 39-0667108100
  Fax: 39-0668806639
  Email: archivio.capitolino@comune.roma.it
  Website: www.archiviocapitolino.it

STATUS

Open Monday–Friday, 9:00 a.m.–4:00 p.m., and closed for Italian national holidays. A valid form of identification and a completed admission form are necessary to gain access to material in the archives. Applications to consult the documents are due before the following times: 9:45 a.m., 11:45 a.m., and 2:00 p.m. on the research day. Material of American interest is mainly in English and Italian. Material post-1939 can be consulted.

HISTORY

While the nucleus of the Archives of the City of Rome dates back to 1143 and the establishment of the municipality of Rome, the archives were created officially in 1874 to preserve the materials pertaining to the city's administration.

DESCRIPTION OF HOLDINGS

The Archives of the City of Rome are currently divided into five main sections: (1) *Archivio del Comune*, (2) *Archivio Notarile Generale Urbano*, (3) *Archivi di Famiglie e di Persone*, (4) *Archivi aggregate*, and (5) *Archivio Fotografico*. The *Archivio del Comune* contains two further sub-sections. The first of these is named *Archivio del Comune Antico* (XV-1847) and includes two parts—*Archivio della Camera Capitolina* and *Archivio del Pronotaro del Senatore*. The second is named *Archivio del Comune Moderno* (1848–) and includes three parts: *Comune Preunitario* (1848–70), *Giunta Provvisoria di Governo* (1870), and *Comune Postunitario* (1871–). A fuller description of the different sections, with a list of the available inventories, is posted at www.archiviocapitolino.it/patrimonio_archivi_elenco.php.

Material of American interest is found in the series *Comune Moderno* (1848) and in *Comune Postunitario* (1871–). An example of the American material found in the section *Comune Postunitario* is provided by the decision of the town council of Rome, which, in mid-December 1918, agreed to confer honorary citizenship on American President Woodrow Wilson (1856–1924) during his visit to Italy in early January 1919.[8]

A further example of the American material is provided by a request that Angelo Annaratone (1844–1922), prefect of Rome, made on behalf of the lawyer Agostino Del Frate. On June 25, 1912, Annaratone wrote to the mayor of Rome, Ernesto Nathan (1845–1921), requesting his authorization of the University of Notre Dame's purchase, which had been made in 1904, of a house located at via dei Cappuccini no. 17.[9] Nathan's affirmative response, dated July 7, 1912, stated that the house bought by Notre Dame could host only six students and that scholars of other nations could not be admitted.[10] The Archives of the

University of Notre Dame contain a large folder concerning this property, which might shed further light on it.

The section *Comune Postunitario* also contains material on the Pontifical North American College. An example is provided by the series *Titolo 61. Campo Verano e Cimiteri* (1871–1922), busta 117, fascicolo 497, pertains to the private chapel that the Pontifical North American College had had at the Verano cemetery since 1874.[11] Of particular interest is the series *Censimento Parrocchiale della Popolazione (1848)*, in the section *Archivio del Comune Moderno Preunitario* (1848–70). In this series is a census from 1848 of the parish of Sant'Andrea delle Fratte; this census indicates the presence of one Jordan Charles, age 16, as an American Catholic student who resided at the Collegio Nazareno, the college founded by Saint José de Calasanz (1557–1648), which opened in 1630 thanks to the generous legacy left by Cardinal Michelangelo Tonti (1566–1622).[12]

BIBLIOGRAPHY

Fiorentino, Daniele, and Matteo Sanfilippo, ed. *Le relazioni fra Stati Uniti e Italia nel periodo di Roma capitale.* Rome: Gangemi, 2008.

Rossini, Daniela. "Americani a Roma nel 1917–19." *Il Veltro* 1–2 (2000): 155–63.

———. "President Wilson and Italy, 1918–1919." *Annales du Monde Anglophone* 14 (2001): 49–59.

———. *Woodrow Wilson and the American Myth in Italy: Culture, Diplomacy and War Propaganda.* Cambridge, Massachusetts: Harvard University Press, 2008.

Sanfilippo, Matteo. "Stranieri e comunità straniere a Roma, 1870–1960." *Archivio della Società romana di storia patria* 134 (2011): 239–52.

Archivio Storico Diplomatico del Ministero degli Affari Esteri /
Diplomatic Archives of the Ministry of Foreign Affairs

Address

Piazzale della Farnesina 1, 00135 Rome

Contact Details

Phone: 39-0636913213

Fax: 39-0636914067

Email: archiviostorico@esteri.it

Website: https://web.esteri.it/archiviostoricodiplomatico

STATUS

Open to researchers; the study room, however, was closed for renovation at the time of this writing, so requested documents were brought to the library. To be granted access and request material, researchers must register online at the website https://web.esteri.it/archivio storicodiplomatico. Registration requires that researchers scan and upload identification, a reference letter, and a permission request from the American Embassy stating the subject of the research. The archives are open Monday–Friday, 9:00 a.m.–2:00 p.m. They close for

Italian national holidays and from the end of July until the end of August. The majority of the material is in Italian.

HISTORY

The early foundations of the archive were laid in 1742, when Carlo Emanuele III of Savoy (1701–73), king of Sardinia, decided that his secretariat of state should have its own archives. With the unification of Italy, the archives of the Ministero degli Affari Esteri were established, though it was only in 1902 that its duties became officially regulated by the Italian government.

DESCRIPTION OF HOLDINGS

At present the archives are divided into five main sections: (1) *Fondi prenunitari*, (2) *Amministrazione Centrale*, (3) *Rappresentanze diplomatiche e consolari*, (4) *Africa*, and (5) *Archivi di personalità*.

Material of American interest is plentifully scattered through various collections of the five sections. The material in the collection *Rappresentanze diplomatiche negli USA* 1848–1901 provides information on two different periods of Italian diplomacy in the United States: The first concerns the activity of the Kingdom of Sardinia's legation and covers the years 1848–61; the second concerns the first period of Italian diplomatic representation in the United States, 1861–1901. A PDF inventory of this collection is posted at www.esteri.it /mae/ministero/servizi/archiviostorico/11washington.pdf.

Further material on Italian diplomatic activity may be found in the collections *Ambasciata d'Italia a Washington, 1901–1909*; *Ambasciata d'Italia a Washington, 1940–1973*; and *Consolati di Chicago, Cleveland, Denver, New Orleans e S. Francisco, 1879–1958*. In the collection of the Italian Embassy in Washington, there is a dossier about the apostolic delegate Diomede Falconio (1842–1917) and the assistance of Italian immigrants.

The above material should be combined with the collection *Affari Politici*, which is divided into four parts that cover the years 1919–1957. PDF inventories are also posted online at the following addresses:

(1) www.esteri.it/mae/ministero/servizi/archiviostorico/1affaripolitici1931-1945.pdf

(2) www.esteri.it/mae/ministero/servizi/archiviostorico/2affaripolitici1946-1950.pdf

This vast collection covers a variety of cultural, diplomatic, political, and religious issues pertaining to the relationships that the United States established with Italy and other countries. One example of the diversity of material in this collection is provided by *Affari Politici, 1931–1945*, *Stati Uniti*, busta no. 21. This collection has sixteen dossiers, of which no. 15, posizione no. 54, deals with Catholic missionaries in the United States and no. 12, posizione no. 53, concerns the American Legion.

In the section *Amministrazione Centrale*, the collection *Z-Contenzioso*, Pos Z 27, busta no. 33, *Stati Uniti 1909–1917* contains details on Italian immigrants during the years 1909–17. A fuller inventory is posted at www.esteri.it/mae/ministero/servizi/archiviostorico/serie _%20z_contenzioso.pdf.

Information on Italian migration to the United States may be found most consistently, however, in the collections *Commissariato generale dell'emigrazione 1901–1927* and *Commissione centrale arbitrale per l'emigrazione 1915–1929*, of which PDF inventories are posted at www.esteri.it/mae/ministero/servizi/archiviostorico/5commissariatogeneraleemigrazione .pdf and www.esteri.it/mae/ministero/servizi/archiviostorico/commissione_centrale _arbitrale.pdf.

BIBLIOGRAPHY

Catani, Patrizia, and Roberto Zuccolini, eds. *I fondi archivistici dei consolati in Chicago, Cleveland, Denver, New Orleans and San Francisco conservati nell'Archivio storico diplomatico*. Rome: Istituto Poligrafico e Zecca dello Stato, 1990.

Colucci, Michele, ed. "La politica migratoria italiani attraverso le fonti governative." Special issue of *Archivio storico dell'emigrazione italiana* 6, no. 1 (2010).

Fogarty, Gerald P. "Archbishop Francis J. Spellman's Visit to Wartime Rome." *Catholic Historical Review* 100, no. 1 (Winter 2014): 72–96.

Ministero degli Affari Esteri, Servizio storico e documentazione. *Inventario della serie Affari Politici 1931–1945*. Rome: Archivio Storico Diplomatico, 1976.

———. *Inventario della serie Affari Politici 1946–1950*. Rome: Archivio Storico Diplomatico, 1977.

Pellegrini, Vincenzo, ed. *Il ministero degli Affari Esteri*. Bologna: Il Mulino, 1992.

Pilotti, Laura. *Il fondo archivistico "serie Z-contenzioso."* Rome: Ministero degli Affari Esteri, 1987.

NOTES

1. Paolo Marella to unknown recipient, March 1922, shelf no. 19, palchetto c, *Miscellanea*, ASSP: "È pieno di Protestanti di ogni setta. Quando vedo i ragazzi per le strade mi fa pena il pensare che gran parte di essi sono eretici. Non c'è qui il chiasso di Roma: gli automobili non suonano la tromba che raramente: il traffico è regolato dai poliziotti."

2. Theodore Roosevelt to Robert Underwood Johnson, January 5, 1906, box 7.2, Archives of the Keats-Shelley House.

3. Harold Woodbury Parson to Harry Nelson Gay, November 21, 1919, box 1.17, Archives of the Keats-Shelley House.

4. Giuseppe Garibaldi to Abraham Lincoln, October 2, 1861, (110/71) 1, Museo Centrale del Risorgimento (MCRR).

5. MCRR, NG VIC22, John R. G. Hassard, *Life of the Most Reverend John Hughes, D.D.: First Archbishop of New York with Extracts from His Private Correspondence* (New York: Appleton, 1866).

6. Fasc. 3bis (anno 1833), b. [busta, or folder] 663, rubr. 298, *Segreteria di Stato, Esteri (parte moderna), 1831–1858*, ASV.

7. Fols. 72–104, fasc. unico [Rappresentanti diplomatici: America], rubr. 279, *Segreteria di Stato, 1848*, ASV.

8. Decision of the municipality of Rome to confer honorary citizenship on the American President Woodrow Wilson, December 12, 1918, fasc. 14, b. 87, *Titolo 18 feste cerimonie e spettacoli, Ripartizione X Antichità e Belle* Arti (1907–1920), Archivio del Comune Postunitario (1871–), Archivio Storico Capitolino (Archives of the City of Rome or ASC).

9. Angelo Annarone to Ernesto Nathan, June 25, 1912, fasc. 113, b. 103, *Titolo 41 Ospizi e Beneficenza (1871–1922)*, Archivio del Comune Postunitario (1871–), ASC.

10. Nathan to Annarone, July 7, 1912, *1912*, fasc. 113, b. 103, *Titolo 41 Ospizi e Beneficenza (1871–1922)*, Archivio del Comune Postunitario (1871–), ASC.

11. Fasc. 497, b. 117, *Titolo 61. Campo Verano e Cimiteri (1871–1922)*, Archivio del Comune Postunitario (1871–), ASC.

12. *Parrocchia di Sant'Andrea delle Fratte, Censimento Parrocchiale della Popolazione (1848)*, 33, Archivio del Comune Moderno Preunitario, (1848–1870), ASC.

CHAPTER 5

Libraries

This chapter contains profiles of the main civic and religious libraries of Rome. One must take into account that each library has its own specific holdings, which, in most cases, still do not have updated and detailed inventories. Due to this, it is likely that some libraries have collections with unknown books or manuscripts of American interest.

Biblioteca Angelica /
Angelica Library
Address
    Piazza di Sant'Agostino 8, 00186 Rome
Contact Details
    Phone: 39-066840801
    Email: b-ange@beniculturali.it
    Website: www.bibliotecaangelica.beniculturali.it/index.php?it/1/home

STATUS
Open to researchers Monday, Friday, and Saturday, 8:15 a.m.–1:45 p.m., and Tuesday–Thursday, 8:15 a.m.–7:00 p.m. From mid-July until early August, the library is open Monday–Saturday, 8:15 a.m.–1:45 p.m. The library closes for Italian national holidays and during the second and third weeks of August. Some form of identification is required, and researchers are advised to consult the online catalog of the manuscripts at manus.iccu .sbn.it//opac_SchedaFondo.php?ID=113.

HISTORY
The Angelica Library was founded by the Augustinian bishop Angelo Rocca (1546–1620), who, in 1605, donated its private collection of volumes to the convent of Saint Augustine. In 1614 the library was opened to the public.

DESCRIPTION OF HOLDINGS

At present the library has a collection of 200,000 volumes, more than 100,000 of which were published between the fifteenth and the nineteenth centuries. Material of American interest mainly concerns the colonial period, particularly Spanish settlements in the Caribbean during the sixteenth and early seventeenth centuries.

BIBLIOGRAPHY

Di Cesare, Francesca. *Catalogo dei manoscritti in scrittura latina datati per indicazione di anno, di luogo o di copista.* Vol. 2: *Biblioteca Angelica.* Turin: Bottega d'Erasmo, 1982.

Fish, Carl Russell. *Guide to the Materials for American History in Roman and Other Italian Archives.* Washington, DC: Carnegie Institution, 1911.

Giorgetti Vichi, Anna Maria. *La biblioteca Angelica: Cenni storici.* Rome: Arti Grafiche f.lli Palombi, 1975.

Sabba, Fiammetta, ed. *Indice degli autori dei manoscritti in scrittura latina della Biblioteca Angelica.* Rome: Istituto Poligrafico e Zecca dello Stato, 2009.

Biblioteca Casanatense /

Casanatense Library

Address

Via Sant'Ignazio 52, 00186 Rome

Contact Details

Phone: 39-066976031

Fax: 39-0669920254

Email: sabina.fiorenzi@beniculturali.it

STATUS

Open to researchers Monday–Friday, 8:15 a.m.–7:15 p.m., and Saturday, 8:15–1:30 p.m. The library closes for Italian national holidays. Because its hours of operation change during the summer, researchers should contact the library in advance.

HISTORY

The Casanatense was originally established in 1701 by Dominicans in the Convent of Santa Maria sopra Minerva. The library was founded on the request of Cardinal Girolamo Casanate (1620–1700), secretary of the Congregation for the Propagation of the Faith (1666–68), and it was opened to the public in 1870. Since 1884, the library has been managed by noneclesiastical staff.

DESCRIPTION OF HOLDINGS

At present the Casanatense Library has a collection of 350,000 printed volumes, 6,000 manuscripts, 2,200 incunabula, 30,000 engravings, 2,000 musical works, 2,000 newspapers, and 70,000 copies of papal bans and edicts dating from the early sixteenth century through 1870.

Several inventories of manuscripts have been posted online: (1) cataloghistorici.bdi.sbn.it /indice_cataloghi.php?OB=Biblioteche_Denominazione&OM=, (2) scaffalidigitali.casanatense .it, and (3) manus.iccu.sbn.it.

Material of American interest is available for the colonial period and the nineteenth century. Concerning the colonial period, the Casanatense Library contains the following items: five letters (MS 367) from Agostino Favoriti, a high official of the Roman Curia, to François de Laval (1623–1708), vicar apostolic of Canada, 1658–74, and bishop of Quebec, 1674–87 (the bishop of Quebec was at that time responsible for the western part of the current United States); a printed dossier on the French and Indian War (MS 5556); an undated manuscript map of North America made by Giovanni Battista Nicolosi (MS 675); and a history of the Jesuits in America (MS 648) by Vincenzo Maria Coronelli (1650–1718), general of the Franciscans from 1701 to 1707.

Amid the material on the nineteenth century, the Casanatense Library contains a small booklet written by Felice Villani, Italian theologian and parish priest of the Church of Our Lady of Loretto in Cold Spring, New Jersey. His work, which was published in 1851 by the printing press of the Congregation for the Propagation of the Faith, provides a vivid account of the state of Catholicism in the United States between the late 1840s and the early 1850s. Speaking of the clergy, Villani stated: "If we throw the eye back, and we consider that in the short space of time that saw the beginning of the American Church, religious orders have taken root and sprouted, everyone will be convinced that the Catholic religion is really respected. It should be added that these convents are not only inhabited by religious strangers, as from the beginning of their foundation, but they are now filling up with American sons and daughters, who will bring with the sanctity of life the most brilliant talents; the clergy has already many American priests and zealous scholars."[1]

Given the immense number of manuscripts this library holds, there is probably additional material of American Catholic interest to be found.

BIBLIOGRAPHY

Ceccopieri, Isabella. *Il fondo manoscritti della Biblioteca Casanatense.* Rome: Palombi, 1988.

Codignola, Luca. "The Casanatense Library." *Annali Accademici Canadesi* 7 (1991): 99–104.

Moneti, Elena, Giovanni Muzzioli, Innocenza Rossi, and Mercedes Zamboni, comps. *Catalogo dei manoscritti della Biblioteca Casanatense.* 6 vols. Rome: Libreria dello Stato, 1949–78s.

Biblioteca dell'Accademia dei Lincei e Corsiniana /

Library of the Accademia dei Lincei e Corsiniana

Address

Via della Lungara 10, 00165 Rome

Contact Details

Phone: 39-06680271

Fax: 39-066893616

Email: segreteria@lincei.it

Website: www.lincei.it/biblioteca

STATUS

Open to researchers Monday, Tuesday, Wednesday, and Friday, 9 a.m.–1 p.m., and Thursday, 9 a.m.–5 p.m. The library closes for Italian national holidays and the whole month of August. Some form of identification is required to gain access to the library. Researchers can consult the online catalog of the manuscripts index at cataloghistorici.bdi.sbn.it/file_viewer .php?IDCAT=19&IDGRP=190001&LEVEL=&PADRE=&PROV=. A fuller description of the holdings can be downloaded as a PDF file at www.lincei.it/files/biblioteca/Guida _patrimonio_documentario.pdf.

HISTORY

The Biblioteca dell'Accademia dei Lincei e Corsiniana is the result of the merging of two libraries: that of the Accademia dei Lincei, founded in 1603 by the Italian scientist Federico Cesi (1585–1630), and that of the Corsini family, which was initially established by Cardinal Neri Corsini (1624–79) and developed by his nephew Cardinal Lorenzo Corsini (1652–1740), who became Pope Clement XII in 1730. In 1883 the Corsini family donated its private library to the Accademia dei Lincei, merging the two libraries.

DESCRIPTION OF HOLDINGS

At present the Biblioteca dell'Accademia dei Lincei e Corsiniana consists of two broad sections: (1) *sezioni principali della biblioteca* and (2) *Fondi archivistici e collezioni librarie particolari*. The former is further subdivided into three main subsections: (a) *sezione Accademica*, (b) *sezione Corsiniana*, and (c) *sezione Orientale*. The latter contains a series of archival collections, mainly of correspondence exchanged by the most prominent members of the Accademia dei Lincei from the early seventeenth century to the second half of the twentieth.

Material of American interest is related to the colonial period, and in particular to the Spanish colonies in Central and South America. In the *Fondi archivistici*, the *Fondo Volterra* contains the correspondence that Vito Volterra (1860–1940), an Italian physicist, exchanged with the mathematician Griffith Conrad Evans (1887–1973) and the astronomer George Ellery Hale (1868–1938), both from the United States.

BIBLIOGRAPHY

Fish, Carl Russell. *Guide to the Materials for American History in Roman and Other Italian Archives*. Washington, DC: Carnegie Institution, 1911.

Pinto, Olga. *Storia della Biblioteca Corsiniana e della Biblioteca dell'Accademia dei Lincei*. Florence: Olschki, 1956.

Biblioteca Nazionale Centrale di Roma /

Rome's National Central Library

Address

    Viale Castro Pretorio 105, 00185 Rome

Contact Details
    Phone: 39-0649891
    Fax: 39-064457635
    Email 1: bnc-rm@beniculturali.it
    Email 2: autom@bnc.roma.sbn.it
    Website: www.bncrm.beniculturali.it

STATUS
Open to researchers Monday–Friday, 8:30 a.m.–7:00 p.m., and Saturday, 8:30 a.m.–1:30 p.m. The library closes for national holidays and during the second and third weeks of August. Researchers should consult the online catalog of manuscripts, available at www.bncrm .beniculturali.it/it/7/cataloghi-storici-digitalizzati, for the precise call numbers of the material they wish to consult.

HISTORY
The Biblioteca Nazionale Centrale di Roma was officially established on March 14, 1876; it incorporated the series preserved in suppressed Roman congregations at the time of the Italian unification.

DESCRIPTION OF HOLDINGS
At present the library has a collection of over seven million printed books, 8,000 manuscripts, 120,000 autographs, 2,000 incunabula, 25,000 editions from the sixteenth century, 20,000 maps, 10,000 photos and drawings, 50,000 newspapers, and 34,000 doctoral theses.

    Material of American interest is found in the manuscript section named *Fondo Gesuitico*, which contains 1,752 manuscripts originally preserved by the Collegio Romano, the Casa Professa del Gesù, and other Jesuit institutions of Rome that were confiscated during the Italian Risorgimento. In particular, this collection contains the following manuscripts: (1) nos. 1253 and 1255, with information on the Jesuit missions in the Americas; (2) no. 1331, titled "USA Missouri, *celebrazione dell'80° anniversario di Pio IX* (Celebrations of the 80th anniversary of Pius IX)"; and (3) no. 1363, dossier no. 4, with various letters written by Felice De Andreis (1778–1820) from 1816 to 1818. De Andreis was a Vincentian missionary who, from 1818 to 1820, operated in the area of Saint Louis, Missouri, where he successfully established the first house of the Congregation of the Mission in the United States.

BIBLIOGRAPHY
Codignola, Luca. *Guide to Documents Relating to French and British North America in the Archives of the Sacred Congregation "de Propaganda Fide" in Rome, 1622–1799*. Ottawa: National Archives of Canada, 1991.
I fondi, le procedure, le storie: Raccolta di studi della Biblioteca. Rome: Tipografia della Biblioteca Nazionale Centrale, 1993.

Ricciardelli, Raffaele. *Vita del servo di Dio Felice de Andreis: Fondatore e primo superiore della Congregazione della Missione negli Stati Uniti d'America*. Rome: Industria Tipografica Romana, 1923.

Tentori, Tullio. "I manoscritti di interesse americanistico esistenti nelle biblioteche ed archivi italiani: I manoscritti della Biblioteca Nazionale Centrale di Roma." Accademia Nazionale dei Lincei, *Rendiconti della Classe di Scienze Morali, Storiche e Filologiche* 8, no. 5–6 (1952): 263–77.

Biblioteca della Pontificia Università Urbaniana /
Library of the Pontifical Urban University

Address

Via Urbano VIII 16, 00120 Vatican City

Contact Details

Phone: 39-0669889676

Fax: 39-0669889663

Email: biblioteca@urbaniana.edu

Website: iscrizioni.urbaniana.edu/Urbaniana/Biblioteca/default.aspx

STATUS

Closed as of July 2016. When the library opens, researchers should check the online catalog (posted at dc03kg0172eu.hosted.exlibrisgroup.com/F?RN=288325713) for the call numbers of desired materials. Most American material is in English.

HISTORY

The library was established in 1627, when the college was founded. In December 1667 Pope Clement IX (1600–69) issued the brief *Conservazioni et manutenzioni librorum bibliothecae Collegi de Propaganda Fide*, which prohibited the removal of books from the library. In 1979 the library of the Urbaniana was merged with that of Propaganda Fide.

DESCRIPTION OF HOLDINGS

At present the library has a collection of 350,000 printed volumes, 12 incunabula, 1,350 books of the sixteenth century, and 3,000 volumes organized in the special collections. The library also holds 50,000 microfiche that come from the following archives: (1) Council for World Mission Archives, 1775–1940; (2) Wesleyan Methodist Missionary Society (London); and (3) IMC/CBMS Archive, Primitive Methodist Missionary Society (London).

Given its concern with Catholic and Protestant world missions from the early sixteenth century on, the library has a very rich collection of worldwide missionary history and of theology from the early sixteenth century until the first decades of the twentieth. Material of American interest consists of various items, such as collections of decrees from diocesan synods, doctoral theses, printed books, and pamphlets. This collection contains, for instance, printed copies of items discussed at the diocesan synods held in New York in 1842.[2]

BIBLIOGRAPHY
Henkel, Willi. "Die Päpstiliche Missionbibliothek der Kongregation für die Evangelisierung der Völker." *Zeitschrift für Missionswissenschaft und Religionswissenschaft* 70 (1986): 261–65.

Biblioteca Vallicelliana /
Vallicelliana Library
Address
   Piazza della Chiesa Nuova 18, 00186 Rome
Contact Details
   Phone: 39-0668802671
   Fax: 39-066893868
   Email: b-vall.servizi@beniculturali.it
   Website: www.vallicelliana.it/index.php?it/94/informazioni

STATUS
Open to researchers Monday, Tuesday, and Friday, 8:15 a.m.–1:30 p.m., and Wednesday and Thursday, 8:15 a.m.–7:15 p.m. On Saturday the library is open 8:15 a.m.–11:30 a.m., although only material previously reserved can be consulted. The library closes for Italian national holidays and the second and third weeks of August. Some form of identification is required to access the library; researchers desiring to consult the manuscript section should make an appointment and bring a reference letter.

HISTORY
The Biblioteca Vallicelliana was established in 1565 by Saint Philip Neri (1515–95). The first collection consisted of Neri's personal books. In 1595 this collection was given to the Congregation of the Oratory, the missionary society Neri had founded in 1575.

DESCRIPTION OF HOLDINGS
At present the Biblioteca Vallicelliana has a collection of almost 130,000 printed books, incunabula, and manuscripts, with a strong general focus on ecclesiastical history. Most material relating to the Americas concerns the Spanish colonies during the sixteenth and early seventeenth centuries. MS no. S-43, fol. 590, contains a reference to the first voyage of Martin Frobisher (1535/1539–94) to what is now northeastern Canada. Additional material on the colonial Americas may be found in MSS G 47, K 13, K 102, K 104, M 13–14, and R 55. Given the abundant material preserved by the Vallicelliana, there is most likely additional material of American interest.

BIBLIOGRAPHY
Codignola, Luca. *Guide to Documents Relating to French and British North America in the Archives of the Sacred Congregation "de Propaganda Fide," in Rome, 1622–1799.* Ottawa: National Archives of Canada, 1991.

Fish, Carl Russell. *Guide to the Materials for American History in Roman and Other Italian Archives.* Washington, DC: Carnegie Institution, 1911.

Vichi, Anna Maria Giorgetti and Sergio Mottironi, eds. *Catalogo dei manoscritti della Biblioteca Vallicelliana.* Rome: Istituto Poligrafico dello Stato, 1961.

Biblioteca della Facoltà Valdese di Teologia /
Library of the Waldensian Faculty of Theology
Address
    Via Pietro Cossa 44, 00193 Rome
Contact Details
    Phone: 39-063204768
    Fax: 39-063201040
    Email: biblioteca@facoltavaldese.org; biblioteca.ill_dd@facoltavaldese.org
    Website: facoltavaldese.org/it/Biblioteca

STATUS

Open to researchers Monday–Friday, 9:00 a.m.–5:00 p.m.; hours of operation change during the month of August and on national holidays. The majority of the material is written in English or Italian.

HISTORY

The origin of the Waldensian Church goes back to the merchant Pietro Valdo (1140–1206), who, during the late decades of the twelfth century, became the key figure of a movement that emphasized the priesthood (and preaching) of all believers and the complete rejection of material wealth. From the thirteenth century to the fourteenth, the Waldensians experienced such severe persecution that very few survived in southern Europe. In 1532 the Waldensians joined the community of the Protestant churches of the Reformation, although they continued to be persecuted and their presence remained confined to the Cottian Alps. Despite the edict issued on February 17, 1848, by Carlo Alberto of Savoia (1798–1849), the Piedmontese king of Sardinia from 1831 to 1849, granting them freedom of religion, many Waldensians emigrated to North and South America.

DESCRIPTION OF HOLDINGS

The holdings of the Library of the Waldensian Faculty of Theology include material on Alessandro Gavazzi (1809–89), a former Barnabite who became a chaplain in the army of Giuseppe Garibaldi (1807–82) and one of the most prominent preachers in Italy from the late 1840s on. In 1870 he became one of the founders and the leader of the Free Italian Church.

    Material of American interest is found in two places. The first is a collection of lectures Gavazzi gave during his visit to the United States, where he remained from early March of 1853 to early January of 1854.[3] The second is a printed letter that William Jay Haskett sent to Gavazzi in mid-May 1853 about the American Temperance organizations. In it Haskett warned Gavazzi:

Your attack upon the Temperance organization of this country was uncalled for, impolitic and ungenerous, and nothing but the burning furor of a heart, maddened by apostasy, can be offered as an apology for so great a wrong to my country. I am an American by birth, and for the last quarter of a century, a humble member of most of these organizations. I know almost every member of note in the Temperance ranks in this country; many of them are my personal friends, and I tell you that I never saw the hand of Jesuitism in any of our organizations. To say that they control them, or that their tendencies are Jesuitical, is perfectly ridiculous.[4]

Further material on Gavazzi's visit to the United States may be found at the Archivio Storico della Tavola Valdese, located in Torre Pellice, fifty-two kilometers west of Turin, in the Piedmont region. The archive is open Tuesday–Thursday, 9:00 a.m.–1:00 p.m. and 2:00 p.m.–6:00 p.m., and on Friday, 9:00 a.m.–1:00 p.m.; it is closed from Christmas Day until January 6. Interested researchers should contact the head of the archive, Dr. Chiara Ballesio, at segreteria@studivaldesi.org or at tvarchivio@chiesavaldese.org. The archive contains the incomplete autobiography of Gavazzi's life, section no. 4 of which describes his journey to and activity in North America. Of particular interest is the part in which Gavazzi writes of Gaetano Bedini (1806–64), the first apostolic delegate sent to the United States, that "his martyrdom is in New York. Bedini had no longer a truce. Anywhere he went, the not-at-all-flattering celebrations of the freemen waited for him."[5] Additional material on Gavazzi's experience in North America is found in the Vatican Secret Archives, the archives of Propaganda, and the library of the Archivio di Stato of Rome.[6]

BIBLIOGRAPHY

D'Agostino, Peter R. *Rome in America: Transnational Catholic Ideology from the Risorgimento to Fascism.* Chapel Hill: University of North Carolina Press, 2004.

Monsagrati, Giuseppe. "Gavazzi, Antonio (in religione Alessandro)." In *Dizionario biografico degli Italiani* 52:719–22. Rome: Istituto della Enciclopedia Italiana, 1999.

Sanfilippo, Matteo. "Alessandro Gavazzi: Oltre l'Italia, l'America." In *Studi Barnabiti* 28 (2011): 245–67.

———. "'Questa mia missione così piena di rose e spine': Il viaggio di Monsignor Gaetano Bedini (1853–1854)." *Miscellanea di Storia delle Esplorazioni* 17 (1992): 171–88.

———. "Tra antipapismo e cattolicesimo: Gli echi della Repubblica romana e i viaggi in Nord America di Gaetano Bedini e Alessandro Gavazzi (1853–1854)." In *Gli Americani e la Repubblica Romana nel 1849*, ed. Sara Antonelli, Daniele Fiorentino, and Giuseppe Monsagrati, 159–88. Rome: Gangemi, 2001.

Santini, Luigi. "Alessandro Gavazzi e l'emigrazione politico-religiosa in Inghilterra e negli Stati Uniti nel decennio 1849–1859." *Rassegna storica del risorgimento* 41 (1954): 587–94.

Sylvain, Philippe. *Alessandro Gavazzi (1809–1899): Clerc, garibaldien, prédicant des deux mondes.* Quebec: Le Centre Pédagogique, 1962.

NOTES

1. *Cenni istorici del progresso del cattolicesimo negli Stati Uniti di America e segnatamente nella diocesi di Nuova York scritti dal teologo Felice Villanis, parroco della chiesa della Madonna di Loreto in Cold Spring nella stessa diocesi e dedicati a Sua Eminenza il Cardinale Giacomo Filippo Fransoni prefetto della Sacra Congregazione de Propaganda Fide* (Rome: Coi Tipi della S. C. de Propaganda Fide, 1851), 23: "Se poi gettiamo l'occhio indietro, e confrontiamo come nel breve spazio di tempo che scorse dal principio della Chiesa Americana, gli ordini religiosi abbiano preso radice e germogliato, ognuno sarà convinto che la Religione Cattolica vi è veramente rispettata. Si aggiunga poi che questi conventi non vengono già abitati solo dai religiosi forestieri, come dal principio della loro fondazione, ma ora vanno riempiendosi di figli e figlie americane, che vi portano colla santità della vita i talenti i più brillanti; Il clero parimenti già conta molti sacerdoti americani zelanti e dotti."

2. *Synodus dioecesana Neo-Eboracensis prima habita anno MDCCCXLII* (New York: Typis Georgii Mitchell, 1842).

3. *Gavazzi Alessandro: The Lectures Complete of Father Giovanni Gavazzi Reported by an Eminent Stenographer, and Revised and Corrected by Gavazzi Himself; Including Translations of the Italian Addresses with Which the Greater Part of the Lectures Were Prefaced* (New York: W. Dodd, 1854).

4. *Letter to Alessandro Gavazzi by William Jay Haskett on Temperance Organizations* (New York: W. H. White, 1853), 1–11.

5. Fol. 31, fasc. 8, Parte IV, *Carte Alessandro Gavazzi*, Archivio Storico della Tavola Valdese: "il suo martirio è in New-York. Il Bedini non ebbe più tregua. Ovunque andasse, lo aspettavano le dimostrazioni niente lusinghiere dei liberi."

6. Fols. 14–15, 43–48, 57–82, 180, fasc. 2, rubr. 251, *Segreteria di Stato, 1854*, ASV; fol. 1831rv, vol. 118, *Udienze*, 1853, Part 2, APF; *Diario Autobiografico di Alessandro Gavazzi*, Biblioteca dell'Archivio di Stato di Roma (Library of the Archives of the State of Rome), MS 504.

CHAPTER 6

Sources for the History
of Italian Immigration
to the United States

This chapter consists of profiles of archives of regular orders and religious institutions in Rome that contain material particularly focused on Italian immigrants in the United States. With the exception of the Archivio Generale Scalabriniano and the Archivio Storico Salesiano, however, the archives described in this chapter were closed at the time of this writing. One of them, the Archivio del Prelato per l'Emigrazione, is being reorganized.

Archivio del Pontificio Consiglio della Pastorale per i Migranti e gli Itineranti /
Archives of the Pontifical Council for the Pastoral Care of Migrants and Itinerant People
Address
    Palazzo San Calisto, 00120 Vatican City
Contact Details
    Phone: 39-0669887131
    Fax: 39-0669887111
    Website: pcmigrants.org

STATUS
Closed.

HISTORY
An increase in European immigration to North America convinced Pope Saint Pius X (1835–1914) of the need to coordinate various efforts to support the immigrants. In 1908 the Segreteria di Stato collected a vast file of information about the immigrants, particularly about the Italian immigrants. (This file is in *Archivio Segreto Vaticano, Segreteria di Stato,*

Età contemporanea, 1914, rubrica 18, fascicoli 3–11.) Three years later, Pius X enjoined all the Italian bishops to protect the departing faithful (*Acta Apostolicae Sedis,* III, 1911, pp. 513–15). For its part, the Congregazione Concistoriale began to draft specific questions about the issue of immigration for all bishops engaged in *ad limina* visitations. Furthermore, the Congregazione Concistoriale advised the pope to establish a charitable institute for the immigrants in all dioceses. In the dioceses, the bishops' task was twofold—to support immigrants and to gather information about them. To coordinate the network of charitable institutes, in 1912 Pius X established the Ufficio per la cura spirituale degli emigranti, a special section of the Congregazione Concistoriale. This was the first body of the papal curia devoted to immigration. Archbishop Pietro Pisani (1871–1960), the first prelate in charge, had jurisdiction all over the Catholic world and supervised immigrants from all continents to prevent conflicts in the dioceses of arrival.

The beginning of World War I arrested the development of the Ufficio per la Cura Spirituale degli Emigranti, and the immigrant situation worsened through World Wars I and II with the rise of totalitarian regimes, the Great Crisis of 1929, and the closing of borders in countries, like the United States, that had traditionally welcomed immigrants. The experience that the Ufficio per la Cura Spirituale degli Emigranti gained between 1908 and 1914, however, laid the groundwork for its restoration. In 1952 the apostolic constitution *Exsul Familia* set new rules for the spiritual assistance to immigrants and confirmed the Congregazione Concistoriale's jurisdiction over a new organization, renamed the Consiglio Superiore per l'Emigrazione. The Second Vatican Council renewed interest in the problems of immigrants. In 1967 Pope Paul VI (1897–1978) transformed the Congregazione Concistoriale into the Congregazione dei Vescovi; in 1970 Paul VI established the Pontificia Commissione per la Cura Spirituale dei Migranti e degli Itineranti within the Congregazione dei Vescovi. In 1988 the commissione was renamed Pontificio Consiglio della Pastorale per i Migranti e gli Itineranti and was given the task of caring for immigrants, Roma people, nomads, and sailors.

DESCRIPTION OF HOLDINGS
The archives of the Pontificio Consiglio della Pastorale per i Migranti e gli Itineranti contain documents from 1912 onward pertaining to immigration on a global level. So far, few researchers have had the opportunity to consult this material, but the findings of those who have provide a good sense of the possibilities these archives offer. Material of American interest is particularly plentiful for the first quarter of the twentieth century, with files on Italian, Polish, and other immigrants in several US dioceses. The archives also contain files on the European priests who were sent to the United States to work among their countrymen and on the establishment of immigrants' associations.

BIBLIOGRAPHY
De Dominicis, Claudio. "Archivio del Pontificio Consiglio per la Pastorale dei Migranti e Itineranti." *Studi Emigrazione/Emigration Studies* 120 (1996): 722–24.

Tomasi, Silvano M. "Fede e patria: The 'Italica Gens' in the United States and Canada, 1908–1936." *Studi Emigrazione/Emigration Studies* 103 (1991): 319–40.

Archivio del Prelato per l'Emigrazione /
Archives of the Prelate for Italian Emigration

Address

    Fondazione Migrantes, Conferenza Episcopale Italiana, Via Aurelia 796, 00165 Rome

Contact Details

    Phone: 39-066617901

    Fax: 39-0666179070

    Email: r.iaria@migrantes.it

    Website: www.migrantes.it

STATUS

Closed at the time of this writing. The archives are being reorganized.

HISTORY

The establishment of the Ufficio per gli Emigranti in the Congregazione Concistoriale was expected to improve coordination with the Opera di Assistenza per gli Italiani Emigrati in Europa (later called the Opera Bonomelli), which had been founded in 1900 by Geremia Bonomelli (1831–1914), bishop of Cremona from 1871 to 1914. It must be noted that Archbishop Pietro Pisani, the first secretary of the Ufficio per gli Emigranti, cooperated with Bonomelli in supporting Italian immigrants to Europe. In 1914 the Pontificio Collegio per l'Emigrazione was established to train diocesan clergy to assist Italian immigrants all over the world. Due to the onset of World War I in 1914, the opening of the college was delayed until 1920. In that same year, Ferdinando Rodolfi (1866–1943), bishop of Vicenza from 1911 to 1943, resigned from Opera Bonomelli, of which he was honorary president and one of the key figures; in doing so, he also left his post as director of the college. The Holy See appointed as the new director Michele Cerrati (1884–1925), bishop of Lydda from 1920 to 1925, who thus became the highest prelate for matters concerning Italian emigration. The rise of the Fascist regime interrupted this reorganization, though, and the jurisdiction of the Holy See over immigration matters became severely limited. Additionally, the Opera Bonomelli was closed; all its activities were taken over by the Scalabrinian missionaries, who were active both in the Americas and in Europe. After World War II, the Pontificio Collegio was entrusted to the Scalabrinians, who in 1963 established within it the Centro di Studi Emigrazione.

DESCRIPTION OF HOLDINGS

Starting in 1949, the archives of the Prelato per l'Emigrazione were hosted by the Scalabrinians in their general archive; the archives were later transferred to the Fondazione Migrantes, where they are presently being reorganized, with a view to reopening. When the archives were housed by the Scalabrinians, they held about 1,500 files, mainly containing accounts of work done by Scalabrinians for Italian immigrants in Europe and the Americas. Of these files, 182 pertained strictly to the United States.

BIBLIOGRAPHY
Ostuni, Maria Rosaria. "Archivio del Prelato per l'Emigrazione Italiana." *Studi Emigrazione/Emigration Studies* 124 (1996): 698–99.
Perotti, Antonio. *Il Pontificio Collegio per l'Emigrazione Italiana, 1920–1970.* Rome: Pontificio Collegio per l'Emigrazione, 1970.
Tomasi, Silvano M. "L'assistenza religiosa agli italiani in USA e il Prelato per l'Emigrazione Italiana 1920–1949." *Studi Emigrazione/Emigration Studies* 66 (1982): 167–89.

Archivio Generale Scalabriniano /
General Archives of the Scalabrinians
Address
Via Calandrelli 11, 00153 Rome
Contact Details
Phone: 39-0658331135
Fax: 39-065803808
Email: segreteriacs@gmail.com
Website: www.scalabrini.org/site/contatti

STATUS
Open Monday–Friday, 9:00 a.m.–5:00 p.m. An appointment is required.

HISTORY
In 1886 the Congregation "de Propaganda Fide" gave to Giovanni Battista Scalabrini (1839–1905), bishop of Piacenza from 1875 to 1905 and cardinal from 1876 to 1905, the task of founding an institute with two key aims: (1) to provide assistance to Italian immigrants in the Americas and (2) to train missionaries to work among the communities of these Italian immigrants. Pope Leo XIII (1810–1903) approved the project on November 25, 1887, and he brought it to the attention of the overseas bishops on December 10, 1888, through the encyclical *Quam aerumnosa.*

Although initially this project was conceived as a five-year effort focusing on Italian immigrants in Brazil and the United States, the pope and the curia soon recognized the need to pay more attention to all immigrants, rather than to Italian immigrants only. Due to a lack of success that beset the priests of Opera Bonomelliana in their work with Italian immigrants, the Scalabrinians progressively extended their activity beyond the Americas and began to work in Europe, Asia, and Australia. They did not limit themselves only to Italians but assisted other immigrants as well, particularly Polish immigrants in the United States.

In the second half of the twentieth century, the Scalabrinians sought to analyze immigration; To that end, they established eight research centers in Rome, Basel, Buenos Aires, Cape Town, Manila, New York, Paris, and São Paulo. Rome's research center, located at 58 via Dandolo, is open to researchers. It shelves over 50,000 books and two hundred academic journals and is open Monday–Wednesday, 9:00 a.m.–12:30 p.m. and 1 p.m.–3:20 p.m., and on Thursday, 1:00 p.m–3:20 p.m. An appointment is required. Contact details are as follows: phone, 39-065809764; fax, 39-065814651; and email, biblioteca@cser.it.

DESCRIPTION OF HOLDINGS

The Archivio Generale Scalabriniano can be divided generally into four key thematic sections: (1) material pertaining to Scalabrini's life and activity and the process of his beatification; (2) documents on the general government of the congregation, including the rules of the individual provinces; (3) documents pertaining to the provinces of the congregation, with material on individual houses and missionary residences; and (4) files on the congregation's members, living and dead. The material is arranged alphabetically in twenty-two series.

Material of American interest abounds and may be found in several series. Of particular interest is series A, *Monsignor Giovanni Battista Scalabrini*, which contains Scalabrini's correspondence with bishops and priests, and therefore includes letters written by the earliest missionaries to arrive in the United States. Another relevant series is E, *Direzioni di Province e di Delegazioni*, which contains material on the province of San Carlo, which includes the eastern parts of Canada and the United States, and the province of San Giovanni Battista, which includes the western parts.

BIBLIOGRAPHY

Brown, Mary Elizabeth. *From Italian Villages to Greenwich Village: Our Lady of Pompei, 1892–1992.* Center for Migration Studies, 1992.
———. *The Scalabrinians in North America (1887–1934).* New York: Center for Migration Studies, 1996.
———, ed. *A Migrant Missionary Story: The Autobiography of Giacomo Gambera.* New York: Center for Migration Studies, 1994.
Caliaro, Marco, and Mario Francesconi. *John Baptist Scalabrini, Apostle to Emigrants.* New York: Center for Migration Studies, 1977.
Francesconi, Mario. *Giovanni Battista Scalabrini vescovo di Piacenza e degli emigranti.* Rome: Città Futura, 1985.
Parolin, Gaetano, and Antonio Lovatin, eds. *L'ecclesiologia di Scalabrini.* Vatican City: Urbaniana University Press, 2007.
Rosoli, Gianfausto. "Archivio dei Missionari di S. Carlo (Scalabriniani)." *Studi Emigrazione/Emigration Studies* 120 (December 1995): 729–34.
———. "Archivio dei Missionari di S. Carlo (Scalabriniani)." *Studi Emigrazione/Emigration Studies* 124 (December 1996): 693–97.
———, ed. *Scalabrini fra Vecchio e Nuovo Mondo: Atti del Convegno Storico Internazionale (Piacenza, 3–5 dicembre 1987).* Rome: CSER, 1989.

Signor, Lice Maria. *John Baptist Scalabrini and Italian Migration: A Socio-Pastoral Project.* New York: Center for Migration Studies, 1994.

Terragni, Giovanni, ed. *P. Angelo Chiariglione missionario scalabriniano "Itinerante."* Naples: Autorinediti, 2014.

———. *Scalabrini e la congregazione dei missionari per gli emigrati: Aspetti istituzionali 1887–1905.* Naples: Autorinediti, 2014.

Tomasi, Silvano M., ed. *For the Love of Immigrants: Migration Writings and Letters of Bishop John Baptist Scalabrini (1839–1905).* New York: Center for Migration Studies, 2000.

———. *A Scalabrinian Mission among Polish Immigrants in Boston, 1893–1909.* New York: Center for Migration Studies, 1986.

Tomasi, Silvano M., and Gianfausto Rosoli, eds. *Scalabrini e le migrazioni moderne: Scritti e carteggi.* Turin: SEI, 1997.

Zizzamia, Alba. *A Vision Unfolding: The Scalabrinians in North America (1888–1988).* New York: Center for Migration Studies, 1989.

Archivio Salesiano Centrale /
General Archives of the Salesians
Address
> Via della Pisana 1111, 00163 Rome

Contact Details
> Phone: 39-06656121
> Fax: 39-066561255
> Email: lcei@sdb.org
> Website: www.sangiovannibosco.net/index.php?id=archivio-salesiano-centrale

STATUS
The archives are open Monday–Friday, 8:30 a.m.–12:30 p.m. and close for Italian national holidays and from mid-July until the end of September. Contact the archivist in advance and fill out a request form to be granted access to the material. A reference letter is also required. Material post-1939 cannot be consulted.

HISTORY
The Salesians are a male religious congregation founded in 1859 by Saint Giovanni Melchiorre Bosco (1815–88) to provide assistance and education to destitute children. The congregation was officially approved by Pius IX on June 23, 1864. From the early 1870s the Salesians served as missionaries in the Americas—first in Argentina, where the Salesians arrived in 1875, and then in the United States, where they established themselves in 1896.

DESCRIPTION OF HOLDINGS
The earliest origins of the Archivio Salesiano Centrale go back to 1885, when Don Gioacchino Berto (1847–1914), secretary to Don Bosco, was mentioned as archivist for the

group of clerics who took part in the general chapter. In 1946 the archives began to be organized, and in 1972 they were transferred from Turin to Rome. In 1985 the general rules of the Archivio Salesiano Generale were officially approved.

The Archivio Salesiano Centrale consists of three sections: (1) *Archivio Storico*, (2) *Archivio Corrente*, and (3) *Archivio Fotografico*. *Archivio Storico* is subdivided into thirty-two series containing a wide array of documents on Don Bosco, the activity of the congregation (inside and outside of the Italian peninsula), the personnel, and the missions established all over the world.

Material of American interest is mainly to be found in the series *Fondo Case Salesiane* (*Documenti*) F380-F737 and *Fondo Case Salesiane* (*Cronache*) F740-F963. These two series contain information about the Salesians' activity in the parish church of Saints Peter and Paul of San Francisco, where they were active from 1896 onward, and in the parish churches of Maria Ausiliatrice and Trasfigurazione of New York, where they were active, respectively, since 1898 and 1902. These two series also provide information about the Salesians' work in the following American parish churches and high schools: (1) the high school of New Rochelle, New York; (2) the parish church of San Antonio of Paterson, New Jersey; (3) the parish church of Rosario in Port Chester, New York; (4) the parish church of Corpus Christi in Port Chester; (5) the parish church of San Giuseppe in Oakland, California; (6) the parish church of Maria Ausiliatrice in Oakland; (7) the parish church of Corpus Christi in San Francisco; (8) the parish church of Saint Patrick in Los Angeles; and (9) the parish church of Saint Elizabeth Ann Seton in San Antonio, Texas.

It must be noted that certain parish churches, such as that of San Giuseppe in Oakland, are no longer in the congregation's hands, and that others, such as Maria Ausiliatrice of the same city, passed from the care of the Italian Salesians to their Portuguese confreres.

BIBLIOGRAPHY
Cei, Luigi. "Archivio Salesiano Centrale." *Studi Emigrazione/Emigration Studies* 124 (December 1996): 700–702.
Motto, Francesco. *Vita e azione della parrocchia nazionale salesiana dei ss. Pietro e Paolo a San Francisco (1897–1930): Da colonia di paesani a comunità italiana.* Rome: Las, 2010.
———, ed. *Insediamenti e iniziative salesiane dopo Don Bosco: Saggi di Storiografia; Atti del 2° Convegno-seminario di storia dell'Opera Salesiana.* Rome: Libreria Ateneo Salesiano, 1996.
Rosoli, Gianfausto. "Impegno missionario e assistenza agli emigranti nella visione e nell'opera di Don Bosco e dei Salesiani." In *Don Bosco nella storia della cultura popolare*, ed. Francesco Traniello, 289–330. Turin: SEI, 1987.

Pontificia Commissione di Assistenza /
Pontifical Aid Commission

STATUS
Closed.

HISTORY

The Pontificia Opera di Assistenza (POA) was officially established by Pope Pius XII (1876–1958) in 1944. After it closed in 1970, its material was transferred to the Fondazione Caritas, which also took over its institutional tasks. In 2009 the POA archives, then housed on the Via della Conciliazione, were handed over to the Vatican Secret Archives. Their material has since been reorganized but cannot be consulted because it pertains chronologically to the pontificate of Pius XII (see the Vatican Secret Archives entry).

DESCRIPTION OF HOLDINGS

It seems that the POA files preserve some material concerning American support of the organization. In fact, the POA was supported by the National Catholic Welfare Conference, thanks also to the intercession of Msgr. Andrew P. Landi, who from Rome directed Catholic Relief Services, which was established by the American bishops. Amid the POA material, correspondence between Msgr. Landi and the Vatican officials on the US funds and overseas relocation of refugees appears to be of special significance. Msgr. Landi also corresponded with the officials who liaised between the POA and several national committees.

It must be noted that the correspondence between Msgr. Landi and the Austrian and German committees is in part contained in the Hudal Papers at the Archives of the Pontifical Institute of Santa Maria dell'Anima (see entry).

At present, the few available details indicate that the POA material, once accessible, will provide relevant information on the Italian diaspora after World War II. This material will continue to shed light on the world of the refugees, Italian and otherwise, who sought to cross the ocean from the late 1950s through the 1970s.

BIBLIOGRAPHY

Di Giovanni, Claudia. "In primo piano la solidarietà con la guerra sullo sfondo." *L'Osservatore Romano*, November 15, 2009, www.vatican.va/news_services/or/or_quo/cultura/265q04d1.html.

Giovagnoli, Agostino. "La Pontificia Commissione di Assistenza e gli aiuti americani, 1945–1948." *Storia Contemporanea* 9, no. 5–6 (1978): 1081–1111.

Gobetti, Erik, ed. *La lunga liberazione 1943–1945*. Milan: Franco Angeli, 2007.

Violi, Roberto. "La Pontificia commissione assistenza nel Sud degli anni Quaranta." *Giornale di storia contemporanea* 1 (1999): 58–88.

Select Bibliography

To aid researchers making use of this guide, we have assembled a select bibliography of relevant books and articles, broken into four categories: other guides to Roman archives, inventories of key collections in Rome, descriptions of archives and libraries in and beyond Rome, and published documentary sources for US Catholic history.

This bibliography does not include specific descriptions of the archives that are found in two monographic issues of *Studi Emigrazione/Migration Studies,* published in 1995 and 1996.

GUIDES

Blouin, Francis X., ed. *Vatican Archives: An Inventory and Guide to Historical Documents of the Holy See.* New York: Oxford University Press, 1998.

Carboni, Luigi. "Gli archivi delle Rappresentanze Pontificie nell'Archivio Segreto Vaticano: versamenti e nuovi ordinamenti." In *Religiosa Archivorum Custodia: IV Centenario della Fondazione dell'Archivio Segreto Vaticano (1612–2012): Atti del Convegno di Studi, Città del Vaticano, 17–18 aprile 2012,* 273–304. Vatican City: Vatican Secret Archives, 2015.

Codignola, Luca. "The Casanatense Library." *Annali Accademici Canadesi* 7 (1991): 99–104.

Fish, Carl Russell. *Guide to the Materials for American History in Roman and Other Italian Archives.* Washington, DC: Carnegie Institution, 1911.

Haskins, Charles H. "The Vatican Secret Archives." *American Historical Review* 2, no. 1 (October 1896): 40–58.

Kowalsky, Nikolaus, OMI, and Josef Metzler, OMI. *Inventory of the Historical Archives of the Congregation for the Evangelization of Peoples or "de Propaganda Fide."* 3rd ed. Rome: Pontificia Universitas Urbaniana, 1988.

Tentori, Tullio. "I manoscritti di interesse americanistico esistenti nelle biblioteche ed archivi italiani: I manoscritti della Biblioteca Nazionale Centrale di Roma." Accademia Nazionale dei Lincei, *Rendiconti della Classe di Scienze Morali, Storiche e Filologiche* 8, nos. 5–6 (1952): 263–77.

INVENTORIES

Codignola, Luca. *Calendar of Documents Relating to North America (Canada and the United States) in the Archives of the Sacred Congregation "de Propaganda Fide" in Rome, 1622–1846.* Rev. ed., 6 vols. Ottawa: Library and Archives of Canada and the Research Centre for Religious History in Canada of Saint Paul University, 2012.

———. *Guide to Documents Relating to French and British North America in the Archives of the Sacred Congregation "de Propaganda Fide" in Rome, 1622–1799.* Ottawa: National Archives of Canada, 1991.

Debeveč, Anton, Mathias C. Kiemen, and Alexander Wyse, eds. *United States Documents in the Propaganda Fide Archives: A Calendar. Second Series.* Vols. 8–10. Washington, DC: Academy of American Franciscan History, 1980–83.

Fish, Carl Russell. "Documents Relative to the Adjustment of the Roman Catholic Organization in the United States to the Conditions of National Independence, 1783–1789." *American Historical Review* 15, no. 4 (July 1910): 800–829.

Hoberg, Hermann. "Aggiunte recenti al fondo 'Missioni' dell'Archivio Vaticano." In *Ecclesiae Memoria: Miscellanea in onore del R. P. Josef Metzler, O.M.I.*, ed. Willi Henkel, 87–92. Freiburg: Herder, 1991.

Kenneally, Finbar, ed. *United States Documents in the Propaganda Fide Archives: A Calendar. First Series.* Vols. 1–7 and index. Washington, DC: Academy of American Franciscan History, 1966–81.

Pizzorusso, Giovanni. "Archives of the Sacred Congregation 'de Propaganda Fide': Calendar of Volume I (1634–1760) of the Series Congressi America Antille." *Storia Nordamericana* 3, no. 2 (1986): 117–64.

Pizzorusso, Giovanni, and Matteo Sanfilippo. *Inventaire des documents d'intérêt canadien dans les Archives de la Congrégation 'de Propaganda Fide' sous le pontificat de Pie IX (1846–1877).* Rome-Ottawa: Centre Académique Canadien en Italie-Université St-Paul, 2001.

Sanfilippo, Matteo. *Inventaire des documents d'intérêt canadien dans l'Archivio Segreto Vaticano sous le pontificat de Léon XIII (1878–1903): Délégation Apostolique du Canada, Délégation Apostolique des États-Unis, Epistolae ad Principes et Epistolae Latinae, et autres séries mineures.* Ottawa-Rome: Archives Nationales du Canada-Centre Académique Canadien en Italie, 1987.

———, ed. "*Fonti ecclesiastiche per la storia dell'emigrazione e dei gruppi etnici nel Nord America: Gli Stati Uniti (1893–1922).*" Monographic issue of *Studi Emigrazione/Migration Studies* 32, no. 120 (December 1995).

DESCRIPTIONS OF ARCHIVES AND LIBRARIES

Arboleda, Hernan, CSsR. "Archivio Storico Generale CSSR." In *Spicilegium Historicum Congregationis Ssmi Redemptoris* 30, no. 1 (1987): 205–8.

Burns, Jeffrey M. "The Archives of the Archdiocese of San Francisco." *U.S. Catholic Historian* 16, no. 1 (Winter 1998): 63–72.

Catani, Patrizia, and Roberto Zuccolini, eds. *I fondi archivistici dei consolati in Chicago, Cleveland, Denver, New Orleans and San Francisco conservati nell'Archivio storico diplomatico.* Rome: Istituto Poligrafico e Zecca dello Stato, 1990.

Ceccopieri, Isabella. *Il fondo manoscritti della Biblioteca Casanatense.* Rome: Palombi, 1988.

Chiappin, Marcel. "L'archivio della Segreteria di Stato: Il periodo napoleonico." In *Religiosa Archivorum Custodia: IV Centenario della Fondazione dell'Archivio Segreto Vaticano (1612–2012); Atti del Convegno di Studi, Città del Vaticano, 17–18 aprile 2012,* 169–94. Vatican City: Vatican Secret Archives, 2015.

Coco, Giovanni. "Il governo, le carte e la memoria: Aspetti della storia degli archivi della Segreteria di Stato in Epoca contemporanea (1814–1939)." In *Religiosa Archivorum Custodia: IV Centenario della Fondazione dell'Archivio Segreto Vaticano (1612–2012); Atti del Convegno di Studi, Città del Vaticano, 17–18 aprile 2012,* 215–72. Vatican City: Vatican Secret Archives, 2015.

Danieluk, Robert, SJ. "Michal Boym, Andrzej Rudomina and Jan Smogulecki—Three Seventeenth-Century Missionaries in China: A Selection of Documents from the Roman Jesuit Archives." In *Monumenta Serica* 59 (2011): 417–24.

Dante, Leonida Enrico, ed. *Catalogo dell'Archivio della Prefettura delle Cerimonie Apostoliche.* Rome, 1956.

De Dominicis, Claudio. *Archives of Apostolic Delegation of United States.* New York: Center for Migration Studies, 1992.

De Nicolò, Paolo. "Profilo storico della Biblioteca Vaticana." In *Biblioteca Apostolica Vaticana,* ed. Leonard E. Boyle and Paolo de Nicolò, 17–36. Florence: Nardini, 1989.

Del Re, Niccolò. *La curia romana: Lineamenti storico-giuridici.* 2nd ed. Rome: Edizioni di storia e letteratura, 1952.

———. *Il vicereggente del Vicariato di Roma.* Rome: Istituto di Studi Romani, 1976.

Di Cesare, Francesca. *Catalogo dei manoscritti in scrittura latina datati per indicazione di anno, di luogo o di copista, 2: Biblioteca Angelica.* Turin: Bottega d'Erasmo, 1982.

Di Giovanni, Claudia. "In primo piano la solidarietà con la guerra sullo sfondo." *L'Osservatore Romano,* November 15, 2009, www.vatican.va/news_services/or/or_quo/cultura/265q04d1.html.

Di Sante, Assunta. "L'Archivio Storico Generale della Fabbrica di San Pietro in Vaticano e i suoi strumenti di corredo." In *La Casa di Dio: La fabbrica degli uomini; Gli archivi delle fabbricerie; Atti del convegno di Ravenna (26 settembre 2008),* ed. Gilberto Zacchè, 49–59. Modena: Enrico Mucchi Editore, 2009.

Di Sante, Assunta, and Simona Turriziani. "L'Archivio Storico Generale della Fabbrica di San Pietro." In *Magnificenze Vaticane: Tesori inediti dalla Fabbrica di San Pietro,* ed. Alfredo Maria Pergolizzi, 189–97. Rome: De Luca Editori d'Arte, 2008.

Dias, Odir Jacques, and Andrea Dal Pino, OSM. *Storia e inventari dell'archivio generale o.sm.* 2nd ed. Rome: Archivum Generale Ordinis Servorum, 1972.

Dieguez, Alejandro M. "Gli archivi delle Congregazioni romane: Nuove acquisizioni e ordinamenti." In *Religiosa Archivorum Custodia: IV Centenario della Fondazione dell'Archivio Segreto Vaticano (1612–2012); Atti del Convegno di Studi, Città del Vaticano, 17–18 aprile 2012,* 305–34. Vatican City: Vatican Secret Archives, 2015.

Doria, Piero. "L'archivio del Concilio Vaticano II all'Archivio Vaticano: Istituzione, inventario e nuove prospettive di ricerca." In *Religiosa Archivorum Custodia: IV Centenario della Fondazione dell'Archivio Segreto Vaticano (1612–2012); Atti del Convegno di Studi, Città del Vaticano, 17–18 aprile 2012,* 497–530. Vatican City: Vatican Secret Archives, 2015.

Ellis, John Tracy. "A Guide to the Baltimore Cathedral Archives." *Catholic Historical Review* 32, no. 3 (October 1946): 341–60.

I fondi, le procedure, le storie: Raccolta di studi della Biblioteca. Rome: Tipografia della Biblioteca Nazionale Centrale, 1993.

Fortini, Reginaldo, OP, Ramón Hernández, OP, and Anny Palliampikunnel, OP. *Catalogus Analyticus Archivi Generalis Ordinis Praedicatorum.* 6 vols. Rome: Sancta Sabina, 2002.

Giorgetti Vichi, Anna Maria. *La biblioteca Angelica: Cenni storici.* Rome: Arti grafiche f.lli Palombi, 1975.

Gualdo, Germano, ed. *Sussidi per la consultazione dell'Archivio Vaticano.* Vatican City: Vatican Secret Archives, 1989.

Guilday, Peter Keenan. "The Sacred Congregation de Propaganda Fide (1622–1922)." *Catholic Historical Review* 6, no. 4 (January 1921): 478–94.

Hanly, John. "Records of the Irish College, Rome, under Jesuit Administration." *Archivium Hibernicum* 28 (1964): 13–75.

———. "Sources of the History of the Irish College, Rome." *Irish Ecclesiastical Record* 102, series 5 (1964): 28–34.

Hanly, John, and Vera Orschel. "Calendar of 17th-and 18th-c. Documents at the Archives of the Irish College, Rome (with Index)." *Archivium Hibernicum* 63 (2010): 7–263.

Henkel, Willi. "Die Päpstiliche Missionbibliothek der Kongregation für die Evangelisierung der Völker." *Zeitschrift für Missionswissenschaft und Religionswissenschaft* 70 (1986): 261–65.

Hoberg, Hermann. "Der Fonds Missioni der Vatikanischen Archivs." *Euntes Docete: Commentaria Urbaniana* 21 (1968): 97–107.

———. *Inventario dell'archivio della Sacra Romana Rota (sec. XIV–XIX).* Vatican City: Vatican Secret Archives, 1994.

Kearns, Conleth. "Archives of the Irish Dominican College, San Clemente, Rome: A Summary Report." *Archivium Hibernicum* 18 (1955): 145–49.

Lamalle, Edmond. "L'Archivio di un grande Ordine religioso: L'Archivio generale della Compagnia di Gesù." In *Archiva Ecclesiae* 24–25, no. 1 (1981–82): 89–120.

Lavenia, Vincenzo, Adriano Prosperi, and John A. Tedeschi, eds. 4 vols. *Dizionario storico dell'Inquisizione.* Pisa: Edizioni della Normale, 2010.

Leumas, Emilie Gagnet. "The Archives of the Archdiocese of New Orleans." *American Catholic Studies* 121, no. 1 (Spring 2014): 47–56.

Lexicon capuccinum: Promptuarium historico-bibliographicum ordinis fratrum minorum capuccinorum (1525–1950). Rome: Bibliotheca Collegii Internationalis S. Laurentii Brundusini, 1951.

Londei, Luigi. "La Segreteria di Stato e la documentazione ad essa afferente conservata presso l'Archivio di Stato di Roma." In *Religiosa Archivorum Custodia: IV Centenario della Fondazione dell'Archivio Segreto Vaticano (1612-2012); Atti del Convegno di Studi, Città del Vaticano, 17–18 aprile 2012,* 195–214. Vatican City: Vatican Secret Archives, 2015.

Manfredi, Antonio, ed. *Le Origini della Biblioteca Apostolica Vaticana tra Umanesimo e Rinascimento (1447–1534),* vol. 1: *Storia della Biblioteca Apostolica Vaticana.* Vatican City: Biblioteca Apostolica Vaticana, 2010.

Metzler, Josef, OMI. "Indici dell'Archivio Storico della SC 'de Propaganda Fide.'" *Euntes Docete: Commentaria Urbaniana* 21 (1968): 109–30.

Millett, Benignus, OFM. "The Archives of St. Isidore's College, Rome." *Archivium Hibernicum* 40 (1985): 1–13.

Ministero degli Affari Esteri, Servizio storico e documentazione. *Inventario della serie Affari Politici, 1931–1945*. Rome: Archivio Storico Diplomatico, 1976.

———. *Inventario della serie Affari Politici, 1946–1950*. Rome: Archivio Storico Diplomatico, 1977.

Moneti, Elena, Giovanni Muzzioli, Innocenza Rossi, and Mercedes Zamboni, comps. *Catalogo dei manoscritti della Biblioteca Casanatense*. 6 vols. Rome: Libreria dello Stato, 1949–78.

Musmanno, Michelangelo. "The Library for American Studies in Italy." In *Rivista d'America e d'Italia* 13–14 (1925).

Orschel, Vera. "Archives of the Pontifical Irish College, Rome: History and Holdings." In *The Irish College, Rome and Its World*, ed. Keogh Dáire and Albert McDonnell, 267–78. Dublin: Four Courts, 2008.

Pagano, Sergio, ed. *Bibliografia dell'Archivio Segreto Vaticano, nuova versione, X (2000–2002)*. Vatican City: Vatican Secret Archives, 2008.

———. "Il fondo di Mons: Umberto Benigni dell'Archivio Segreto Vaticano." *Ricerche per la storia religiosa di Roma* 8 (1990): 347–402.

———. "Ospizio dei Convertendi di Roma fra carisma missionario e regolamentazione ecclesiastica (1671–1700)." *Ricerche per la storia religiosa di Roma* 10 (1998): 313–90.

———. "Paolo V e la fondazione del moderno Archivio Segreto Vaticano (1611–1612)." In *Religiosa Archivorum Custodia: IV Centenario della Fondazione dell'Archivio Segreto Vaticano (1612–2012); Atti del Convegno di Studi, Città del Vaticano, 17–18 aprile 2012*, 305–34. Vatican City: Vatican Secret Archives, 2015.

Pandzic, Basilio, OFM. "L'archivio generale dell'ordine dei frati minori." In *Il Libro e le biblioteche: Atti del primo congresso bibliologico francescano internazionale, 20–27 febbraio 1949*, 223–37. Rome: Pontificium Athenaeum Antonianum, 1950.

Parsons, Wilfrid, SJ. "Researches in Early Catholic Americana." *The Papers of the Bibliographical Society of America* 33 (1939): 55–68.

Pellegrini, Vincenzo, ed. *Il ministero degli Affari Esteri*. Bologna: Mulino, 1992.

Perzynska, Kinga. "Catholic Archives of Texas: Sense and Sensibility of Catholic History Preservation and Research." *U.S. Catholic Historian* 16, no. 1 (Winter 1998): 35–46.

Piazzoni, Ambrogio M., Antonio Manfredi, and Dalma Frascarelli. *La Biblioteca Apostolica Vaticana*. Rome: Vatican Museums, 2012.

Pilotti, Laura. *Il fondo archivistico "serie Z-contenzioso."* Rome: Ministero degli Affari Esteri, 1987.

Pinto, Olga. *Storia della Biblioteca Corsiniana e della Biblioteca dell'Accademia dei Lincei*. Florence: Olschki, 1956.

Pizzo, Marco, ed. *L'Archivio del Museo Centrale del Risorgimento: Guida ai fondi documentari*. Rome: Gangemi Editore, 2007.

Pizzorusso, Giovanni. "Archives du Collège Urbain de Propaganda Fide." *Annali Accademici Canadesi* 7 (1991): 93–98.

———. "I Cattolici nordamericani e la sovranità temporale dei romani pontefici propugnata nella sua integrità dal suffragio dell'Orbe cattolico regnante Pio IX l'anno XIV." In *Gli Stati Uniti e l'unità d'Italia*, ed. Daniele Fiorentino and Matteo Sanfilippo, 113–24. Rome: Gangemi, 2004.

———. "Un diplomate du Vatican en Amérique: Donato Sbarretti à Washington, La Havane et Ottawa (1893–1910)." *Annali Accademici Canadesi* 9 (1993): 5–33.

———. "Le fonds Benigni aux Archives Secrètes du Vatican." *Annali Accademici Canadesi* 8 (1992): 107–11.

———. "Le fonti del Sant'Uffizio per la storia delle missioni e dei rapporti con Propaganda Fide." In *A dieci anni dall'apertura dell'archivio della Congregazione per la Dottrina della Fede: storia e archivi dell'Inquisizione (Roma, 21–23 febbraio 2008)*, 393–423. Rome: Accademia dei Lincei Scienze e Lettere, 2011.

———. "Grassi, Giovanni Antonio." In *Dizionario biografico degli Italiani* 57, 625–28. Rome: Istituto della Enciclopedia Italiana, 2002.

———. "Una presenza ecclesiastica cosmopolita a Roma: Gli allievi del Collegio Urbano di Propaganda Fide." *Bollettino di Demografia Storica* 22 (1995): 129–38.

———. "Tre lettere di Giovanni Battisti Scalabrini (1889–1892) sull'assistenza spirituale agli italiani negli Stati Uniti nel fondo 'Udienze' dell'Archivio storico della Congregazione 'de Propaganda Fide.'" *Archivio Storico dell'Emigrazione Italiana* 6 (2010): 151–57.

Pizzorusso, Giovanni, and Matteo Sanfilippo. *Dagli indiani agli emigranti: L'attenzione della Chiesa romana al Nuovo Mondo, 1492–1908*. Viterbo: Edizioni Sette Città, 2005.

Pyne, Tricia T. "The Archives of the Second Vatican Council Fathers Project: A Report from the United States." *U.S. Catholic Historian* 30, no. 3 (Summer 2012): 51–63.

———. "The Associated Archives at St. Mary's Seminary and University: A New Model for Catholic Archives." *American Catholic Studies* 118, no. 2 (Summer 2007): 69–78.

Rigotti, Gianpaolo. "L'archivio della Congregazione per le Chiese Orientali: Dalla Costituzione apostolica Romani Pontifices (1862) alla morte del card. Gabriele Acacio Coussa (1962)." In *Fede e martirio: Le chiese orientali cattoliche nell'Europa del Novecento; Atti del Convegno di storia ecclesiastica contemporanea, Città del Vaticano, 22–24 ottobre 1998*, ed. Aleksander Rebernik, Gianpaolo Rigotti, and Michel Van Parys, OSB, 247–95. Vatican City: Libreria Editrice Vaticana, 2003.

Sabba, Fiammetta, ed. *Indice degli autori dei manoscritti in scrittura latina della Biblioteca Angelica*. Rome: Istituto Poligrafico e Zecca dello Stato, 2009.

La Sacra Congregazione per le Chiese Orientali nel Cinquantesimo della fondazione. Rome: Tipografia Italo-Orientale "San Nilo," 1969.

Sanfilippo, Matteo. "L'Archivio Segreto Vaticano come fonte per la storia del Nord America anglo-francese." In *Gli Archivi della Santa Sede come fonte per la storia moderna e contemporanea*, ed. Matteo Sanfilippo and Giovanni Pizzorusso, 237–64. Viterbo: Edizioni Sette Città, 2001.

———. "Gli ordini religiosi nell'Archivio della Congregazione per la Dottrina della Fede." In *Gli archivi per la storia degli ordini religiosi*, vol. 1: *Fonti e problemi (secoli XVI–XIX)*, ed. Massimo Carlo Giannini and Matteo Sanfilippo, 63–76. Viterbo: Edizioni Sette Città, 2007.

———. "Roman Sources for the History of American Catholicism." *American Catholic Studies Newsletter* 37, no. 1 (2010): 1–22.

Saraco, Alessandro, ed. *La Penitenzieria Apostolica ed il suo Archivio*. Rome: Edizioni Paoline, 2012.

Spatzenegger, Hans. "Das Archiv von Santa Maria dell'Anima in Roma." *Römische historische Mitteilungen* 25 (1983): 133–54.

Tamburini, Filippo. "Archivio della Sacra Penitenzieria Apostolica." In *Guida delle fonti per la storia dell'America Latina negli archivi della Santa Sede e negli archivi ecclesiastici d'Italia*, ed. Lajos Pásztor, 349–52. Vatican City: Tipografia Poliglotta Vaticana, 1970.

———. "Sacra Penitenzieria Apostolica." In *Dizionario degli Istituti di Perfezione*, 8:169–81. Rome: Edizioni Paoline, 1988.

Tedeschi, John A. "The Dispersed Archives of the Roman Inquisition." In *The Inquisition in Early Modern Europe: Studies on Sources and Methods*, ed. G. Hennigsen, John Tedeschi, and Charles Amiel, 13–32. DeKalb: Northern Illinois University Press, 1986.

———. "The Organization and Procedures of the Roman Inquisition: A Sketch." In *The Prosecution of Heresy: Collected Studies on the Inquisition in Early Modern Italy*, ed. John Tedeschi, 47–88. Binghamton, NY: Medieval and Renaissance Texts and Studies, 1991.

Vian, Paolo. "I carteggi di Giuseppe Toniolo alla Biblioteca Vaticana: Genesi, consistenza e fortuna del fondo." In *Giuseppe Toniolo: L'uomo come fine; Con saggi sulla storia dell'Istituto Giuseppe Toniolo di studi superiori*, ed. Aldo Carera, 273–301. Milan: Vita e Pensiero, 2014.

Vichi, Anna Maria Giorgetti, and Sergio Mottironi, eds. *Catalogo dei manoscritti della Biblioteca Vallicelliana*. Rome: Istituto Poligrafico dello Stato, 1961.

Vignodelli, Rubrichi Renato. "Il fondo detto 'L'Archiviolo' dell'archivio Doria Landi Pamphilj in Roma." In *Miscellanea della Società Romana di Storia Patria* 22 (1972): 7–18.

Wolf, Hubert. *Storia dell'Indice: Il Vaticano e i libri proibiti*. Rome: Donzelli, 2006.

Wuest, Joseph. *Annales Congregationis SS. Redemptoris, Provinciae Americanae*. 5 vols., 1888–1924. Ilchester: Congregationis Sanctissimi Redemptoris, 1914.

PUBLISHED DOCUMENTARY SOURCES FOR US CATHOLIC HISTORY

Abell, Aaron I., ed. *American Catholic Thought on Social Questions*. Indianapolis: Bobbs-Merrill, 1968.

Appleby, R. Scott, Patricia Byrne, CSJ, and William L. Portier, eds. *Creative Fidelity: American Catholic Intellectual Traditions*. Maryknoll, NY: Orbis, 2004.

Archambault, Marie Therese, OSF, Mark G. Thiel, and Christopher Vecsey, eds. *The Crossing of Two Roads: Being Catholic and Native in the United States*. Maryknoll, NY: Orbis, 2003.

Armato, Maria Michele, and Mary Jeremy Finnegan, eds. *The Memoirs of Father Samuel Mazzuchelli, O.P.* Chicago: Priory Press, 1967.

Avella, Steven M., and Elizabeth McKeown, eds. *Public Voices: Catholics in the American Context*. Maryknoll, NY: Orbis, 1999.

Bahr, Howard M., ed. *The Navajo as Seen by the Franciscans, 1898–1921: A Sourcebook*. Lanham, MD: Scarecrow Press, 2004.

Bechtle, Regina, and Judith Metz, eds. *Elizabeth Bayley Seton: Collected Writings*. Vol. 1: *Correspondence and Journals, 1793–1808*. Vol. 2: *Correspondence and Journals, 1808–1820*. Vol. 3: *Spiritual Writings, Notebooks, and Other Documents*. Hyde Park, NY: New City Press, 2000–2008.

Brown, Roberta Stringham, and Patricia O'Connell Killen, eds. *Selected Letters of A.M.A. Blanchet, Bishop of Walla Walla and Nesqualy (1846–1879)*. Seattle: University of Washington Press, 2013.

Brownson, Henry F., ed. *The Works of Orestes A. Brownson, Collected and Arranged by Henry F. Brownson.* 20 vols. Detroit, 1882–1907.

———. *The Works of Orestes A. Brownson.* 20 vols. New York: AMS Press, 1966. Reprint of previous entry.

Brumleve, Barbara, ed. *The Letters of Mother Caroline Friess, School Sisters of Notre Dame.* Saint Louis: School Sisters of Notre Dame, 1991.

Burns, Jeffrey M., Ellen Skerrett, and Joseph M. White, eds. *Keeping Faith: European and Asian Catholic Immigrants.* Maryknoll, NY: Orbis, 2000.

Butler, Anne M., Michael E. Engh, SJ, and Thomas W. Spalding, CFX, eds. *The Frontiers and Catholic Identities.* Maryknoll, NY: Orbis, 1999.

Callahan, Nelson J., ed. *The Diary of Richard L. Burtsell, Priest of New York: The Early Years, 1865–1868.* New York: Arno Press, 1978.

Campeau, Lucien, SJ. *Monumenta Novae Franciae.* 9 vols. Rome: Apud Monumenta Hist. Soc. Iesu, 1967–2003.

Carey, Patrick W., ed. *American Catholic Religious Thought.* New York: Paulist Press, 1987.

———. *The Early Works of Orestes A. Brownson.* Vols. 1–7. Milwaukee: Marquette University Press, 2000–2007.

Chinnici, Joseph P., OFM, ed. *Devotion to the Holy Spirit in American Catholicism.* New York: Paulist Press, 1985.

Chinnici, Joseph P., OFM, and Angelyn Dries, OSF, eds. *Prayer and Practice in the American Catholic Community.* Maryknoll, NY: Orbis, 2000.

Cosacchi, Daniel, ed. *The Berrigan Letters: Personal Correspondence between Daniel and Philip Berrigan.* Maryknoll: Orbis Books, 2016.

Culberson, Diana, ed. *Rose Hawthorne Lathrop: Selected Writings.* New York: Paulist Press, 1993.

Curran, Robert Emmett, ed. *American Jesuit Spirituality: The Maryland Tradition, 1634–1900.* New York: Paulist Press, 1988.

———. *Intestine Enemies: Catholics in Protestant America, 1605–1791; A Documentary History.* Washington, DC: Catholic University of America Press, 2017.

Davis, Cyprian, OSB, and Jamie Phelps, OP, eds. *"Stamped with the Image of God": African Americans as God's Image in Black.* Maryknoll, NY: Orbis, 2003.

De Smet, Pierre-Jean. *Oregon Missions and Travels over the Rocky Mountains in 1845–46.* Fairfield, WA: Ye Galleon, 1978.

Diomedi, Alexander. *Sketches of Indian Life in the Pacific Northwest,* ed. Edward Kowrach. Fairfield, WA: Ye Galleon, 1978.

"Documents on American Catholic Attitudes toward Peace and War, 1789–1983." *U.S. Catholic Historian* 4, no. 1 (1984): 100–121.

Donnelly, Joseph P., ed. *Wilderness Kingdom: Indian Life in the Rocky Mountains, 1840–1847; The Journals and Paintings of Nicolas Point, S.J.* New York: Holt, Rinehart, Winston, 1967.

Ellis, John Tracy, ed. *Documents on American Catholic History.* 2 vols. Chicago: H. Regnery, 1967.

———. *Documents of American Catholic History.* 3 vols. Wilmington, DE: Michael Glazier, 1987.

Ellsberg, Robert, ed. *All the Way to Heaven: The Selected Letters of Dorothy Day.* New York: Image Books, 2010.

———. *Dorothy Day, Selected Writings: By Little and by Little.* Maryknoll, NY: Orbis, 1992.

———. *The Duty of Delight: The Diaries of Dorothy Day.* New York: Image Books, 2011.

Espinosa, Manuel, ed. *The Pueblo Indian Revolt of 1696 and the Franciscan Missions in New Mexico: Letters of the Missionaries and Related Documents.* Norman: University of Oklahoma Press, 1988.

Estevez, Felipe, ed. *Letters to Elpidio/Felix Varela.* New York: Paulist Press, 1989.

Faulkner, Anselm, OFM. "Letters of Charles Bonaventure Maguire, O. F. M. (1768–1833)." *Clogher Record* 10 (1979–81): 284–303; 11 (1982–83): 77–101, 187–213.

Foley, Thomas, ed. *At Standing Rock and Wounded Knee: The Journals and Papers of Father Francis M. Craft, 1888–1890.* Norman, OK: Arthur H. Clark, 2009.

Gallin, Alice, ed. *American Catholic Higher Education Essential Documents, 1967–1990.* Notre Dame, IN: University of Notre Dame Press, 1992.

———. *Ex Corde Ecclesiae: Documents Concerning Reception and Implementation.* Notre Dame, IN: University of Notre Dame Press, 2006.

Garcia, Mario T., ed. *The Gospel of Cesar Chavez: My Faith in Action.* Lanham, MD: Sheed and Ward, 2007.

Geiger, Maynard, OFM, ed. *As the Padres Saw Them: California Indian Life and Customs as Reported by the Franciscan Missionaries, 1813–1815.* Santa Barbara, CA: Santa Barbara Mission Archive Library, 1976.

Gleason, Philip, ed. *Documentary Records of Early American Catholicism.* New York: Arno Press, 1978.

Gower, Joseph F., and Richard M. Leliaert, eds. *The Brownson-Hecker Correspondence.* Notre Dame, IN: University of Notre Dame Press, 1979.

Greer, Allan, ed. *The Jesuit Relations: Natives and Missionaries in Seventeenth-Century North America.* New York: Bedford Books of Saint Martin's Press, 2000.

Griffin, Martin Ignatius Joseph, ed. "The Beginnings of the Hierarchy in the United States: The Appointment of a Superior; Benjamin Franklin's Recommendation of Rev. John Carroll, His Companion on the Embassy to the Canadians." *American Catholic Historical Researches* 19, no. 4 (October 1902): 155–59.

———. "Documents Relating to the Appointment of Coadjutors of the Right Rev. John Carroll, First Bishop of Baltimore, of the Years 1793 and 1794." *American Catholic Historical Researches* 5, no. 4 (October 1888): 188–93.

———. "Letter of Bishop Challoner to the Propaganda in 1763, Giving an Account of the American Missions under his Jurisdiction." *American Catholic Historical Researches* 12, no. 1 (January 1895): 44–45.

———. "Memoir of the Louisiana Missions by Father Philibert Francis Watrin, S.J." *American Catholic Historical Researches* 17, no. 2 (April 1900): 89–93.

———. "A Pastoral Letter, from the Apostolic Vice-Prefect, Curate of the Holy Cross at Boston." *American Catholic Historical Researches* 6 (January 1889): 2–6.

———. "Reverend Ferdinand Farmer, S.J.: A Priest of Pennsylvania, 1752–1786." *American Catholic Historical Researches* 7, no. 3 (July 1890): 120–28.

———. "Rev. John Thayer, the First New England Convert Priest." *American Catholic Historical Researches* 7, no. 2 (April 1911): 97–100.

Guilday, Peter, ed. *The National Pastorals of the American Hierarchy (1792–1919)*. Westminster, MD: Newman Press, 1954.

Hanley, Thomas O'Brien, SJ, ed. *The John Carroll Papers*. 3 vols. Notre Dame, IN: University of Notre Dame Press, 1976.

Healy, Kathleen, ed. *Sisters of Mercy: Spirituality in America, 1843–1900*. New York: Paulist Press, 1992.

Hennessy, Thomas C., ed. *How the Jesuits Settled in New York: A Documentary Account*. New York: Something More Publications, distributed by Fordham University Press, 2003.

Herr, Dan, and Joel Wells, eds. *Through Other Eyes: Some Impressions of American Catholicism by Foreign Visitors from 1777 to the Present*. Westminster, MD: Newman Press, 1965.

Hudson, Gertrude Reese, ed. *Browning to His American Friends: Letters between the Brownings, the Storys and James Russell Lowell*. London: Bowes and Bowes, 1965.

Hughes, Thomas, SJ. *History of the Society of Jesus in North America: Colonial and Federal*. 4 vols. New York: Longmans, Green, 1907–17.

Kane, Paula, James Kenneally, and Karen Kennelly, CSJ, eds. *Gender Identities in American Catholicism*. Maryknoll, NY: Orbis, 2003.

Kehoe, Lawrence, ed. *Complete Works of the Most Rev. John Hughes, D.D., Archbishop of New York*. 2 vols. New York: American News, 1865.

Kelly, Ellin, and Annabelle Melville, eds. *Elizabeth Seton: Selected Writings*. New York: Paulist Press: 1987.

Kupke, Raymond J., ed. *American Catholic Preaching and Piety in the Time of John Carroll*. Lanham, MD: University Press of America, 1991.

Mahoney, Joseph F., and Peter Wosh, eds. *The Diocesan Journal of Michael Augustine Corrigan, Bishop of Newark, 1872–1880*. Newark and South Orange: New Jersey Historical Society and New Jersey Catholic Historical Records Commission, 1987.

Matovina, Timothy, and Gerald E. Poyo, eds. *¡Presente! U.S. Latino Catholics from Colonial Origins to the Present*. Maryknoll, NY: Orbis, 2000.

Mazenod, Charles-Joseph-Eugène de. *Lettres aux correspondants d'Amérique*. Vols. 1–2. Rome: Postulation générale OMI, 1977.

McCants, Dorothea Olga, DC, ed. *They Came to Louisiana: Letters of a Catholic Mission, 1854–1882*. Baton Rouge: Louisiana State University Press, 1970.

McCloskey, Neil G., SJ, ed. *Catholic Education in America: A Documentary History*. New York: Teachers College, Columbia University, 1965.

McNeil, Betty Ann, ed. *Balm of Hope: Charity Afire Impels Daughters of Charity to Civil War Nursing*. Chicago: Vincentian Studies Institute, DePaul University, 2015.

Meconi, David, SJ, ed. *Catherine de Hueck Doherty: Essential Writings*. Maryknoll, NY: Orbis, 2009.

———. *Frank Sheed and Maisie Ward: Spiritual Writing*. Maryknoll, NY: Orbis, 2010.

Messmer, Sebastian G., ed. *The Works of the Right Reverend John England, First Bishop of Charleston*. 7 vols. Cleveland: Arthur H. Clark, 1908.

Nolan, Hugh J., ed. *Pastoral Letters of the American Hierarchy, 1792–1970*. Huntington, IN: Our Sunday Visitor, 1971.

O'Brien, David J., and Thomas A. Shannon, eds. *Catholic Social Thought: Encyclicals and Documents from Pope Leo XIII to Pope Francis*. Maryknoll, NY: Orbis, 2016.

———. *Renewing the Earth: Catholic Documents on Peace, Justice, and Liberation.* Garden City, NY: Image Books, 1977.

Pastoral Letters of Archbishop Carroll to the Congregation of Trinity Church, in Philadelphia, 1797, and of Archbishop Maréchal, to the Congregation of Norfolk, Virginia, 1819. Baltimore: Joseph Robinson, 1820.

Quigley, Margaret, and Michael Garvey, eds. *The Dorothy Day Book.* Springfield, IL: Templegate, 1982.

Randall, Catharine, ed. *Black Robes and Buckskin: A Selection from the Jesuit Relations.* New York: Fordham University Press, 2011.

Reardon, Maurice E., ed. *Mosaic of a Bishop: An Autobiographical Appreciation of His Grace, the Most Reverend John T. McNicholas . . . Gained from His Addresses, Sermons and Correspondence.* Paterson, NJ: Saint Anthony Guild Press, 1957.

Reynolds, Ignatius, ed. *The Works of the Right Rev. John England.* 5 vols. Baltimore: J. Murphy, 1849.

Rybolt, John E., ed. *Frontier Missionary: Felix De Andreis, CM, 1778–1820; Correspondence and Historical Writings.* Chicago: Vincentian Studies Institute, 2005.

Samway, Patrick, SJ, ed. *The Letters of Robert Giroux and Thomas Merton.* Notre Dame, IN: University of Notre Dame Press, 2015.

Scutchfield, F. Douglas, and Paul Evans Holbrook Jr., eds. *The Letters of Thomas Merton and Victor and Carolyn Hammer: Ad Majorem Dei Gloriam.* Lexington: University Press of Kentucky, 2014.

Shannon, William H., ed. *The Hidden Ground of Love: The Letters of Thomas Merton on Religious Experience and Social Concerns.* New York: Farrar, Straus and Giroux, 1985.

Spalding, Thomas W., ed. *John Carroll Recovered: Abstracts of Letters and Other Documents Not Found in the John Carroll Papers.* Baltimore: Cathedral Foundation Press, 2000.

Stock, Leo F., ed. *Consular Relations between the United States and the Papal States: Instructions and Despatches.* Washington, DC: American Catholic Historical Association, 1945.

———. *United States Ministers to the Papal States: Instructions and Despatches, 1848–1868.* Washington, DC: Catholic University of America Press, 1933.

Tancrell, Luke, OP, ed. *Edward Dominic Fenwick Papers, 1803–1832: Founding American Dominican Friar and Bishop.* New York: Dominican Publications, 2005.

Thiel, Mark, and Christopher Vecsey, eds. *Native Footsteps along the Path of Saint Kateri Tekakwitha.* Milwaukee: Marquette University Press, 2013.

Thwaites, Reuben G., ed. *The Jesuit Relations and Allied Documents: Travels and Explorations of the Jesuit Missionaries in New France, 1610–1791.* 73 vols. Cleveland: Burrows Brothers, 1896–1901.

Tomasi, Silvano M., ed. *For the Love of Immigrants: Migration Writings and Letters of Bishop John Baptist Scalabrini (1839–1905).* New York: Center for Migration Studies, 2000.

Torres y Vargas, Don Diego de. *Report on the Island and Diocese of Puerto Rico (1647),* trans. Jaime Vidal. Scranton, PA: University of Scranton Press, 2010.

Treutlein, Theodore E., ed. *Missionary in Sonora: The Travel Reports of Joseph Och, S.J., 1755–1767.* San Francisco: California Historical Society, 1965.

Walling, Regis M., and N. Daniel Rupp, eds. *The Diary of Bishop Frederic Baraga, First Bishop of Marquette, Michigan,* trans. Joseph Gregorich and Paul Prud'homme, SJ. Detroit: Wayne State University Press, 1990.

Weber, Francis J., ed. *The Writings of Francisco García Diego y Moreno, Obispo de Ambas Californias.* Los Angeles: Dawson's Book Shop, 1976.

White, Andrew, SJ. "A Briefe Relation of the Voyage vnto Maryland." In *The Calvert Papers* 3, 26–45. Baltimore: Baltimore Historical Society Fund Publication, 1899.

———. *Relatio Itineris in Marylandiam: Declaratio Coloniae Domini Baronis de Baltimore; Escerpta ex Diversis Litteris Missionariorum Ab anno 1635, ad annum 1638*, ed. Edwin A. Dalrymple. Baltimore: Maryland Historical Society Fund Publication, 1874.

White, James D., ed. *Diary of a Frontier Bishop: The Journals of Theophile Meerschaert.* Tulsa, OK: Sarto Press, 1996.

Wild, Robert A., ed. *Compassionate Fire: The Letters of Thomas Merton and Catherine de Hueck Doherty.* Notre Dame, IN: Ave Maria Press, 2009.

Yzermans, Vincent A., ed. *Days of Hope and Promise: The Writings and Speeches of Paul J. Hallinan, Archbishop of Atlanta.* Collegeville, MN: Liturgical Press, 1973.

Zanca, Kenneth J., ed. *American Catholics and Slavery, 1789–1866: An Anthology of Primary Documents.* Lanham, MD: University Press of America, 1994.

Index

MATTEO BINASCO
was a postdoctoral fellow at the Cushwa Center
at the University of Notre Dame from 2014 to 2017,
and is now an adjunct professor at the Università per
Stranieri di Siena and at the Università degli Studi di Genova.

Kathleen Sprows Cummings
is director of the Cushwa Center and an associate professor of history
and American studies at the University of Notre Dame.

Contributors include Matteo Sanfilippo and Luca Codignola.

CPSIA information can be obtained
at www.ICGtesting.com
Printed in the USA
LVHW06*2154270618
582087LV00011B/195/P